The
Incarnation
of
Jesus Christ

by
Jacob Böhme

The Incarnation of Jesus Christ

Set out in three parts. viz.:

I. How the eternal Word has become man; and of Mary the Virgin, who she was from her first beginning, and what sort of mother she became by conception of her son Jesus Christ.

II. How we must enter into the suffering, dying and death of Christ; and out of his death rise again with him and through him, and become like his image, and live eternally in him.

III. The tree of Christian faith. A true instruction, showing how many may be one spirit with God, and what he has to do to work the works of God.

Written according to divine illumination.

by
Jacob Böhme

in the year 1620

Translated from the German by
John Rolleston Earle, M.A.

CONTENTS

PART I

CHAPTER I. That the person of Christ, as well as his incarnation, cannot be known by the natural understanding without divine illumination

CHAPTER II. Manifestation of the Deity by the creation of angels and men from divine essence

CHAPTER III. The gate of the creation of man

CHAPTER IV. Of the paradisaic sphere and dominion

CHAPTER V. Of the lamentable fall of man

CHAPTER VI. Of Adam's sleep

CHAPTER VII. Of the promised seed of the woman

CHAPTER VIII. Of the Virgin Mary, etc.

CHAPTER IX. Of the virginity of Mary

CHAPTER X. Of the birth of Jesus Christ, the Son of God

CHAPTER XI. On the practical application

CHAPTER XII. Of the pure virginity

CHAPTER XIII. Of the twofold man

CHAPTER XIV. On the new birth

PART II

CHAPTER I. Of the origin of life from fine

CHAPTER II. The tree and highly precious gate of the Holy Trinity

CHAPTER III. The very earnest gate

CHAPTER IV. Of the origin of the world of fire

CHAPTER V. Of the Principle in itself

CHAPTER VI. Of our death

CHAPTER VII. Of spiritual seeing

CHAPTER VIII. The pilgrim's path from death unto life

CHAPTER IX. Further particulars regarding the third citation

CHAPTER X. Of the image of God which is man

PART III

CHAPTER I. What faith is, and how it is one Spirit with God

CHAPTER II. Of the origin of faith, and why faith and doubt dwell together

CHAPTER III. Of the property of faith, how it goes out from the will of the natural craving into the freewill of God

CHAPTER IV. What the work of faith is and how the will may walk therein and concerning its guide

CHAPTER V. Why the ungodly are not converted, which is the most painful part of conversion, of the false shepherds, how we must enter into God's kingdom, of the destruction of the devil's kingdom, of the three forms and what we have inherited from Adam and Christ

CHAPTER VI. What lust can do; how we in Adam have fallen and in Christ have been born again, and that it is not such an easy matter to become a true Christian.

CHAPTER VII. To what end this world with all Being was created, also concerning two eternal mysteries; of the exceedingly fierce struggle in man for the image, and wherein the tree of the Christian faith stands, grows, and bears fruit

CHAPTER VIII. In what manner God forgives sin, and how you become a child of God

PART I

HOW THE ETERNAL WORD HAS BECOME MAN, ETC.

CHAPTER I

THAT THE PERSON OF CHRIST, AS WELL AS HIS INCARNATION, CANNOT BE KNOWN BY THE NATURAL UNDERSTANDING OR THE LETTER OF THE HOLY SCRIPTURE, WITHOUT DIVINE ILLUMINATION. ITEM, OF THE ORIGIN OF THE ETERNAL DIVINE BEING

1. WHEN Christ asked his disciples: Whom do men say that the Son of man is? they said: Some say that thou art Elias, some that thou art John the baptist or one of the prophets. He said to them But whom say ye that I am? Then answered Simon Peter and said: Thou art Christ, the Son of the living God. And Jesus answered and said unto him: Of a truth flesh and blood hath not revealed this unto thee, but my Father which is in heaven. Thereafter he announced to them his sufferings, death and resurrection (Matt. xvi. 13-21). By this he meant to indicate that individual reason in the knowledge and wisdom of this world could not in its own reason know or comprehend the person who was God and man; but that he would be known rightly only of those who would give themselves up wholly to him, and for his Name would endure the cross, tribulation and persecution, and would cleave with earnestness to him. And such in fact was the case, so that he, while yet living visibly among us in this world, was known in least measure by the wise in reason. And though he walked in Divine wonders, yet outward reason was so blind and foolish that those great wonders or miracles were attributed by the wisest in the art of reason to the devil. And as at the time when he lived visibly in this world, he remained unknown of individual reason and knowledge, so he is and remains even now unrecognized and unknown of outward reason.

2. From thence has arisen so much wrangling and dispute about his person, as outward reason always believed it fathomed what God and man is, and how God and man can be one person. This dispute has filled the earth, for individual reason always supposed it had grasped the pearl, and did not reflect that God's kingdom is not of this world and that flesh and blood cannot know or comprehend it, much less fathom it.

3. Accordingly it behoves everyone who would speak of the Divine mysteries or teach them, that he have the Spirit of God, and that he know in the Divine light what he would give out as true; and not suck it from his own reason, nor take his stand upon the mere letter without Divine knowledge and drag in Scripture by the hair, as reason does. Wherefrom a great deal of error has arisen, because men have sought for Divine knowledge in their own understanding and art, and have thus passed from the truth of God into individual reason, and regarded the incarnation of Christ as something strange and remote, whereas we must all be born again of God in this incarnation, if we will escape the wrath of the Eternal Nature.

4. Seeing then it is for the children of God an intimate and indigenous work, with which they should daily and hourly be occupied, and enter continually into the incarnation of Christ, go out from the earthly reason, and thus during this life of sorrow be born in the birth and incarnation of Christ, if they wish to be God's children in Christ: I have proposed to write this high mystery according to my knowledge and gifts, for a memorial, in order that I may thus have an occasion to recreate and to refresh myself cordially with my Immanuel,-for I am also along with other children of Christ in this birth,-that I might have a memorial and support, in case the dark and earthly flesh and blood would put upon me the poison of the devil and obscure my image. I proposed it as an exercise of faith, whereby my soul may thus, as a twig in its tree Jesus Christ, refresh itself from his sap and power. And this, not with sage and high discourses of art, or springing from the reason of this world, but according to the knowledge that I have of my tree which is Christ, that my twig

also may bud and grow beside others in the tree and life of God. And though I ground highly and deeply, and shall expound it clearly, this nevertheless must be told the reader, that without the spirit of God it will be to him a mystery, and unapprehended. Therefore let everyone take heed what judgment he passes, lest he fall into the judgment of God and be seized by his own turba, and his own reason overthrow him. This I say from a good intent and affection, and give it to the reader to consider of.

5. If we will write of the incarnation and birth of Jesus Christ the Son of God, and speak of it correctly, we must reflect upon the cause, and consider what moved God to become man, seeing that He was not in need of this for the realization of his being. And it can by no means be said that God's own being was changed in the incarnation. For God is un

changeable, and yet has become what He was not; but his proprium has at the same time remained immutable. It was only for the sake of the salvation of fallen man, that He might bring him again into Paradise. And here we are to consider the first man, as to how he was before his fall, on account of which the Deity has put itself in motion.

6. We know what Moses says, that God created man in his likeness, in an image according to him (Gen. i. 27). Understand, then, that God, who is a Spirit, beheld himself in an image, as in a likeness. Not the less has he created also this world, that thus he might manifest the Eternal Nature in essence and substance as well as in living creatures and figures, that all this might be a likeness and outbirth from the Eternal Nature of the first Principle. Which likeness, before the times of the world, stood in the wisdom of God as a hidden magia, and was seen in the wisdom by the Spirit of God, who at the beginning of this world moved the Eternal Nature and brought forth and disclosed the likeness of the hidden divine world. For the fiery world was just as if swallowed up and hidden in the light of God, the light of Majesty ruling alone in itself. We are not, however, to think that the fiery world existed not. It did exist; but it separated into its own principle, and was not manifest in the light of God's Majesty.

As we may conceive of this in fire and light, that fire is indeed a cause of light, and the light dwells in the fire, but without being laid hold of by it, and has another life than the fire. For fire is fierceness and consumes, and light is gentleness, and from its power arises substantiality, as the water or sulphur of a thing, which the fire draws into itself and uses for its strength and life, and thus forms an eternal bond.

7. This fire and divine light have from eternity stood still in themselves, each in its order, in its principle, and have neither ground nor beginning. For the fire has in itself its own form for its source, namely Desire, from and in which all the forms of nature are generated, one being a cause of another, as has been told in detail in the other writings. And we find in the light of nature that the fire in its own essence, in the sour desiring source in itself, was a darkness, and was as if swallowed up in the gentleness of God, without enkindling; and though it burned, yet as a special principle of its own was in itself only perceptible. For there have been from eternity only two principles: one in itself, the fiery world, and the other similarly in itself, the lightflaming world; although they were not separated, as fire and light are not separated, the light dwelling in the fire, without being laid hold of by it.

8. We are thus to understand two kinds of spirit united in one another, namely, a fiery spirit, in conformity with the essence of the sour and severe nature proceeding from the hot and cold fierce essential fire, which is regarded as God's spirit of wrath, and belongs to the Father's property, according to which he calls himself an angry, jealous God and a consuming fire, whereby is understood the first Principle. And, secondly, a gentle light-flaming spirit, which from eternity receives its transformation in the centre of the light; for in the first Principle, in the Father's property, it is a fiery spirit, and in the second Principle, in the light, a gentle light-flaming spirit, which from eternity is generated in this way, and is one, not two. But it is understood in a twofold source, viz. in fire and light according to the property of each source, as may be understood sufficiently in any outward

fire, that the fire's source gives a fierce consuming spirit, and the light's source furnishes a gentle lovely spirit, and yet originally there is but one spirit.

9. In like manner we are to consider of the Being of eternity or the Holy Trinity, which in the light of Majesty we recognize to be the Deity, and in the fire to be the Eternal Nature. For the all-powerful Spirit of God with the two Principles has from eternity been itself All; there is nothing prior to it, it is itself the ground and unground. And yet the holy divine Being is regarded specially as a single existence in itself, and dwells out of the fiery nature and property in the light's property, and is called God; not from the fire's property, but from the light's property, though the two properties are unseparated. As we see in this world, that a hidden fire lies concealed in the deep of nature and in all beings, else no outward fire could be produced. And we see how the gentleness of the water keeps this hidden fire imprisoned in itself, so that it cannot be revealed; for it is as it were swallowed up in the water, and nevertheless is, not indeed substantially but essentially, and at its awakening comes to be known and qualifying; and all were a nothing and a groundlessness without fire.

10. Thus, we understand also that the third Principle, or the source and the spirit of this world, has from eternity been hidden in the Eternal Nature of the Father's property, and was seen by the lightflaming Spirit in the holy Magia, in God's wisdom and the divine tincture. Consequently the Deity has moved itself according to the nature of the genetrix, and brought forth the great mystery, wherein lay all that the Eternal Nature can do. It was, however, only a mysterium, and resembled no creature, but there was in it everything as in a chaos together. The fierce wrathful nature has generated a dark chaos, and the light-flaming nature in its proprium has generated flames in the Majesty and the gentleness, which from eternity has been the water-fountain and cause of the holy divine essentiality. It was power and spirit only, without parallel, nor was anything discerned there but the Spirit of God in a twofold source and form, viz. the hot and cold

severe source of fire, and the gentle source of love, after the manner of fire and light.

11. This has like a mystery entered one into the other, and yet one has not comprehended the other, but has at the same time remained in two principles. Here then the sourness or the father of nature has always seized the essence in the mystery, where this then has been formed as it were into an image, and yet there was no image, but as a shadow of an image. All this in the mystery has indeed thus always had an eternal beginning, as it cannot be said that something has arisen which has not had its figure as a shadow in the great eternal Magia; but there was no being, but only a spiritual play one in another, and it is the Magia of the great wonders of God, where always there has been origination where

there was nothing but an ungrounded existence. This nothing has in the nature of the fire and the light advanced into a ground, and yet issues from nothing but the spirit of the source, which is not a being either, but a source which gives birth to itself in itself in two properties, and likewise separates into two principles. It has no separator or maker, nor any cause of its own creativeness, but is itself the cause.

12. Thus, we are now able to recognize the creation of this world, including both the creation of angels, and also of man and all creatures. It has all been created out of the great mystery. For the third Principle stood before God as a magia, and was not made wholly manifest. Hence God has not had any likeness, in which he might have beheld his own being, but the wisdom only. That has been his longing, and was there in his will with his spirit as a great wonder in the light-flaming divine magia of the Spirit of God. For it was the dwelling of the Spirit of God, and was not a genetrix, but the revelation of God, a virgin, and a cause of the divine essentiality, for in it lay the light-flaming divine tincture for the heart of God, as for the Word of life of the Deity, and it was the revelation of the Holy Trinity. Not that it has manifested God by its own power and productivity, but the divine centre, viz. God's heart or being, manifests itself in it. It is like a mirror of

the Deity; for every mirror keeps still and produces no image, but it receives the image. Accordingly this virgin of wisdom is a mirror of the Deity, in which the Spirit of God beholds itself, as well as all the wonders of the magia, which have come into being with the creation of the third Principle. All has been created from the great mystery, and this virgin of the wisdom of God stood in the mystery, and in it has the Spirit of God seen the forms of the creatures. For it is that which is uttered, what the Father utters by the Holy Spirit out of his centre of the light-flaming divine property, out of the centre of his heart, out of the Word of the Deity. It stands before the Deity as a reflection or mirror of the Deity, wherein the Deity beholds itself, and in it lies the divine kingdom of joy of the divine will, i.e. the great wonders of eternity, which have neither beginning nor end, nor number, but all is an eternal beginning and an eternal end, and together resembles an eye which sees, where however there is nothing in the seeing, and yet the seeing does spring from the essence of the fire and light.

13. Thus, understand in the fire's essence the Father's proprium and the first Principle, and in the light's source and property the Son's nature or the second Principle, and the ruling Spirit which proceeds from these two properties understand as the Spirit of God, which in the first Principle is wrathful, severe, sour, bitter, cold and fiery, and is the impelling spirit in the wrath. And therefore it rests not in the wrath and fierceness, but goes forth and blows up the essential fire, uniting itself again to the essence of the fire, for the fiery essences draw it again into themselves, as it is their source and life; and again in the enkindled fire in the light it proceeds from the Father and Son, and reveals the fiery essences in the source of the light, whereby the fiery essences burn in a great desire of love, and the rigorous austere source is not known in the source of the light, so that the severity of the fire is only a cause of the light-flaming majesty and the desiring love.

14. And thus we are to understand the Being of the Deity and also of the Eternal Nature. And we understand always the divine Being in the light of majesty, for the gentle light makes the

Father's severe nature gentle, lovely and merciful, by which God is called a Father of mercy in accordance with his heart or Son. For the Father's proprium stands in fire and in light. He is himself the Being of all beings. He is the unground and the ground, and in the eternal birth divides into three properties, or into three persons, or into three principles, although in eternity there are but two in being, and the third is as a mirror of the first two, from which this world has been created as a palpable existence in a beginning and end.

CHAPTER II

MANIFESTATION OF THE DEITY BY THE CREATION OF ANGELS AND MEN FROM DIVINE ESSENCE

1. SEEING then there has thus been a mystery from eternity, we are now to consider its manifestation. We can speak of eternity only as of a spirit, for the whole has been spirit only; and yet from eternity has generated itself into substance by desire and longing. We can in no wise say that in eternity there has not been substance, for no fire exists without substance. So also there is no gentleness without the production of substance. For the gentleness produces water, and the fire swallows this up and transforms it in itself, one part into heavens and firmament, and the other part into sulphur, wherein the fire-spirit with its wheel of essences makes a mercury, then awakens Vulcan (that is, strikes fire), by which the third spirit or air is generated. In the middle is found the noble tincture, as a lustre with colours, and has its rise originally from the wisdom of God. Every colour remains with its essence in the gentleness of the waterfountain, black excepted, which has its origin from the sour fierceness.

2. Each form longs after the other, and by the desirous longing one form is impregnated from the other, and one brings the other to being, in such a way that eternity stands in a perpetual magia, where nature is in process of growth and struggle, and the fire consumes this and gives it as well, and thus forms an eternal bond. But the light of the Majesty and Trinity of God is immutable; for the fire cannot seize it, it lives free in itself.

3. We recognize and find, however, that the light of the love is desirous, viz. of the wonders and figures in wisdom, and in such desire this world as a model [mirrored form] has been perceived from eternity in wisdom, in the deep and hidden magia of God; for the desire of the love searches the ground and the unground. And here likewise from eternity has been intermixed the desire of the wrath, that is, of the sour severe source in the nature and proprium of the Father. And hence the image of angels and men

in the divine property, as also in the wrath's property the devils, have been seen in God's wisdom from eternity: yet not in any being, but only after the manner in which a thought arises in the depth of the mind, and is brought before its own mirror of the soul, where often an object appears which has no being.

4. Thus the two genetrixes, that of the wrath in fire and that of the love in light, have brought their form into wisdom, where then the heart of God has longed in the love to make this mirrored form into an angelic image composed of divine essence, so that they should be a likeness and image of the Deity and dwell in the wisdom of God, in order to fulfil the longing of the Deity and for the eternal delight of the divine kingdom of joy.

5. And now we are to consider the* verbum fiat, which has grasped them and brought them into a substance and corporeal being, for the will to this image has arisen from the Father, out of the Father's proprium in, the Word or heart of God from eternity, as a desiring will to the creature and for the manifestation of the Deity. Because, however, from eternity God has not put himself in motion till the creation of the angels, so no creation has taken place till the creation of the angels. But the reason and cause of this we are not to know; God has reserved in his might as to how it was that he put himself in motion once, since he is indeed an unchangeable God. We must explore no further here, for it confuses us.

6. But of the creation we have power to speak, for it is a work in the being of God. And we understand that the will of the Word or heart of God has laid hold of the sour fiat in the centre of the nature of the Father, with its seven spirits and forms of the eternal Nature, and that in the form of a throne, whereby the sour fiat has appeared not as a maker, but as an agent in the property of every essence, that is, in the great wonders of wisdom. As the figures had been beheld from eternity in wisdom, they were now grasped by the fiat in the Will-spirit of God, and not taken from alien matter, but from God's essence, or from the nature of the Father. And they were with God's Will-spirit introduced into the light of Majesty, where they were then children of God and not

strangers, and were born and created from the Father's nature and property, and the spirit of their will was directed to the Son's nature and property. They could eat and were to eat of God's love and essentiality in the light of Majesty, whereby their fierce property which proceeds from the Father's nature was transformed into love and joy. And this they all did with the exception of one throne and kingdom, which turned itself away from the light of love, and wished in the severe fire-nature to rule over God's gentleness and love. And therefore it was driven out of the proprium of the Father, out of its creaturely proper place into the eternal darkness, into the abyss of the harsh fiat; there it must remain in its own eternity; and thus the wrath of the Eternal Nature has also been satisfied.

7. But it must not be thought that King Lucifer, could not have stood firm. He had the light of Majesty before him just as the other throne-angels. If he had imagined thereinto, he would have remained an angel; but he withdrew himself from God's love into the wrath, and accordingly he is an enemy of the love of God and of all the holy angels.

8. Further, we are to consider here the hostile enkindling of the expelled spirits, when as yet they were in the proprium of the Father, how they have kindled by their imagination the nature of the essentiality, so that from the heavenly Essence earth and stones were produced, and the gentle spirit of water in the qualification of fire became the burning firmament. Thereupon ensued the creation of this world as the third Principle; and to the place of this world another light was given, viz. the sun, and thus the devil was deprived of his pomp, and he was shut up in darkness as a prisoner between the kingdom of God, and the kingdom of this world, so that his dominion in this world extends no further than the turba, where the wrath and anger of God is awakened, and there he is an executioner. He is a perpetual liar, calumniator and deceiver of the creatures; he turns all that is good into what is bad, so far as opportunity is afforded him. Whatever is terrible and resplendent, in it he exhibits -his might, and is wishing always to be above God. But the heaven which is created

out of the midst of the waters as a gentle firmament abates his pomp and pride, so that he is not sovereign prince in this world, but prince of wrath.

9. But seeing the devil was cast out from his place, this place or throne (destitute of its angelic host) was in great desire for its prince; but he had been cast out. God then created for it another prince, viz. Adam, the first man, who was also a throne-prince before God. And here we are to consider aright his creation, as well as his fall, on account of which the heart of God moved itself and became man.

10. It is not a trivial matter, then, the creation of man, on account of whose fall God became man, that He might restore him. And hence his fall does not consist in the mere act of biting an apple; nor was his creation accomplished in the way outward reason supposes, as it understands the first Adam in his creation to be a mere clod of earth. No, my dear soul, God did not become man for the sake of a clod of earth; neither was it a question merely of a disobedience, at which God was so angry that his anger could not have been appeased unless he revenged himself upon his Son and slew him.

11. To us men, after the loss of our paradisaic image, this is a mystery and has remained hidden, except to some who have again attained the heavenly mystery; to these has something of it been disclosed according to the inner man. For in Adam we are dead to Paradise, and we must by the death and corruption of the body bud forth again in Paradise as in another world, in the life of God in the heavenly essentiality and corporeity. And though it be in some, that they have again acquired in respect of the soul God's essentiality (viz. Christ's body), yet the corrupt earthly Adam has covered up the holy and pure mystery, so that the great secret has remained hidden to reason. For God dwells not in this world in the external Principle, but in the inner Principle. Certainly he dwells in the place of this world, but this world apprehends him not. How in fact should the earthly man apprehend the mysteries of God? And if a man should apprehend them, he would

apprehend them according to the inner man, who is born again of God.

12. But seeing the divine Mystery will henceforth uncover itself entirely, and is thus presented comprehensibly to man, so that he comprehends the secret quite clearly, there is need to reflect well on what that signifies,-nothing else than the harvest of this world. For the beginning has found the end, and the middle is put into separation. Let this be told you, ye children, who would inherit the kingdom of God: It is a time of great seriousness; the floor must be purged; evil and good must be separated; the day dawns; this is highly recognized!

13. If we will speak of man, rightly understand him, and understand from what he has been made, we must consider the Deity with the Being of all beings, for man was created in the likeness of God from all the three Principles, a complete image and likeness as regards every sphere of existence. He was not to be only an image of this world, for the image of this world is animal, and for the sake of no animal image has God become man. Nor did God create man to live thus in the animal property, as we now live after the fall, but He created him in Paradise, unto the eternal Life. Man had no such animal flesh, but heavenly flesh; but at. the fall it became earthly and animal. We are not to understand, however, that he had nothing of this world in him. He had the kingdom and dominion of this world in him, but the four elements ruled not in him, but they were included in one, and the earthly kingdom lay hidden in him. He was to live in the heavenly quality; and though all was awake in him, yet he was to rule with the heavenly quality of the second Principle over the earthly quality, and the kingdom and quality of the stars and elements was to be subject to the paradisaic quality. No heat nor frost, no sickness nor mishap, nor any fear, was to touch him or terrify him. His body could pass through earth and stones without any breaking of them or itself. For that would be no eternal man whom terreity could control, who would be fragile.

14. Therefore we must consider man aright. It is not a matter of sophisticating or imagining, but of knowing and understanding in

the spirit of God. It is said: Ye must be new-born, if ye will see again the kingdom of God, out of which ye are gone. Art will not avail, but the spirit of God, which opens the door of heaven to the image of man, that he may see with three eyes. For man lives in a threefold life if he be God's child; if not, he lives only in a twofold. And it is sufficiently known to us, that Adam has with the right holy image, which was the likeness according to the Holy Trinity, gone out from the Divine Being and imaginated into earthliness, and introduced the earthly kingdom into the divine image, which has corrupted and darkened it; hence we then lost also our paradisaic seeing. Further, God has withdrawn Paradise from us, whereby we have become feeble, weak and powerless; and at once the four elements and the stars became powerful in us, so that with Adam we have fallen under their influence. And this also was the cause of the woman, that God divided Adam when he could not stand firm, and brought him into two tinctures which are in accordance with fire and water, one giving soul and the other spirit. After the fall man became an animal entity, who has to propagate himself by an animal property, since Heaven, Paradise and the Deity have become a mystery to him; though however what is eternal in man has remained, viz. the noble soul, but covered with an earthly garment, darkened and infected with earthly quality, and poisoned by false imagination, so that it was no longer recognized as God's child; and on account thereof God became man, that he might release the soul from the dark earthliness and introduce it again into the heavenly essentiality, into Christ's flesh and blood which fills the heavens.

CHAPTER III

THE GATE OF THE CREATION OF MAN

1. THOUGH we have explained this almost sufficiently in the other books, as everyone has them not at hand, it is necessary to give a short summary description of the creation of man, in order that the incarnation of Christ may afterwards be better understood. Also because of the pearls which in the course of his seeking fall more and more to man, are imparted and disclosed to him. And it affords me a special joy to recreate myself thus with God.

2. The creation of man has been carried out in all the three Principles, that is, in the Father's eternal nature and property, in the Son's eternal nature and property, and in this world's nature and property. There was breathed into man, whom the verbum fiat created, the threefold spirit for his life, from three principles and sources. By a triple fiat was he created, understand what is corporeal and essential; and the will of the heart of God introduced into him the spirit according to all the three Principles. Understand this as follows

3. Man was created entirely in the likeness of God. God manifested himself in humanity in an image which was to be as himself. For God is all, and all has arisen from him; and because all is not good, all, therefore, is not called God. For, as regards the pure Deity, God is a light-flaming spirit, and dwells in nothing but in himself only; there is nothing like unto him. But as regards the property of fire, wherefrom light is generated, we know the property of fire to be nature, which is a cause of life, movement and spirit, else there were no spirit, no light, nor any being, but an eternal stillness; neither colours nor virtues, but only a groundlessness without being.

4. And though the light of Majesty dwells in the unground (groundlessness) and is not laid hold of by the fiery nature and property, we are to consider the fire and light withal in the following way The fire has and makes a terrible and consuming

source. Now, there is in the source a sinking down, like a dying, or freely giving itself up. And this free surrendering falls into freedom out of the source, as into death, and yet there is no death; but it descends thus a degree deeper into itself and is delivered from the torment of the fire's anguish, and yet holds in keeping the sharpness of the fire,-not indeed in anguish, but in freedom.

5. And now the freedom and unground is a life, and becomes in itself a light; for the freedom receives the flash of the anguishful source and becomes desirous of substantiality, and the desire makes itself pregnant with substantiality from out of the freedom and gentleness. For that which sinks down or turns away from the source of anguish, rejoices that it is free from the anguish and draws the joy into itself, and passes with its will out of itself, and this the life and spirit of joy. To express which we should require an angelic tongue. But in this connection we will give to the reader that loveth God a short intimation to reflect upon, in order to understand the heavenly substantiality.

6. For in God all is power, spirit and life; but what is substance is not spirit. That which sinks down from fire, as in powerlessness, that is substance. For spirit stands in fire, but separates into two sources, namely one in fire, and one in the sinking down into freedom in the light. The latter is called God, for it is gentle and lovely, and has within it the kingdom of joy. And the angelic world is understood in the delapsing freedom of the substantiality.

7. And because we were gone out from the freedom of the angelic world into the dark source, with fire as its abyss, there was no remedy for us unless the power and Word of the light, as a Word of the divine Life, became a man, and brought us out of the darkness through the torment of fire, through the death in fire, again into the freedom of the divine Life, into the divine essentiality. Therefore Christ had to die, and with the soul's spirit pass through the fire of the eternal Nature, that is, through the hell and wrath of the eternal Nature, into the divine essentiality, and make our soul a way through death and wrath, in which path we might with him and in him enter through death into the eternal divine Life.

8. But regarding the divine essentiality, that is, regarding the divine corporeity, we are to understand as follows: The light gives gentleness as a love; now the fire's anguish desires gentleness that it may allay its great thirst; for the fire is desiring and the gentleness is giving, for it gives itself. Thus in the desire of the gentleness being is produced, as a substantial essentiality which has escaped from the fierceness, which freely gives its own life: such is corporeity. For through the power in the gentleness it becomes substantial, and is attracted and retained by the sourness, viz. by the eternal fiat. And it is therefore called substantiality or corporeity because it is fallen down to the fire-source and spirit, and is relatively to spirit as dumb, dead or powerless, although it is an essential life.

9. You must understand us aright. When God created the angels, two Principles only were manifest and in being, viz. the existence in fire and light, to wit, as involving the fierce essentiality in the severe, sour fiat, along with the forms of the fiery nature, and, secondly, as involving the heavenly essentiality from the holy power along with the water-fountain of gentleness of the life of joy, in which, as in love and gentleness, the divine sulphur was generated; its fiat was God's desiring will.

10. From this divine Essence, as from God's nature, the angels as creatures were created. Their spirit or source of life stands in fire; for without fire no spirit exists. But it passed out of the fire into the light; there it received the source of love. And the fire was only a cause of its life; but the fire's fierceness was extinguished by the love in the light.

11. Lucifer despised this, and remained a spirit of fire. Thus, he elevated himself and kindled in his locus the essentiality, from which earth and stones were produced; and he was cast out. Here commenced the third corporeity and the third Principle, along with the kingdom of this world.

12. As the devil was cast out of the third Principle into the darkness, God created another image in his likeness for this region. But if it was to be God's likeness according to all the three Principles, it had to be taken from all three, and from every entity

of this region, so far as the fiat had at the creation put itself forth in the ether in connection with Lucifer's princely throne. For man came in Lucifer's place; and hence the great envy of the devils, that they

beteem not man that honour, but lead him continually by the evil corrupt way, in order that they may augment their kingdom. And they do this in defiance of gentleness or God's love. Further, they suppose, because they live in the fierceness of the strong might, they are higher than God's Spirit, which consists in love and gentleness.

13. Thus the Will-spirit of God or the holy Spirit has disposed the twofold fiat into two principles, namely, the inner in the angelic world and the external in this outer world, and has created man (Mesch or Mensch) as a mixed person. For he was to be an image of the outer and inner world, and was to rule by the inner quality over the outer in this way he would have been God's likeness; for the outer nature was suspended to the inner. Paradise budded forth through the earth, and man was in this world, on earth, in Paradise. Paradisaic fruit also grew for him till the fall. When the Lord cursed the earth, Paradise passed into mystery, and became for man a mystery or secret; although if he be born again of God, he dwells by the inner man in Paradise, but by the outer man in this world.

14. And we are further to consider the coming and origin of man. God created his body from the matrix of the earth, from which the earth was created. All was mixed up, and yet was divided into three Principles coextensive with three kinds of essence, and nevertheless that in the fierce wrath was not known. If Adam had but remained in innocency, he would have lived all the time of this world in two Principles only, and would have ruled by one over all; the fierce wrathful kingdom would never have been known or manifest in him, although he had in himself this kingdom.

15. Adam's body was created by the inner fiat from the inner element, wherein lies the inner firmament and heaven with the heavenly essences; and, secondly, it was created by the outer fiat

from the four elements of the external nature and from the stars. For in the matrix of the earth this was mixed up. Paradise was therein, and the body moreover was created for Paradise. It had divine and also earthly essentiality in itself; but the earthly was as it were swallowed up in the divine or powerless. The substance or matter from which the body was made or created was a mass, or a water and fire with the essence of both Principles; although the first was also contained in it, but was not active. Each Principle was to remain in its seat and not mix with the others, just as is the case in God: in this way man would have been a complete likeness of the being of God.

Of the insufflation of soul and spirit

16. The body is a likeness according to the substantiality of God, and the soul and spirit is a likeness according to the Holy Trinity. God gave to the body his substantiality from the three Principles, and spirit and soul from the fountain of the threefold Spirit of the omnipresent Deity. And we are to understand that the soul with its image and its outward spirit has come from three principles, and. has been inbreathed and introduced into the body, as Moses attests: God breathed into man's nostrils the breath of life, and man became a living soul (Gen. ii. 7).
17. Now the breath and spirit of God includes three kinds of sources. In the first Principle it is a fire-breath or spirit, which is the true cause of life and stands in the Father's quality, as in the centre of the fiery nature. In the second Principle God's breath or spirit is the light-flaming love-spirit, the true spirit of the very Godhead, which spirit is called God the Holy Spirit. In the third Principle, as in the similitude of God, God's breath is the air-spirit, upon which the Holy Spirit sweeps along, as David says: The Lord walketh upon the wings of the wind (Ps. civ. 3); and Moses says: The Spirit of God moved upon the face of the waters, upon the gulf where the air [spiritus mundi] arises (Gen. i. 2).
18. This threefold spirit has the total God inbreathed and introduced into the created image from all the three Principles.

First, the fire-spirit, which He introduced into man from within, not by the nostrils, but into the heart, into the twofold tincture of the inner and outer blood, although the outer was not known, but was mystery. The inner, however, was in evidence and had two tinctures, one derived from fire and the other from light. This fire-spirit is the true essential soul, for it has the centrum naturae with its four forms as its fire-power. It kindles itself the fire, and makes itself the wheel of the essences.

19. It is not indeed the true image according to the Deity, but a magical everlasting fire, which has never had any beginning, neither will it have any end. Understand that God has introduced the eternal unoriginated fire (which from eternity has existed in itself, in the eternal Magia, viz. in the will of God, in the desire of the eternal Nature, as an eternal parturient centre); for this image was to be a likeness according to Him.

20. Secondly, at the same time as the soul's essential fire the Holy Spirit introduced the light-
flaming love-spirit out of itself into man, moreover in the second Principle only, wherein the Deity is understood; not at the nostrils, but as fire and light are suspended to one another and are one, although in two sources. Thus the good love-spirit was introduced into his heart with the essential fire-spirit, and each source brought with it its own tincture as a special life of its own. And in the love-tincture is understood the true spirit, which is the image of God, a likeness according to the clear true Deity, and resembles the whole man, likewise fills the whole man, but in its Principle.

21. The soul is in and by itself an eye of fire or a mirror of fire, in which the Deity has manifested itself according to the first Principle, that is, according to nature; for it is a creature, yet not created into a likeness. But its image, which it generates out of its eye of fire into light, is the true creature, for the sake of which God became man and brought it again into the holy Ternary out of the wrath of the eternal Nature.

22. The soul and its image are certainly together one spirit; but the soul is a hungry fire and must have substance, else it becomes

a hungry dark abyss, as the devils are become such. The soul makes fire and life, and the gentleness of the image makes love and heavenly essentiality. Thus the soul's fire is attempered and filled with love; for the image has water from God's fountain, and it flows forth into life eternal; this water is love and gentleness, and it draws it out of the Majesty of God. As may be seen in a kindled fire, that the fire in itself has a fierce fervent quality, and the light a gentle gracious quality; and as in the deep of this world water is produced from light and air, so in like manner also here.

23. Thirdly, God had breathed into man's nostrils at the same time and at once the spirit of this world with the source of the stars and elements, that is, the air [spiritus mundi]. He was to be a ruler in the outer kingdom and open up the wonders of the outer world, to which end God created man also unto the outward life. But the outward spirit was not to encroach upon the image of God, nor was the image of God' to lodge within it the outward spirit and suffer that to rule over it, for its aliment was from God's Word and power. And the outer body had paradisaic food,-not taken into the worm-bag or carcass, for this appendage he had not. Further, he had neither masculine nor feminine form, for he was them both, and had both tinctures, viz. of soul and spirit, of fire and light, and was to produce another man from himself according to his likeness. He was a chaste virgin in pure love; he loved himself and made himself pregnant by imagination, and in such wise was his reproduction. He was a lord over the stars and elements, a likeness, according to God. As God dwells in the stars and elements, and nothing seizes Him, He rules over everything: so was man created. The earthly source was not fully active in him. He had indeed the air-spirit, but heat and cold were not to affect him, for God's essentiality penetrated all. As Paradise pressed and budded through the earth, so did the heavenly essentiality grow up in the external being of his body and outward spirit. What seems strange to us in the earthly life is assuredly possible in God.

24. Fourthly, by the introduction of his fair heavenly image into the Spirit of God, Adam received also the living Word of God,

and this was the nutriment of his soul and image. The same living Word was surrounded with the divine Virgin of wisdom; and the soul's image stood in the virgin image which in the Deity had been seen from eternity. The pure image of Adam came from the wisdom of God. For God willed to see and manifest himself thus in an image, and that was the likeness according to God's Spirit, according to the Triad, an image entirely chaste, like the angels of God. In this image Adam was the child of God,-not only a likeness, but a child, born of God, of the Being of all beings.

25. Thus it has been briefly stated what kind of image Adam was before his fall and how God has created him, in order to attain a better understanding why God's Word became man, how that has come to pass and what it has brought about.

CHAPTER IV

OF THE PARADISAIC SPHERE AND DOMINION, SHOWING HOW IT WOULD HAVE BEEN IF MAN HAD REMAINED IN INNOCENCY

1. THE devil has many objections whereby he seeks to excuse himself, saying that God has created him thus, although his primitive angelic form, his source and his image always convict him of being a liar. And so is he also to poor fallen man: he continually introduces into him the earthly kingdom with its power and faculty, that he may have a permanent mirror before him and also accuse God of having created him earthly and evil. But he leaves out of view what is best, namely Paradise, in which man was created, and also God's omnipotence, that man liveth not by bread only, but by the power and Word of God, and that Paradise has reigned with its source over earthliness. He shows man only his hard, miserable, fleshly, naked form; but the form in innocence, when Adam knew not that he was naked, he covers in order to deceive man.
2. Seeing then this is so much concealed to us poor children of Eve, and indeed the earthly wretch is not worthy of knowing it, and yet such knowledge is very necessary to our minds; it is highly needful for us to flee to the true janitor (who has the key to open), to supplicate him, and give ourselves up wholly to him, that he be willing to open to us the gate of Paradise in the inner centre of our image, so that the paradisiacal light may shine upon us in our minds and that we may thus become desirous to dwell again with our Immanuel according to the inner and new man in Paradise; for without this opening we should understand nothing of Paradise and of our primitive image in innocence.
3. But as Christ, the Son of God, has generated us again to the paradisaic form, we ought not to be so indolent as to rely upon art and earthly reason. We shall not find Paradise and Christ (who must become man in us, if we would see God) in our reason; there all is dead and blind. We must go out from reason and enter

into the incarnation of Christ; in this way we shall be taught of God. Then we shall have power to speak of God, Paradise and the Kingdom of Heaven. In the earthly reason, which comes only from the stars, we are fools before God if we try to speak of the Mystery in a heavenly manner, for we speak of a thing which we have never known or seen. But a child knows its mother. So likewise

everyone who is born again of God knows his mother, not with earthly eyes, but with divine eyes, and with the eyes of the mother of whom he is born. We give in all sincerity to the reader to reflect as to what he is to do, and from what spirit and understanding we will write.

4. The reason of the outer world insists on maintaining that God has created man unto, the outer dominion, unto the source of the stars and four elements. If that were, he would have been created unto anguish and death, for the astral heaven has its term; when it reaches that, it abandons the creature of which it was the leader. Then the dominion and being of the creature, who is subject to the outer heaven, passes away; and we see indeed how we decay and die when the outer heaven with the elements abandons us, so that even a child in the womb is already old enough to die, moreover often perishes while it is yet without life and in the fiat of the outer dominion, in the process of growth of body, before the centrum naturae kindles the fire of the soul. We undoubtedly know death and dying through the fall of Adam, that Adam (as soon as he became earthly) died to Paradise and became dead as to the kingdom of God; therefore we were in need of regeneration, otherwise we could not revive.

5. But because God did forbid Adam to touch the earthly fruit, which was mixed, and besides did create but one man, with masculine and feminine property, with the two tinctures, viz. of fire and light in love, and brought him at once into Paradise (yea, he was created in Paradise), we cannot admit the conclusions of Reason which, in consequence of the devil's infection, says that man has been created earthly. For whatever is created solely and alone from the earthly life or source is animal, has beginning and

end, and attains not eternity, for it issues not from thence. Now, that which issues not from the Eternal is transitory, and a mere mirror, in which the eternal wisdom has beheld itself as in a figure and likeness. There remains of it nothing but a shadow without life or being; it passes like a wind, which has risen and again subsides. For the sake of such a creature the Word of God did not become man; the Eternal has not entered into the perishable nature on account of what is transitory. Neither has it entered into what is earthly on the ground that it will raise and introduce the earthly and perishable into the power of Majesty; but for the sake of that which had arisen from the power of Majesty, but had become evil and earthly, and as it were eclipsed in death, that it might again quicken, awaken and raise it into the power of Majesty, into the abode in which it was, before it was a creature.

6. We must understand man differently than we have done hitherto in regarding him as an animal. He has indeed become animal, according to the property of this world; by dying in Adam, he lives thereafter to this world and not to God. But if he entered with the spirit of his will into God, the willspirit would obtain again the noble image and would live according to this image in God, and according to the animal property in this world. Thus he was in death and yet was alive. And so then the Word of God became man in order that it might unite him again to God, that he might be entirely born again in God, and that Paradise might become perceptible within him.

7. Thus, we are to consider the paradisaic image. We say and know that Adam was created good, pure and without blemish, as well as Lucifer with his hosts. He had pure eyes, and that doubly. For he had both kingdoms in himself, viz. God's kingdom and the kingdom of this world. As God is Lord of all, so also was man, in the power of God, to be lord of this world. As God has rule over everything and passes through everything, imperceptibly to the thing;

so was the hidden divine man able to pass into and see into all things. The external man was indeed in the external, but lord of the external; it was subject to him and restricted him not. He could without effort have broken rocks. The tincture of the earth was discernible to him; he would have found out all the marvels of the earth. For to this end Adam was created also unto the outward life, that he should manifest in figures and carry into works what had been seen in the eternal wisdom; for he had virgin Wisdom in him.

8. Gold, silver and the precious metals have indeed also, passing out of the heavenly magia, been shut up in this way by the enkindling. What we have here is something different from the earth. Man loves it well and employs it for his support, but he knows not its ground and origin. It is not for nothing that it is loved by the mind; it has a high origin, if we reflect on it. But we properly say nothing of it in this place, because without that man loves it too much, and thereby withdraws himself from the Spirit of God. One ought not to love the body more than the spirit, for the spirit is the life.

9. But know that it was given to man for his sport and ornament, he had -it by right of nature; it belonged to him, namely to the outer body, for the outer body with its tincture and the metalline tincture are near akin. But when the tincture of the outer body was corrupted by the evil desire of the devil, the metalline tincture also became concealed from the human tincture and was hostile to it; for it is purer than the corrupted tincture in the outer man.

10. And let this be plain to you, ye seekers of the metalline tincture: If you would find the lapis philosophorum, set yourselves to attain the new birth in Christ, else it will be difficult for you to apprehend it. For it has considerable fellowship with the heavenly substantiality, which would be well seen if it were released from the fierce wrath. Its lustre indicates something which we should certainly recognize, if we had paradisaic eyes. The affective foundation (das Gemüth) shows us that indeed, but the understanding and full cognition are dead as to Paradise. And because we use what is noble to the dishonour of God and to our own perdition, and honour not God thereby, and enter not with our spirit into the Spirit of God, but abandon the spirit and

cleave to the substance, the metalline tincture has become a mystery to us, for we have become alienated from it.

11. Man was created to be a lord of the tincture, and it was subject to him; but he became its servant, and moreover alien to it. Thus, he seeks only for gold and finds earth. Because he abandoned the spirit and went with his spirit into substance, substance has taken him prisoner and shut him up in death. As the tincture of the earth is shut up in the wrath till the judgment of God, so also is the spirit of man shut up in the wrath, unless he go out and be born in God. For the devil wished to be sovereign prince with his wrath in the heavenly Essentiality; therefore it became closed to him and took the form of earth and stones, so that he is not a prince, but a prisoner in the wrath, and the Essentiality profits him nothing. For he is spirit and despised the heavenly Essentiality, and kindled the mother of nature, which forthwith made all corporeal; and this the Spirit of God brought together into an amassment. It could however be known to man. He had power to disclose the tincture and bring forth the noble pearl for his sport and joy, as well as to the honour and mirificence of God, if he had remained in innocency.

1 Bury in his translation, in a note on the word Gemilth, says: ' St-Martin n'a rien trouve de mieux pour le rendre en français que I'expression base affective. C'est en effet la base, le centre d'ou emanent nos pensees, et, dans l'ordre inferieur de notre etre, la base de nos inclinations; en elle aussi se produisent les sensations morales et s'opbre la regeneration.'

12. As regards man's eating and drinking, by which he was to furnish substance and aliment to his fire, it was thus: He had two kinds of fire in himself, the soul's fire and the outer fire of the sun and stars. Now, every fire must have sulphur or substance, else it does not subsist, that is, it burns not. We have sufficient of this to understand the divine nature which would have been man's food. For, as stated above,, the soul's fire is fed with God's love, gentleness and essentiality, with all that the Word as the divine centre brings forth. For the soul comes from the eternal magical fire; it must have also magical food, that is, by the imagination. If

it has God's image, it imaginates into God's love, into the divine essentiality, and eats of God's food, of the food of the angels. But if not, then it eats of that into which its imagination enters, viz. of the earthly or hellish source. And into this matrix it also falls, not with itself as a substance, but it is filled with such, and the same begins to operate in it like a poison does in the flesh.

13. We know also sufficiently the alimentation of the outer body. The outer man indeed was; yet he was as it were half swallowed up by the inner man. The inner ruled through and through, like fire in glowing iron, and each life took its food from its property. The image of God, or the soul's spirit, ate of the heavenly divine essentiality, and the outer body ate paradisaic fruit in the mouth and not in the belly. For as the outer body was as it were half swallowed up in the inner, so in like manner was the fruit of Paradise. The divine essence budded through the earthly essence, and had as it were half swallowed up the earthly essence in the paradisaic fruit, so that the fruit was not known to be earthly. And therefore this was called Paradise, as a budding through the wrath, since the love of God budded in the wrath and bore fruit.

14. And we are to understand further how God dwells in this world, and the world is as it were swallowed up in Him. It is in Him unpowerful and He himself all-powerful. So was man, and so did he eat: his earthly eating was heavenly. Just as we know that we must be born again, so was the paradisaic fruit born from the wrath again in heavenly essence; or as we see that from the bitter earth grows a good sweet herb, which the sun qualifies in a different manner than the earth has qualified it. In such a way did the holy man qualify the paradisaic fruit in his mouth, so that the earthliness was swallowed up as a nothing, and touched not man; or as we know that in the end the earth will be swallowed up, and no longer be a palpable body.

15. Thus was even man's external eating. He ate the fruit with his mouth, and required no teeth to do that, for at this point appeared the separation of power. There were two centres of power in Adam's mouth, each of them took its due. What was earthly became transformed into heavenly quality, as we, know

that we shall in our body be changed, and be made a body of heavenly power. So likewise was the transmutation in the mouth; and the body received the power, for the kingdom of God stands in power. And hence man stood in the kingdom of God, for he was immortal and a child of God. But if he should have brought his eating into the intestines and had such a stench in the belly as we have now, I will ask Reason whether that can be Paradise, and whether God's Spirit can dwell in that; inasmuch as the Spirit of God was to dwell in Adam as in the creature of God.

16. His work in Paradise, on the earth, was childlike, but with celestial wisdom. He might plant trees and herbs, all at his pleasure. There grew for him in all paradisaic fruit, and all was pure to him. He did what he pleased, and he did aright. He had no law but that of imagination or desire; these he was to place with his spirit in God; then he would' have remained thus eternally. And even though God had changed the earth, yet man would have remained without want or death; all would have been transformed for him into heavenly essence.

17. In like manner with regard to his drinking. The inner man drank the water of eternal life from God's nature, and the outer man drank water on the earth. But as the sun and the air absorb water and yet are not filled therewith, so it was in the mouth of man: such absorption separated into mystery. All that was earthly had by man's mouth to enter again into that which it was before the creation of the world. The spirit and virtue thereof pertain to man, and not an earthly body; for God created for him once for all a body, which was eternal. He needed not another creative act. He was a princely throne (understand Adam), made out of heaven, earth, stars and elements, as well as out of God's essence, a lord of the world and a child of God.

18. Observe it, ye Philosophers i It is the true ground and highly known. Mix no verbiage of the schools with it, it is clear enough. Opinion will not do; but the true spirit, born of God, knows it aright. All opinion without knowledge is a terrestrial fool, understanding earth and four elements; but the Spirit of God understands but one element, wherein four lie hidden. Not four

were to rule in Adam, but one over four; the heavenly element over the four elements of this world. Accordingly we must rebegin to be if we would possess Paradise; and on that account God became man.

19. Let it be told you, ye academic disputers: you walk round the circle and enter not, like a cat, which fears the heat, walks round the hot broth; thus are ye afraid and ashamed before the fire of God. And as little as the cat enjoys the broth by smelling only round the rim, so little also does man enjoy the paradisaic fruit, unless he go out from Adam's skin, which the devil has soiled, and enter into the new birth of Christ. He must enter into the circle, and cast off the skin of reason; then he obtains human understanding and divine knowledge; no learning will avail, but only being born.

CHAPTER V

OF THE LAMENTABLE AND MISERABLE FALL OF MAN

1. IF we are to describe clearly the incarnation of Jesus Christ, it will be necessary to expound to you the causes for which God has become man. It is not a small thing or a nothing as the Jews and Turks regard it, and even with the Christians is half meaningless; it cannot but be a very considerable cause, for which the immutable God put himself in motion. Mark then this, we will expound to you the causes.

2. Adam was a man, and an image of God, a complete likeness according to God, although God is no image. He is the kingdom and the power, also the glory and eternity, all in all. But the ungrounded deep desired to manifest itself in similitudes; and indeed such a manifestation has taken place from eternity in the wisdom of God, as in a virgin figure, which however was not a genetrix, but a mirror of the Deity and eternity as present in the ground and unground, an eye of the glory of God. And according to the same eye and in it were created the thrones of princes as angels, and lastly man, who had again the throne in himself; just as he had been created from the eternal magia, from God's Essence, from nothing into something, from spirit into body. And as the eternal magia had generated him out of itself, in the eye of the wonders and wisdom of God, so likewise he could and was to bring forth out of himself another man in a magical way, without dilaceration of his body; for he was conceived in God's longing, and had been generated and brought to light by the desiring of God. And consequently he had the same longing in himself for his own gravidation. For the tincture of Venus is the matrix, and it becomes pregnant with substance, as with sulphur in the fire, which yet attains to substance in, the water of Venus. The tincture of fire gives soul, and the tincture of light gives spirit, and water or substance gives body, and Mercury or the centrum naturae gives the wheel of the essences and the great life in fire

and water, heavenly and earthly; and Salt, heavenly and earthly, maintains this in being, for it (Salt) is the fiat.

3. For as man has in himself the external constellation, which is his wheel of essences of the outer world and the cause of the affective foundation (Gemuth); so also he has the internal constellation, of the centre of the fiery essences, and, in the second Principle, that of the light-flaming Divine essences. He had the whole magia of the Being of all beings in himself. The possibility was in him: he was able to beget in a magical way, for he loved himself, and in turn from out of his centre desired likeness. As he had been conceived from God's desiring, and brought to light by the genetrix in the fiat, so likewise was he to bring to light his angelic or human host.

4. But whether all were to be generated from one, i.e. from the princely throne, or one from another, it is not necessary to know, for the purpose is broken. It suffices us to know what we are and what our kingdom is. I find, however, in the deep, in the centre, that one was to arise from another; for the heavenly centre as well as the earthly has its minutes, which are always striking, since the wheel with the essences in all the three Principles is ever going, and discloses continually one wonder after another. Thus was constructed and composed the image of man in the wisdom of God, wherein lie innumerable wonders; these were to be opened up by the human host. And undoubtedly in the course of time a greater wonder would have been revealed in one than in another, all according to the wonderful variations of the heavenly and earthly begetting; as indeed is the case even to-day, so that more art and understanding of the wonders is found in one individual than in another. Therefore I conclude that one man was to have arisen and been born from another, in connection with the great wonders and for man's joy and delight, as each man would have brought forth the fellow of himself. Accordingly the human race would have remained in process of birth till God had placed the third Principle of this world in its ether again, for it is a globe with beginning and end. When the beginning reaches the end, so that the last comes into the first, all is finished and complete.

Then will the middle be repurified and enter again into that which it was before the times of this world, except the wonders which persist in God's wisdom, in the great magia, as a shadow of this world.

5. Seeing then Adam was such a glorious image, and moreover, in the place of Lucifer who had been cast out, the devil grudged him this position, was violently envious of him, and set his mark and craving continually before Adam, slipped with his craving into the earthliness of the fruit, and made Adam believe that great glory resided in his enkindled earthliness. Albeit Adam knew him not; for he did not come in his own form, but in that of the serpent, as in the form of an artful beast; he practised apish tricks like a fowler, who beguiles birds and catches them. He had moreover with his itch of pride infected and half killed the earthly kingdom, by which it became so thoroughly tainted and vain, though it would gladly have been delivered from vanity. And as it felt that Adam was a child of God and possessed glory and power, it longed vehemently after him. The enkindled wrath of God also longed after Adam, in order to delectate itself in this living image.

6. Thus all drew Adam and desired to have him. The kingdom of heaven desired to have him, for he was created for it. In like manner the earthly kingdom desired to have him, for it had a part in him; it wanted to be his master, because he was but a creature. So likewise the fierce wrath opened wide its jaws, and wished to be creaturely and essential, in order to satisfy its great and fierce hunger. Adam, then, was tried forty days, as long as Christ was tempted in the wilderness, and Israel at mount Sinai, when God gave them the law, to see whether it were possible that this people could stand firm in the qualification of the Father, in the law, before God; whether man could remain in obedience, in such a sense that he would place his imagination in God, so that God would not need to become man: on which account God did such wonders in Egypt, that man should see that there is a God, and should love and fear Him. But the devil was a liar and deceiver, Israel was led away by him, so that they made a calf and worshipped it as God. It was thus not possible now to stand firm.

Moses therefore came down from the mount with the tables upon which the law was written, and brake them, and slew the calf-worshippers. So then Moses was not to bring the people into the promised land; this might not be. Joshua had to do it and ultimately Jesus, who in the temptation stood firm before the devil and the wrath of God, who overcame the anger and broke death to pieces, as Moses did the tables of the law. The first Adam then could not stand firm, though the kingdom of God was before his eyes and he was in Paradise. God's wrath was much enkindled, and drew Adam; for it was much enkindled in the earth by the devil's imagination and strong will.

7. Reason says: Had then the devil such power? Yes, dear man, and man has it too; he can overturn mountains, if he enter strongly with his imagination. The devil has issued from the great magia of God and was a prince or king of this throne. He entered into the strongest might of fire, with the intention to be lord over all the host of heaven. Thus the magia became enkindled and the great turba generated, which struggled with Adam to see if he would be strong enough to possess the devil's kingdom and rule there in another source. Adam's spirit of reason, it is true, did not understand this; but the magical essences, from whence desire and will arise, contended one against another, till Adam began to imaginate after earthliness and wished to have earthly fruit. So it was done. For his noble image, which was to eat only of the Word of God, became infected and obscured: the earthly tree of temptation grew up at once, for Adam's lust had desired and permitted this. He had to be tempted, to see if he could stand firm. Then came the severe command from God, and said to Adam: Thou shalt eat of every tree in Paradise, but of the tree of knowledge of good and evil shalt thou not eat, for in the day that thou eatest thereof thou shalt die the death, that is to say, die to the kingdom of heaven and become earthly (Gen. ii. 16, 17). Adam knew the command well, ate not thereof, but he imaginated thereinto and was taken prisoner in his imagination, and wholly without vigour, feeble and weak, he was vanquished; then he dropped down into sleep.

8. Thus he fell to the magia and his glory was lost. For sleep indicates death and a subjugation. The earthly kingdom had subjugated him, it wished to rule over him. The sidereal kingdom desired to have Adam and accomplish its wonders by him, for no other creature had been so highly elevated as man, who was able to attain the sidereal kingdom. Therefore Adam was drawn and duly tempted, to try whether he could be a lord and king of the stars and elements. The devil was at work and thought also to overthrow man and bring him into his power, in order that this throne might remain finally his kingdom; for he knew well that if man would go out from God's will, he would become earthly. He also knew well that the abyss of hell lay in the earthly kingdom; therefore he was now so busy. For if Adam had brought forth magically, Paradise would have remained on earth. That did not suit the devil, he liked not that, he had no fancy for it in his kingdom; for it smelt not of brimstone and fire, but of love and sweetness. Then the devil thought: Thou wilt not eat this herb, for thou wouldst cease to be a lord in fire.

9. Thus the fall of Adam lay entirely in the earthly essence. He lost the heavenly essence, from which springs Divine love, and acquired earthly essence, from which springs anger, malice, poison, disease and misery; and also lost the heavenly eyes. Further, he could no longer eat in the paradisaic way, but imaginated after the forbidden fruit, in which evil and good are mixed, as are still in the present day all the fruits on earth. And hence the four elements became active and effectually operative in him, for his will by imagination took in the earthly kingdom to lodge in the soul's fire. Thus he went out from God's Spirit into the spirit of the stars and elements; these received him and rejoiced in him, for they came to be living and powerful in him. Previously they were compelled to be submissive and in constraint; now they obtained the dominion.

10. Whereupon the devil will have laughed and mocked at God; but he knew not what was behind; he knew as yet nothing of the serpent-bruiser, who was to take away his throne and destroy his kingdom. And so Adam sank down into sleep, into the magia, for

God saw that he could not stand firm. Therefore he said: It is not good that man should be alone. We will make him an help, to bear him company (Gen. ii. 18), through whom he may raise up offspring and propagate himself. For he saw the fall and came to his aid in another way, as he did not wish that his image should perish.

11. Reason says: Why did God let the tree grow, by which Adam was tempted? It must thus have been His will that Adam was tempted. Reason will, then, refer also the fall to God's will, and thinks that God willed that Adam should fall. God, according to it, willed to have a certain number of individuals in heaven and a certain number in hell, else he would have prevented the evil and have preserved Adam, so that he would have remained good and in Paradise. Thus the present world judges. For, it says, if God had made nothing that was bad, there would be nothing bad, since all comes from him, and he alone is the creator, who has made all. Accordingly, he has made what is bad and what is good, else this could not be so. Reason insists on maintaining this position absolutely. It thinks also that if there had been nothing with which the devil and also man had been captivated, and come to be evil, the devil would have remained an angel and man in Paradise.

12. Answer: Yes, dear Reason, now you have hit the mark; you cannot, then, fail of success if you are not blind. Hearken: why sayest thou not to the light, wherefore sufferest thou the fire? how delightful thou wouldst be, if thou didst not dwell in the fire. I would set up my tent with thee, but thou dwellest in the fire; I cannot. Do but say to the light: go out from the fire, then thou wilt be excellent and delightful. And if the light obey you, you will find a great treasure. How you will rejoice if you can dwell in the light, so that the fire does not burn you. Thus far goes Reason.

13. But see aright with magical eyes, understand with divine and also with natural eyes, then shall it be shown to you, if you are not quite blind and dead. Behold, I give you this to understand by similitude, seeing that Reason is a fool and understands nothing of the Spirit of God. I suppose, then, that I have the power to

take away the light from the fire (which however cannot be) and see what would follow upon it. Consider! If I take away the light from the fire, (1) the light loses its essence, by which it shines; (2) it loses its life and becomes a powerlessness; (3) it is seized and overcome by the darkness, extinguished in itself and becomes a nothingness, for it is the eternal freedom and a groundlessness; while it shines, it is good, and when it is extinguished, it is nothing.

14. Consider further! What have I remaining of the fire if I take away the light and lustre from it? Nothing but a dry hunger and a darkness. It loses essence and life, is anhungered and becomes likewise a nothingness. Its former sulphur is a death; it consumes itself as long as the essence exists. When the essence is no more, there is a nothingness or

groundlessness, where no vestige remains.

15. And so, dear seeking soul, meditate thereon thus: God is the eternal light, and his power and source dwell in the light. The light produces gentleness, and from the gentleness being is produced; this being is God's being, and the source of the light is the Spirit of God, which is the origin. There is no other God than this very God. In the light is the power, and the power is the kingdom. But now the light and the power have only a love-will, which desires nothing bad; it desires indeed being, but from its own essence, understand from love and sweetness, for that is like the light. But now the light arises from fire, and without the fire it would be nothing, it would have no essence without fire. Fire causes life and movement and is nature, but has a different will from the light. For it is a rage or greed, and desires only to consume. It takes only, and mounts in pride; whereas the light takes not, but gives, so that the fire is preserved. The source of fire is fierceness, its essences are bitter, its sting is hostile and disagreeable. It is an enmity in itself, it consumes itself; and if the light comes not to its aid, it devours itself, so that it becomes a nothing.

16. Therefore, dear seeking soul, consider this, and thou wilt soon attain to peace and to the goal. God is from eternity the

power and the light, and is called God according to the light and according to the power of the light, according to the spirit of light and not according to the spirit of fire. For the spirit of fire is called his wrath, anger, and is not denominated God, but a consuming fire of the might of God. The fire is called nature and the light is not called nature; it has indeed the fire's property, but transmuted, from wrath into love, from devouring and consuming into bringing forth, from enmity and bitter woe into gentle beneficence, amiable desire and 'sempiternal fulness; for the love-desire draws the gentleness of the light into itself, and is a pregnant virgin, that is, pregnant with the understanding and wisdom of the power of the Deity.

17. Thus, we are able highly to recognize what is God and nature, the ground and the unground, and also the deep of eternity. We recognize, then, that the eternal fire is magical and is generated in the desiring will. If then the eternal and unfathomable is magical, that also is magical which is born from the eternal, for from desire all things have arisen. Heaven and earth are magical, likewise the mind with the senses; if we would but once know ourselves.

18. Now what can the light do if the fire lays hold of and swallows up something, when, however, the object laid hold of by the fire is also magical? If it has a life and the power and understanding of the light, why does it then run into the fire? The devil was an angel and Adam an image of God; they both had the fire and the light, moreover, the divine understanding in them. Why did the devil imaginate into the fire and Adam after the earth? They were free. The light and power of God drew not the devil into fire, but the wrath of nature. Why did his spirit consent? What Magic has made for itself, that it has had. The devil made for himself hell, and that he had. Adam made himself earthly, and that he is. God is not a creature nor a maker, but a Spirit and a Revealer. On creation taking place, the position may be considered and apprehended thus: Fire and light have at the same time awakened in desire, and have desired a mirror or image according to eternity; yet we find by real knowledge that

fierceness or the fire's nature is not a maker; it has made nothing substantial from itself, for that cannot possibly be; but it has made spirit and source. Now, no creature has its subsistence in essence only. If a creature is to exist, it must be by means of substance, as by power or sulphur, it must consist of spiritual salt; and then from the fire-source arises a mercury and a true essential life; it must besides have lustre, if intelligence and cognition are to be found within.

19. Thus, we know that every creature has its subsistence in spiritual sulphur, mercury and salt, but spirit alone does not accomplish this; there must be sulphur, wherein is the fiat, viz. the sour matrix for the centrum naturae, in which the spirit is upheld, that is, there must be substance. For where there is no substance, there is no shaping. A creaturely spirit is not a comprehensible being; it must draw substance into itself by its imagination, else it would not subsist.

20. If the devil drew fierceness into his spirit, and man earthliness, what could the love of the essentiality of God do to that? For the love and gentleness of God with the divine essence was presented and offered to the devil, as well as to man. Who shall accuse God? That the wrathful essence was too strong in the devil, so that it vanquished the loveessence: what can God do to that? If a good tree be planted, and yet perishes, what can the earth do? It imparts to it nevertheless sap and energy. Why does the tree not draw them to itself? Thou wilt say: Its essences are too feeble. But what can the earth do, or even he who planted the tree? His will is only that he wishes to raise for his pleasure a good tree, and thinks to enjoy its fruit. If he knew that the tree would perish, he would never plant it.

21. We are then to recognize that the angels were created, not as a tree that is planted, but from the motion of God, from both principles, viz. light and darkness, in which darkness fire lay hidden. Fire burned not at creation and in the motion, as it burns not at this day, for it has its own principle. Why did Lucifer awaken it? The will arose from his creaturely being, and not outside of him. He wished to be a lord over fire and light; he

wished to extinguish the light, and despised gentleness; he wished to be a fire-lord. Seeing then he despised the light and his birth in gentleness, he was justly cast out. Thus he lost fire and light, and has to dwell in the abyss in darkness. If he will have fire, he must kindle it for himself, and inflame it with his malice in the imagination. Yet such fire does not properly burn for him, but only in the fierce essential source, according as the four forms in the centrum naturae furnish it in themselves. The first form is sour, hard, rough and cold; the second form in the centre is bitter, stinging, hostile; the third form is anxiety, pain and torment; and with the anxiety, as in movement and life, he [Lucifer] strikes fire in, the hard sourness, between the hardness and bitter sting, so that it shines forth like a flash of lightning, which is the fourth form. And if there be no gentleness or essence of gentleness, it gives no light, but only a flash; for the anguish will have freedom, but is too sharp, and attains it only as a flash, that is to say, fire, yet possesses no stability or foundation. Hence the devil must dwell in darkness, and has only the fiery flash in himself; moreover the whole figure of his dwelling is like a fiery flash, as if there were thunder pealing: thus does the hellish proprium present itself in the source.

22. In like manner we are to understand regarding the tree of temptation which Adam awakened by his imagination: he desired, and the matrix naturae presented to him what he desired. God forbad him to touch it; but the earthly matrix would have Adam, for it recognized in him the divine power. Because it had become earthly by the devil's enkindling, although not quite dead, it longed after that which it was before, viz. after Freedom, to be delivered from vanity; and in Adam was freedom.

23. Accordingly it drew Adam, so that he began to imaginate; and thus Adam lusted against God's command and will, as Paul says: The flesh lusts against the spirit, and the spirit against the flesh (Gal. v. 17). Adam's flesh was half heavenly and half earthly, and thus Adam's spirit had also brought by imagination a power into the earth, and so the matrix naturae gave him what he wished. He had to be tempted, to see whether he would stand steadfast as an

angel in the place of Lucifer. Therefore God created him not merely as an angel, so that, if he should fall and not remain firm, He might help him, that he might not perish in the fierce wrath like Lucifer. On this account Adam was created from

matter, and his spirit was introduced into matter, viz. into a sulphur of water and fire, that God might be able to ingenerate in him a new life again: as a fair sweet-smelling flower grows from the earth. Hence also the purpose of God, because He knew that Adam would not stand. Therefore Paul also says: We are foreordained in Christ Jesus before says
the foundation of the world; that is, when Lucifer fell, the foundation of the world was not yet laid, and yet man was already seen in the wisdom of God. If, however, he was to be created from the three Principles, there was already danger, on account of the enkindled sulphur of the materials. And though he was created above the earth, yet the sulphur was extracted from out of the matrix of the earth, as a fair blossom out of the earth, and danger already existed. And here the sweet name Jesus has formatively introduced itself as a saviour and regenerator; for man is the greatest mystery that God has produced. He has the figure in which it is shown how the Divine Nature has from eternity progenerated itself out of the fierceness, out of fire, by sinking down, by dying, into another principle of another source. So also is he rebegotten out of death, and grows up out of death in another principle of another source and power, where he is wholly freed from earthliness.

24. And it is very beneficial to us that we have as regards the earthly part fallen to the share of the earth, if at the same time, however, we obtain the divine part. For thus we are made quite pure, and come again into God's kingdom wholly perfect, apart from any craving of the devil. We are a much greater mystery than the angels. We shall also surpass them in heavenly essence. For they are flames of fire, illustrate with the light; but we attain the great

fountain of gentleness and love which springs in God's holy Essence.

25. Therefore they deal falsely and wrongly who say, that God willeth not to have all men in heaven. He willeth that all should be saved; it is the fault of man himself, in that he will not suffer himself to be saved. And though many a one be of evil tendency, this is not from God, but from the matrix naturae. Wouldest thou accuse God? Thou liest; God's Spirit withdraws itself from no one. Cast thy wickedness away, and enter into gentleness, into truth, into love, and give thyself up to God; then thou wilt be saved; for Jesus is therefore born, because he willeth to save. Thou sayest: I am held, so that I cannot. Yes forsooth! thou dost will to have it so; likewise did the devil will to have it. If thou art a Knight, why fightest thou not against evil? But if thou fightest against the good, thou art an enemy of God. Dost thou suppose that God will put an angelic crown upon the devil? If thou art an enemy, thou art not a friend. If thou wilt be a friend, abandon enmity and go to the Father, then thou art a son. Wherefore whoever accuses God is a liar and murderer like the devil. Thou art in fact thine own maker, why dost thou make thyself bad? Even though thou be a bad kind of material, God hath given thee his heart and spirit. Use these gifts for the making of thyself, and thou wilt make thyself good. But if thou usest covetousness and pride, and also the pleasure of the earthly life, what can God do to that? Shall God moreover seat himself in thy contemptible pride? No, that is not his source. But thou wilt say: I am an evil source, and cannot, I am held. Well now, let the evil source alone, and enter with thy will-spirit into the love-spirit of God, give thyself up to his mercy; thou shalt certainly be delivered one day from the evil source. The evil source is born of the earth. When the earth receives the body, it can take to itself the badness belonging to it; but thou art and remainest a spirit in the will of God, in his love. Let the evil Adam die; a new and good one will bud forth to thee from the old, as a fair flower grows forth out of stinking dung. Only have a care to maintain the spirit in God. There need be no great concern for the evil body, which is full of

evil effects. If it be wickedly inclined, do it so much the less good; give it not occasion to exercise lewdness. To keep it in restraint is a good remedy; but to be high with drink and full of high feeding is to cast the evil ass up to the neck into the mire, whereas it befouls itself sufficiently in the mud, like a swine. To be sober, to lead a temperate life, is an excellent purgative for the evil ass; not to give it what it longs for, to let it fast often, so that it does not hinder prayer, is beneficial to it. It refuses indeed; but the Understanding must be lord and master, for it bears God's image.

26. This in truth is not relished by the world of Reason in the sphere of carnal pleasure. But because it relishes it not, and instead thereof draws in and drinks up naught but evil earthly sensuality, the wrath stirs within it, constantly makes it pass with Adam out of Paradise, and with Lucifer into the abyss. There thou wilt eat and drink thy fill of what in this present life thou hast voluntarily drawn into thee. But God thou shouldest not accuse; otherwise thou art a liar and an enemy of truth. God willeth not any evil, nor is there any evil thought in him. He hath but one source, that is, love and joy; but his fierce wrath, viz. nature, hath many sources. Therefore let everyone take heed what he doeth. Every man is his own God and also his own devil: the source to which he inclines and to which he gives himself up, impels and guides him: he becomes its workman.

27. It is a great misery that man is so blind that he cannot recognize what God is, though he lives in God. There are men again who forbid this, saying that inquiry should not be made as to what God is, and would at the same time be regarded as teachers from God. Such are indeed teachers from the devil, that he and his kingdom of hypocritical falseness may not be revealed and known.

CHAPTER VI

OF ADAM'S SLEEP, SHOWING HOW GOD DID MAKE OUT OF HIM A WOMAN, AND HOW HE BECAME ENTIRELY EARTHLY, AND HOW GOD BY THE CURSE WITHDREW PARADISE FROM HIM

1. WHEN man is weary and tired, he falls into a sleep as into the magia. It is as if he were not in this world, for all his sense-perceptions cease, the wheel of the essences enters into a state of repose, it is as if he were essential and not substantial. He resembles only the magia, for he knows nothing of his body; he lies as it were dead, and yet is not dead; but the spirit stands still. Then the essences have their fulfilment, and the spirit of the soul alone sees. Then is represented in the sidereal spirit all that the astral heaven brings about, and is set magically in the mind as a mirror, in which the spirit of the great world is taken much with beholding, and conducts what it sees in the mirror into the essences, and the essences spring therein, as if they accomplished the work in the spirit; they pourtray moreover that in the spirit, as dreams and prefigurements.
2. We are tp recognize, then, that when earthliness struggled with Adam and he imagined into it, he was at once infected thereby, and became in his soul dark and fierce; for the earthliness began to be operative like a water that begins to seethe, the astral source was aroused and was now lord of the body. Moses says then quite correctly: God caused a deep sleep to fall upon Adam. That is, seeing that his will-spirit longed after earthliness, God let him fall. For with the longing he introduced earthliness into the heavenly essentiality, and that, the Spirit of God, which is a Spirit of light, would not have. For Adam's spirit was a creature, and went out from God's love-spirit. Certainly He abandoned him not willingly, but earthliness had already caught him. And when He abandoned him, he sank down into a powerlessness, and fell into the power of the third Principle, viz. to the stars and to the four elements; thus he was involved in the earthly magia. Yet he became not

wholly earthly; he lay in mystery, hidden between God's kingdom and the kingdom of this world, since the two fiats, the divine and the earthly, were active in him; and the two kingdoms, the kingdom of God and the kingdom of hell, were now for the first time in conflict respecting man. If now the precious name Jesus had not been imprinted in Adam, even prior to his creation, as in the essentiality of God, wherein was the Virgin of the wisdom of God, and in which Adam was created, he would assuredly still be sleeping and be in the earthly death.

3. And this is the reason why the second Adam, Christ, had to rest till the third day in the earth in the sleep of the first Adam, and raise up again the first Adam out of earthliness. For Christ had also a soul and spirit from Adam, and the precious Word of the Deity with the Spirit of God raised up again in Christ's flesh the dead essentiality of the sulphur, or the body which in Adam was dead, and restored it into the power of the Majesty of God, and therewith us all.

4. All who by their faith and desire enter into Christ's flesh and blood, into his death and rest in the earth, all these bud forth with their spirit and will in the divine Essentiality, and are a fair flower in the Majesty of God. And God, the eternal Word and the power, will at the last day raise up in himself, by his Spirit, the dead body, which in Adam has fallen into the power of the earth. For Christ's soul and flesh, which is also our soul and flesh, that is, the part which Adam received from the divine Essentiality, has God through and in the death of Christ separated from the earthly nature, and raised it up and again introduced it into the divine Essentiality, as it was before the times of the world, and us in and by Him.

And with us at present there is a lack of surrender or submission, in that we allow ourselves to be held by the devil; for our death is broken, our sleep has become a life, and that in Christ, and through Christ in God, and through God into eternity, with our ground removed into the unground, that is, into the Majesty without the nature of fire.

5. Ah blindness, that we know not ourselves! O thou noble Man! if thou knewest thyself, who thou art, how wouldst thou rejoice! How wouldst thou turn the dark devil out, who day and night strives to make our mind earthly, so that we should not recognize our true native land from which we have gone out! O miserable corrupt Reason, if thou perceivedst but a spark of thy former glory, how wouldst thou long after it! How gracious is the aspect of the divine Essence! How sweet is the water of eternal life that springs from God's Majesty! O most worthy Light, bring us back again, we are now with Adam fallen asleep in the earthly source! O come, thou most worthy Word, and awaken us in Christ! O most worthy Light, since thou hast shone forth, destroy the power of the devil, who holds us captive! Break the power of Antichrist and covetousness, and deliver us from evil! Awaken us, Lord; for we have slept long in the devil's net, in the earthly source! Let us once again see thy salvation, bring forth the new Jerusalem! It is day, why should we sleep in the day? Come then, thou breaker through of death, thou powerful hero and champion, and destroy the devil's kingdom on earth! Give us (thy sick Adam) a further cordial from Zion, that we may refresh ourselves and return into our true native land! Lo, all the mountains, hills and valleys are full of the glory of the Lord: He shoots up as a plant, who shall prevent it? Hallelujah!

6. Now, when Adam had fallen asleep, he lay in mystery as in God's wonders; what He did with him was done. Thus, the imprinted name Jesus put the fiat in motion yet again in two forms, that is, in both tinctures of fire and water. For this first image had fallen under the power of the name Jesus in the Word of life, and now the Word of life was the second creator (understand with the imprinted name Jesus, which was to become man). This second creator separated the two tinctures of fire and light from each other, yet not wholly in power, but only in essence; for in the essence of the tincture of light was the sulphur veneris of love, in which Adam was destined and was able to make himself pregnant. The tincture of fire gave soul, and the light's tincture gave spirit, as an image according to the outer image. The

fire-life longed after the light-life, and the light-life after the fire-life, that is, after the essential power from which the light shines; such a position was in Adam one, for he was man and woman. And the Word of life took the tincture of Venus with the heavenly and earthly fiat from Adam, also a rib from his side, and the half-cross T in the head, which is the mark of the Holy Trinity, stamped with the Word of life, as with the severe name of God, which has such a characterization. T indicates the cross of Christ, on which he was to suffer death, and generate Adam anew, and in the name Jesus introduce him into the Holy Ternary. All this did the fiat take into itself, with all the essences of human quality, though likewise the proprium of the soul's fire, but in the tincture of Venus, not according to the might of the centre; and divided into the entire form of man.

7. Thus was the woman made, with all the members and feminine properties, as she still has them; for the spirit majoris mundi had now the strongest fiat, and figurized the woman according to such a form as this could be. For the angelic form had departed; generation had to be carried out now in an animal way. Hence also there was given to Adam, seeing that he had fallen into the power of the earthly magia, an animal form and figure of masculine members; and Adam's begetting was assigned to the fiat, and it made out of him a likeness according to itself. If he had remained heavenly minded, he would have begotten himself in a heavenly way. It was done then by the earthly fiat, and his outer body became an animal; he lost also the heavenly understanding and the virtue of the All-power.

8. Thus, dear reader, thou must know that Christ, the second Adam, has not in vain suffered himself to be crucified and pierced in his side with a spear, nor has his blood been shed in vain. Here we have the key. Adam was broken open in his side in connection with the rib for the formation of the woman. Into this same side must come the spear of Longinus with God's wrath, for it had entered into Adam and through Mary's earthliness also into the side of Christ, and the blood of Christ had to drown the wrath and take it away from the first Adam; for the second Adam had

also heavenly blood, and it had to drown the earthly turba, in order that the first Adam might be made whole again.

9. Let this be told you, ye children of men, for it has been known in the Holy Ternary, and not in opinions or conceits. Your soul and body are at stake. Take heed what you do.

10. Human reproduction began then in an animal way. For Adam retained the limbus, and his Eve the matrix of Venus, as the tinctures had separated. Now, each tincture is a complete magic, as a desirous craving, in which the centrum naturae is born, and that in sulphur. So then the desiring magic with the tincture is to be found again in sulphur, and yet cannot attain to life unless the tincture of fire enter into the tincture of Venus. The tincture of Venus is unable to awaken a fire, it is too feeble. And seeing such cannot be in it, and at the same time both the tinctures desire life, the violent longing of the man and woman begins, so that the one desires to mingle with the other; for the force of the essences wishes to be vital, and the tincture impels thereunto and also desires that. For the tincture belongs to the eternal Life, but is shut up with substance. Thus, it desires to live as it has done from eternity; and therefore the man longs for the matrix of the woman and the woman for the limbus of the man.

11. The woman has a watery tincture, and the man a fiery tincture. The man sows soul, and the woman spirit, and both sow flesh, that is, sulphur. Accordingly man and woman are one body, and the two make one child; and therefore they ought to remain together, if they once commix, for they have become one body. But he who commixes with others, or separates, he breaks the order of nature, resembles a brute beast, and considers not that in his seed lies the eternal tincture, wherein is hidden the divine essentiality, which hereafter will be awakened in the wrathful part. Further, this [viz. fornication] is a work which follows the shadow of man, and in the end awakens its pang in the conscience. For the tincture in the seed has its origin from eternity; it is imperishable, appears in the form of spirit and enters into man's magic, from whence man has produced it and poured it forth.

12. Mark this, ye strumpets and libertines: what you pursue in secret, often with great duplicity, enters into your conscience and becomes for you an evil gnawing worm. The tincture is an eternal being, and would fain live in God's love. But if, under the impulse of the astral region through infection of the devil, you pour it into a false and foul vessel in abomination and disorder, it will hardly attain God's love; but rather passes by longing again into the first place, viz. into you. If it has become false in a false vessel, so that it cannot rest, then it will gnaw you and come in the hellish abyss into the conscience. This is neither fiction nor jest. Be not then wholly animal; for an animal gets its tincture only from this world, but you get it from eternity. What is eternal dies not. Though you corrupt the sulphur, yet the will-spirit in the sulphur enters with the noble tincture into the mystery, and each mystery takes what belongs to it. And at the last day, when the Spirit of God will move itself in all the three Principles, the mystery shall be revealed: there you will see your fine works.

13. Thus the great mercy of God in regard to the human race is highly recognizable by us; for God has willed to help man thus. Otherwise, if God had desired the animal property, he would have created at once in the beginning a male and a female; he would not have made one alone, furnished with both tinctures. But God did well know the fall of man, as also the fraud of the devil, which thus through Eve was turned into derision. When Adam fell down into sleep, the devil thought: Now am I lord and prince on the earth; but the woman's seed was to him an hindrance of that.

14. We are to understand the awakening of Adam out of his sleep. He fell asleep to the heavenly world, and woke up to the earthly world. The spirit of the great world awakened him. Then he saw the woman, and knew that she was his flesh and his bone, for the Virgin of the wisdom of God was still in him. And he looked upon her and carried his imagination or desire into her, for she had his matrix, moreover the tincture of Venus, and straightway by desire one tincture seized the other. Therefore Adam took her unto him and said: She shall be called woman, because she was

taken out of man. Eve is not to be regarded as a pure virgin, nor any of her daughters either. The turba has destroyed the virginity, and made the pure love earthly; the earthly desire destroys the true virginity. For God's wisdom is a pure Virgin, in which Christ was conceived and in a true virgin vessel became man, as will be seen later.

15. Accordingly the earthly virgin could not remain in Paradise. Though both man and woman were still in Paradise, and both of them still had the paradisaic nature, yet this was mixed with earthly craving. They were naked, and had their bestial members for procreation, though these they did not yet know, neither were they ashamed; for the spirit of the great world had not dominion over them until they ate of the earthly fruit. Then their eyes were opened, for the heavenly Virgin of the wisdom of God withdrew from them; then they first came to know the kingdom of the stars and elements. When God's Spirit went out, the earthly spirit in the fierce fervent source entered in. Here the devil got admittance, and infected them and led them into wrath and badness, as this is going on still in the present day. For the wrath of God which arises from the eternal Nature, and which the devil had kindled and awakened, lay in the earthly centre. Nor can any life be born unless the centre be awakened; for the Principle stands in fire, wherein every life is rooted, and the centrum naturae has in its forms fierceness or ferventness. Therefore it is said: Bow down, and enter into meekness, and leave life its right. For life is fire, and life's image, which is the likeness of God, has being in light, that is, in the fire of love; the light-fire, however, gives not the centrum naturae. Hence the devil still thinks that he is a greater lord than the creature in the love-fire. Certainly he is more austere; but he lives in darkness and devours the harsh essentiality, wherefore also he is an enemy of love.

16. We are to recognize that the devil is the cause that man was created in his place, and. that he is to blame for man's fall, although Adam and his Eve, when God had divided Adam, could not stand firm. They were indeed in Paradise and were to eat paradisaic fruit in an angelic manner, but they enjoyed it not,

because the tree of the knowledge of good and evil was more agreeable to them; and Eve, as soon as she was made, imaginated into the tree of temptation. And though Adam revealed to her the command, desire was nevertheless only directed towards the tree; for the earthly essences were not yet manifest in Adam and Eve, they were as yet bound; therefore it was that they shot forth thus into desire, for they wished to be lord and master. This came about through the infection of the devil, through his ascendant false imagination. Accordingly he laid himself in the serpent's form on the tree, and praised the fruit to Eve, to the effect that it made one wise. Yes forsooth I wise to know evil and good; misery enough; two kinds of sources to rule in one creature. Not knowing were better. He told her lies and truth together, she should be wise and her eyes should be opened. Oh yes, sufficiently. She soon saw that by the earthly source she had fallen unto the spirit of this world, that she was naked; she recognized her bestial members, acquired guts in the body and a stinking worm-bag, full of sorrow and misery, in anguish and trouble, as is set forth in the book De tribes principiis. We have then before our eyes what sort of angels of Paradise we are, how we must generate and support ourselves in anguish, sorrow and misery, which should be done in a different way.

17. Thus, we know sufficiently Adam's fall and why he could not remain in Paradise, and what Paradise was, which exists yet to this day. But it bears not now paradisaic fruit, and we have not the paradisaic nature and eyes; we see it not. For God has cursed the earth for man's sake, so that Paradise no longer buds through the earth. It has become to us a mystery, and nevertheless still is; and into this mystery depart the souls of the saints, when the earthly body separates from the soul. It is in this world and also out of this world, for this world's source touches it not. The whole world would have been as a paradise if Adam had remained in innocency; but when God cursed the earth, Paradise vanished; for God's cursing is a flight. His flight is not a receding, but it is entering into another Principle, into himself. The Spirit of God goes out from God into essence; but when this essence became

earthly, and the devil, who was an enemy of God, began to dwell in it, then the Spirit of God entered into its own Principle, viz. into love, and withdrew from the earthliness. There it is presented to man in the light of life. Now, he who desires to enter into God's love, goes by his willspirit into Paradise. Thus Paradise buds again in his will-spirit, and he receives again in connection with his image heavenly essentiality, in which the Holy Spirit rules.

18. Let this be a pearl to you, ye children of men; for it is the true foundation. He who seeks and finds it, hath utter delight in it. It is the pearl that lies hid in the field, of which Christ says, that a man sold all his goods and bought the pearl (Matt. xiii. 45, 46).

19. And we are to regard the Cherubin, which drove Adam and Eve out of Paradise, as the stern angel, which signifies the abscinder of the earthly life from Paradise, so that body and soul have to separate.

20. We know indeed that Adam and Eve had been driven forth from the place where the tree of temptation stood, for paradisaic fruit was there; this they were no more to see nor eat, for what is heavenly belongs not to the earthly. The animals also were driven forth on account of the evil tree; they were besides not capable of enjoying paradisaic fruit; but any animal could eat of this tree, for it was earthly. Thus Adam and Eve were compelled to leave Paradise, for God had, through the spirit of the great world, clothed them with the skins of beasts in lieu of the heavenly robe of brightness, and had pronounced to them sentence as to what should be their doings in this world, what they should henceforth eat, and how they should get their bread in sorrow and misery, till they should return unto earth, from which as regards one part they were extracted.

CHAPTER VII

OF THE PROMISED SEED OF THE WOMAN AND BRUISER OF THE SERPENT

1. ADAM and Eve being in Paradise as man and wife and still in possession of heavenly life and joy, although mixed, the devil could not suffer this, for his envy was too great. Seeing that he had caused Adam to fall and deprived him of his angelic form, he now beheld Eve as the woman taken from Adam, and thought that they might beget children in Paradise, and remain in Paradise. [He said to himself:] Thou wishest to deceive her, so that she eateth of the forbidden fruit, then will she become earthly and thou mayest reach into her heart and bring thy desire into her, so gettest thou her into thy kingdom and still remainest prince on the earth in the third Principle. This he accomplished indeed, and persuaded her to indulge in the false fruit, so that she took hold of the tree, plucked an apple and did eat, and gave also to Adam. And when Adam saw that Eve did not at once fall down and die, he ate also, for the desire existed in both of them.

2. Such was the morsel whereby Heaven and Paradise vanished, as the Cherubin or abscinder stepped with naked flaming sword before the door of Paradise, and no longer allowed them into Paradise. His sword was the destroying angel, which cuts man now with heat, cold, sickness, want and death, and at last severs the earthly life from the soul.

3. When this sword was to be broken in the death of Christ, the earth did quake and the sun was darkened; and the rocks were rent before the strong might of God, who thus broke death to pieces. And the graves of the saints were opened, and their bodies arose again from death; for the sword was broken and the angel who guarded Paradise removed. And the bodies of the saints went again into Paradise.

4. When Adam and Eve ate here of the earthly fruit, they fell among murderers, who beat them and stripped them, and left them half dead. Their going out from Paradise is the going from

Jerusalem to Jericho, for they went out of heaven into this evil corrupt world, into the house of sin, where forthwith in their soul, in the centrum naturae, the wheel of the senses began to qualify in the earthly source; where each sense was adverse to the other, where envy, pride, covetousness, anger and repugnancy sprang in profusion; for extinguished was the noble light of love, which made the fierce source pleasant, friendly and gentle, in which the Spirit of God worked and the fair Virgin of the wisdom of God rested: they went out from fair wisdom.

5. God had created Adam in and unto the chaste Virgin of His wisdom. But he got instead an evil, contrarious, earthly spouse, with whom he had to live in an animal form, in constant sorrow, anxiety and distress. And from his fair garden of delight, which he had in himself, there arose to him an adverse garden of thorns and thistles, where yet in a way he sought for the virgin fruit. It was with him as with a thief, who was in a fair garden to keep and preserve it, but was on account of theft driven out of it, and nevertheless would fain eat of the fruit in question, yet cannot get in, but walks round outside, stretches forth his hand to seize the fruit, which the gardener however snatches from him, and he is forced to go off in an ill humour, and cannot satisfy his desire. So it is with man in regard to the woman.

6. When Adam was yet in God's love, and the woman was in him a chaste virgin, in God's sweetness and wisdom, he ate the fruits of her, and could certainly delight himself with his own love in the matrix of Venus. For the tincture of fire has a great joyous delectation in the tincture of light, and Adam had such in himself: he was man and woman. Now he must walk round this garden on the outside and touch the tincture of Venus with one member only; the internal tinctures then receive one another in the seed, and work so as to produce a life. But the outer body is not worthy to enjoy the inqualifying or assimilating of the internal kingdom of joy, in which the soul's life is sown. Only the internal essences have enjoyment of that, for they are of the Eternal. But the outer animal man accomplishes only a bestial desire. He knows not of the joy of the essences, when one tincture enters into the other;

which takes place where there is yet something of Paradise; but the earthly essence intermeddles immediately, and it is only a joyous glance or lustre wherein is generated the will to life, which keeps on in that direction and becomes pregnant with sulphur, till it can reach the Principle and strike fire in the centre: then it amounts to a true life, and another soul is born.

7. Now when the fair image withdrew thus from God's love, it knew itself, that it had passed into a different state. Then began fear and terror of the wrath of God, which commenced to make itself felt in them. They looked upon each other and became aware of their animal form, and that they were naked. The devil will have danced then, and mocked at God. They were afraid and hid themselves among the trees, took fig leaves, wove them together, and held them before their shame; for the heavenly Virgin was gone. They recognized the fall and were ashamed; that is, the soul, which is of the Eternal, was ashamed of the bestial nature: as is the case still in the present day, that we are ashamed of the bestial members. And hence it is that the woman covers her shame with a white cloth, that the spirit of the soul, which shows in the eyes, be not troubled, for it knows the matrix of Venus and begins at once in the male to imaginate regarding it; which, if the woman clothed herself in black and veiled her eyes, would not easily happen, save only by imagination; whereas the two tinctures of the man and the woman seize one another immediately at the eyes, where the spirit shows.

8. Now when Adam and Eve stood thus in terror before the wrath of God, God called Adam and said unto him: Where art thou? And he said: Here I am; I am afraid, because I am naked. And He said: Who told thee that thou art naked? Hast thou not eaten of the tree, whereof I commanded thee that thou shouldest not eat? And the man said: The woman gave me of the tree, and I ate. And the Lord God said unto the woman: Wherefore hast thou done this? And the woman said: The serpent deceived me, so that I ate (Gen. iii. 9-13).

9. In this connection we understand the great love of God, that God recalled Adam, so that he should know, seek and find

himself, and turn again to God. For Adam had been in God, but had gone out from God's love, from the second Principle, from the holy paradise of God into the outer earthly kingdom of this world of the stars and elements, into the third Principle. Therefore God said: Where art thou, Adam? Seest thou not that thou art no longer in heaven? He turned His gracious countenance again to one part in Adam, namely, to the part which he had received from the heavenly essentiality, and aspected it again with His spirit, and said to the serpent, unto the old devil: Because thou hast done this, be thou accursed. And to the creaturely serpent, which now had to be a creature (for the devil had changed himself into the form of a serpent, and so it is that the serpent had to remain), He said Upon thy belly shalt thou go, and earth shalt thou eat. Because the serpent had seduced man, so that he had become earthly, the devil's image had also to be earthly and eat the wrathful earthly quality, viz. poison: that was to be its characteristic.

10. And here we are to know that the devil formed for himself the image of the serpent from the stars and elements by his imagination, for he had great power until the Lord cursed him utterly, and placed the precious name Jesus as separating mark: then his great power fell. For God said to Adam and Eve: The seed of the woman shall bruise the serpent's head, and thou, the serpent, shalt sting him in the heel (Gen. iii. 15); that is, in the wrath of God thou shalt slay him, but he will bud forth out of death and bruise thy head, that is, will take away thy power and overcome the wrath with love. And in this place the Word of the promise of the woman's seed, that is, the highly precious name Jesus, has imprinted itself with its sign in the vital light; and in this same sign the highly precious Virgin of the wisdom of God, in which Christ, as the breaker down of death, was to become a true man, deprive death of its power and destroy the devil's sting; he was to tread the winepress of the fierceness and wrath, and enter into the wrath as into the centre of fire, and extinguish the fire with his heavenly blood and with the water of meekness which springs from the fountain of the Spirit of God.

11. And know for a certainty if the Word of promise had not imprinted itself in the life's light, when Adam and Eve fell into the earthly source, the spirit of the soul would have become a fierce devil and the body an evil beast, as it also indeed is. If the [holy] elementary water did not abate the pride of the fierceness, we should see well enough how many a one would be a ferocious devil.

12. Now we are to consider that the world, before the incarnation of Christ, was saved in this imprinted Word and name Jesus. Those who have inclined their will into God, they have received the Word of promise, and the soul was taken thereinto. For the whole law of Moses regarding sacrifice is absolutely nothing but a type of the humanity of Christ. What Christ in his humanity did by his sacrifice, in drowning with his blood and his love the wrath of God, that Moses did by his sacrifice with the blood of beasts. For the Word of promise was in the covenant, and God meanwhile set before himself the figure and allowed himself to be reconciled in the covenant by a similitude. The name Jesus was in the covenant, and it reconciled through desire the anger and wrath in the nature of the Father. The Jews certainly did not understand this, but the covenant understood it; for the animal man was not worthy to know it, till Christ was born. Then went forth the sound, which however after a short time was covered up again by Antichrist in Babel, for the animal man of iniquity is not worthy of the precious name Jesus; neither does it belong to the animal part, but only to the divine part. The animal must remain on the wild earth, and at the last day be consumed by the fire of God. But the heavenly part ought to be introduced into the divine power; hence it is an abomination before God that man thus proudly pranks with the animal. The animal is not God's image, even as the sacrifice of Moses was not the reconciliation, nor is there any but the covenant of grace and the Word of life in the covenant.

13. The circumcision of the Jews, it being obligatory on them to circumcise male children only, contained this law in itself as follows: Adam was the one man that God created, and in him was

God's image. Eve, as his wife, God did not will to create; the image was to be born from one only. But seeing that he fell, and that God had to make the woman for him, the covenant with the promise passed again upon one, so that all should be regenerated and new-born from one, viz. from the second Adam; not from the woman Mary, but from Christ as the heavenly Adam. For the first man's or Adam's first blood, which he received from God's essentiality, was to avail, and not the woman's earthly blood, in which Adam became earthly and a woman had to be contrived for him. And therefore also only the male kind was circumcised, and in the same member that is an abomination before God and a shame of the soul, for impregnation was not destined to be bestial. Circumcision was thus a sign and figure, intimating that this member should be cut off from man and not appear with him in eternity. And Christ had to take on him the form of a man, though inwardly he stood in a virgin image, that the purpose of God might stand. For the man's or the fire's property must rule, and the woman's or the light's property must soften his fire and bring it into the gentle image of God.

14. The woman's blood would not have reconciled the wrath of God, it was necessary that the man's blood only should do this. For the woman belongs to the man, and will in the kingdom of God be a masculine virgin, just as Adam was, not a woman. The woman is saved in the covenant of the man; for the covenant was made for the sake of the man, i.e. of the masculine virgin, that it might be reconciled. Therefore Paul says: The woman is saved in childbearing, if she continue in faith and in love, and in sanctification with sobriety (I Tim. ii. 15). And not only that, but also in the covenant of the man, for she is a part taken from Adam. Hence each individual woman ought to be subject to the man, and he ought to be lord. God gives moreover to the man Virgin Wisdom; he ought to govern the woman, not as a tyrant, but as his own life. He ought to love his wife as his own body, for she is his flesh and body, an image taken from him, his helpmeet, his rose-garden. Though she be earthly and weak, yet he is to

understand that he himself is the cause thereof, and have patience with her, nor allow his wrath the ascendency, to destroy her.

15. The woman also is to understand that she is saved in the [first, virgin] man's covenant and blood, and that she is Adam's and the man's rib and tincture, and is proper to the man. She ought to be humble. As a member serves the body, so should the woman serve the man and love him as herself. She should cast her love unto him absolutely, for thus she obtains the heavenly Virgin with divine Wisdom, and the spirit of the covenant.

16. But to unmarried virgins and wifeless men, as well as to widows, it is said that they have the covenant of Christ as spouse: before it they ought to be chaste and humble. For Christ is the bride of the man, his chaste virgin, which Adam lost; and He is also the bridegroom of the virgins and widows His masculinity is their masculinity, so that they appear accordingly before God as a masculine virgin. For our image is being generated now in will and faith. Where then our heart and will is, there also is our treasure and image.

17. Therefore guard yourselves from whoredom and false love, for the true image is thereby destroyed. Whoredom is the greatest wickedness that man works in himself. Other sins pass out of him into a figure; but the whore remains in him; for he [she] produces a false image in which the Virgin of God is not known, but only a bestial form. Let it be told thee, thou man: There is so great a horror behind, that heaven shudders at it, as one who enters not easily into the bestial imagination.

CHAPTER VIII

OF THE VIRGIN MARY, AND THE INCARNATION OF JESUS CHRIST THE SON OF GOD

1. MANY have taken upon themselves to write of the Virgin Mary, and have believed that she was not a daughter of the earth. To them indeed has been presented a reflection of the eternal Virginity, but they have come short of the true mark. Some have simply supposed that she was not the daughter of Joachim and Anna, for Christ is called the seed of the woman, and indeed is, and he himself attests that he came from above, from heaven; he must therefore, according to them, be born of a wholly heavenly Virgin. But this would profit little to us poor children of Eve, who have become earthly and carry our souls in an earthly vessel. Where were our poor soul, if the Word of eternal life had not taken it into itself? If Christ had brought a soul from heaven, where were our soul and the covenant with Adam and Eve, by which the woman's seed was to bruise the head of the serpent? If Christ had willed to come and to be born wholly from heaven, he would not have needed to be born a man upon earth. But where were the covenant, in which the name of promise, viz. Jesus, incorporated itself in the light of life, in the tincture of the soul, immediately in Paradise when Adam fell, nay, before Adam was created? As Peter says (I Pet. i. 20): We are foreseen in Christ, before the foundation of the world was laid. For God in his wisdom knew the fall; hence the name Jesus incorporated itself there forthwith in the Word of life, surrounded with the Virgin of wisdom, in Adam's image with the cross. For the soul also is a crucial birth: when the fire of the soul is enkindled, it makes in the flash a cross, that is, an eye with a cross and three Principles, in accordance with the character of the Holy Trinity.

2. We are to understand that Mary, in whom Christ became man, was by the outer flesh truly the daughter of Joachim and Anna, and was begotten from the seed of Joachim and Anna according to the outer man; but by the will she was the daughter of the

covenant of promise, for she was the goal to which the covenant pointed. In her lay the centre of the covenant; therefore she was highly known of the Holy Spirit in the covenant, and highly blessed before and among all women, even from Eve; for the covenant disclosed itself in her.

3. You must understand us in a very high and lofty way: The Word with the promise, which with the Jews stood in prefigure, as in a mirror, into which God the angry Father imaginated and thereby extinguished his wrath, this Word and promise now moved itself in an essential manner, which had not happened from eternity. For when Gabriel brought Mary the message, that she should become pregnant, and she consented and said: Be it unto me according to thy word, then the centre of the Holy Trinity moved itself and disclosed the covenant, that is, disclosed within her in the Word of life the eternal virginity which Adam had lost. For the Virgin of the wisdom of God surrounded the Word of life or the centre of the Holy Trinity. Thus the centre was moved, and the heavenly Vulcan kindled the fire of
love, so that the principle of the flame of love was generated.

4. Understand it aright. In Mary's essence, in the virgin essence, corrupted in Adam and from which he was to have produced a virgin image according to the wisdom of God, divine fire was struck and the principle of love enkindled; thou must understand, in the seed of Mary, when she became pregnant with the soul's spirit or with the tincture of Venus, for in the tincture of Venus, that is, in the source of love, Adam's first fire was kindled in the Word of life, and in the child Jesus both tinctures were perfect as in Adam; and ' the Word of life in the covenant, understand the Holy Trinity, was the centre, and the principle appeared in the sphere of the Father. Christ became man in God and also in Mary and herewith at the same time in the earthly world, that is, in all the three Principles. He took upon him the form of a servant that he might get the upper hand of death and the devil, for he was to be a prince in the locus of this world, in the angelic princely throne, in the seat and authority of the erstwhile angel and prince Lucifer, over all the three Principles. If then (I) he was to be lord

of the external world, he must also dwell in the external world, and have its nature and property; if (2) he was to be God's Son, he must necessarily also be born of God; if (3) he was to extinguish the wrath of the Father, he must also be in the Father; if (4) he was to be the Son of Man, he must also be of the essence and nature of man, and have a human soul and body, as we all have.

5. And it is recognizable that Mary, his mother, as well as Christ through his mother, were both of them of human essence, in body, soul and spirit, and that Christ received a soul from Mary's essence, but without the intervention of man's seed. The great mystery of God was there revealed. The first man in his hiddenness, who fell into death, was here begotten again vitally, understand in God's principle. For on this account the Deity put itself in motion and kindled fire in the Father's principle; thus the dead sulphur, which had died in Adam, was again quickened; for the Word possessed heavenly essentiality in itself, and revealed itself in heavenly essentiality in the virgin image of the Deity. The same is the pure chaste Virgin, in which the Word of life became man; and thus the outer Mary was adorned with the highly blessed heavenly Virgin, and was blessed among all the women of this world. In her was again revived what was dead and shut up in humanity; and therefore she was exalted highly, like the first man before the fall, and became mother of the Royal Prince. This however occurred to her not by her own power, but by God's power. If the centre of God had not put itself in motion within her, she would have been in no way different from all the daughters of Eve. But the Word of life had set up the goal in this place, in connection with the covenant of promise; therefore is she blessed among all women and above all the children of Eve. Not that she is a goddess, whom we should honour as God, for she is not the goal; and indeed she said: How shall this be," seeing I know not a man? But the Word of life in the centre of the Father, which by the motion of the Deity gave itself to humanity and was disclosed in human essence, is the goal: that is the goal toward which we must run for the attainment of the new birth.

6. This is a greater wonder than was done in the case of the first Adam. For the first Adam was created from three principles, and his spirit was introduced into him by the Spirit of God: in this case the Heart of God needed not to move specially; the Spirit of God from God's Heart only moved. But now was put in motion the centre or the Heart of God, which had rested from eternity, and the divine fire became kindled and inflamed.

The precious Gate

7. We must understand aright the incarnation of Christ, the Son of God. He has not become man in the Virgin Mary only, as if his deity or divine nature sat cooped up there. As little as God dwells in one place only, but is to be regarded as the fulness of the whole of things, so little also has God moved himself in one separate part only; for he is not divisible, but everywhere entire, and where he manifests himself, there he is wholly manifest. So in like manner God is not measurable, nor is any place found for him, unless he make for himself a place in a creature; but thus he would be at the same time along with the creature and outside of the creature.
8. When the Word put itself in motion for the revelation of life, it revealed itself in the divine essentiality, in the water of eternal life; it entered into it and became sulphur, that is, flesh and blood; it made heavenly tincture, which surrounds and fills the Deity, in which the wisdom of God stands eternally with the divine magia. Understand it aright: The Deity has longed to become flesh and blood; and although the pure clear Godhead remains spirit, it has become the spirit and life of the flesh, and works in the flesh; so that when we enter by our desire into God and give ourselves up wholly to him, we may say that we enter into God's flesh and blood and live in God, for the Word has become man, and God is the Word.
9. We do not thus abolish the creature of Christ, as if he was to be supposed not a creature. We may compare the sun to the creature of Christ, and the whole deep of the world to the eternal

Word in the Father. We see indeed that the sun shines in the whole deep, and gives it heat and power; yet we cannot say that in the deep, independent of the body of the sun, the sun's power and lustre does not exist. For if it did not exist, neither would it seize the sun's power and lustre, since only one power and lustre seizes another. The deep is as to its lustre merely hidden; but if God pleased, the whole deep would be nothing but sun. It were but to kindle it, so that the water would be swallowed up and become a spirit, then would the sun's brightness shine everywhere; and, accordingly, the centre of fire would have to inflame itself, as in the locus of the sun.

10. Further, know this: We understand that the heart of God has rested from eternity; but by motion and entrance into essence it has become manifest in all places, though in God there is no place nor limit, except in the creature of Christ. There the entire holy Trinity has manifested itself in a creature, and thus through the creature also in the whole of the heavens. He has gone hence and prepared for us the place where we shall see in his light, live in his essentiality and eat of it; his essentiality fills the heavens and Paradise. In the beginning we were made out of God's Essence, why should we not also live in it? As air and water fill this world, and we all enjoy them, so exists hiddenly the divine essentiality, which we enjoy, if in real earnest we imagine thereinto and along with the will give ourselves up to it. This then is Christ's flesh and blood in the divine power; for the flesh and blood of the creature of Christ is found there, and is a reality, a power, a spirit, a God, a plenitude, without being separated by any place, yet in its own principle. A hoggish man may say: Eh but how shall we eat him? Thou ass, first get so far as to reach him, for thou wilt not eat him with the outer mouth. He is a principle deeper, and yet is the outer One. He was in the Virgin Mary and also by his birth in this world; and he will at the last day appear in all the three Principles before all men and devils.

11. He has really taken earthly nature on him; but in his death, when he vanquished death, the divine nature swallowed up the earthly and took away its dominion. Not that Christ has laid

aside something, but the external nature was overcome and as it were swallowed up; and the life which he now lives, he lives in God. So also was Adam to have been, but he resisted not. Therefore the Word had to be born man and give itself to substance, in order that we might receive power, so that we might be able to live in God.

12. Christ has then brought again what Adam had lost, yea and much more. For the Word has become man everywhere, that is, it is revealed everywhere in the divine essentiality, in which lies our eternal humanity. For in eternity we shall live in the same corporeal essence in which the Virgin of God stands; and we must put on God's Virgin, for Christ has put her on. He has become man in the eternal Virgin and also in the earthly virgin, although the latter was not a right virgin. But the heavenly divine Virgin made her a virgin in the blessing, that is, in the disclosing of the Word and covenant. That part in Mary which she had inherited from Adam out of the heavenly essentiality, which Adam however made earthly, that part was blessed. Thus the earthly element only died in her, the other lived eternally and became again a chaste Virgin, not in death, but in the blessing. When God revealed himself in her, she put on the fair Virgin of God, and became a virile virgin by the heavenly part.

13. Thus Christ was born of a right, pure, chaste, heavenly Virgin, for in the blessing she received the limbus of God into her matrix, into her seed. Nothing foreign indeed, but the limbus of God opened itself within her, in God's power. This limbus in Adam was dead, and it was made living by God's motion. In the Word of life God's essence entered into her and opened the centre of the soul, so that Mary became pregnant with a soul and also with a spirit, both of them heavenly and earthly. And that was a true image of God, a likeness according to and founded on the Holy Trinity on all the three Principles.

CHAPTER IX

OF THE VIRGINITY OF INIARY, SHOWING WHAT SHE WAS BEFORE THE BLESSING, AND WHAT SHE BECAME BY THE BLESSING

1. IT is very necessary for us poor children of Eve to know this, as in it lies our eternal salvation. For it is the gate of Emanuel; the whole Christian faith rests upon it, and it is the gate of the greatest mystery. For here lies hidden the secret of man, in which he is the likeness and image of God.

2. Our whole religion consists in three points, which we cultivate and teach. First, as to the creation, of what essence, nature and property man is; whether he be eternal or not eternal, and how that is possible; from whence he came in the beginning and what property the origin of man is.

3. Secondly, what his fall has been, on account of which we are mortal and subject to malignity and the source of wrath.

4. Thirdly, what the new birth is, seeing that God is willing to receive us again into grace; and on that account He has given laws and doctrine, and confirmed them with great miracles. In what power and spirit we may be new-born and rise again from death.

5. We find all this represented in two figures, viz. in the eternal, holy Virginity, and in the earthly, perishable virginity; while the new birth is found in the figure of Christ quite plain and clear. For in the eternal Virginity, in the essentiality of God, where the image and likeness of God has been seen as in a mirror from eternity and known of the Spirit of God, was Adam the first man created. He had the Virginity for a possession as the true love-tincture in the light, which desires the fire's tincture or the property of the essences, that it may become a burning life in power and glory, and be in the fire's essence a genetrix, which is not possible in the light's essence without fire.

6. We recognize then a Virginity in the wisdom of God, in the desiring will of the divine Essence, from eternity. Not a woman who brings forth, but a figure in the mirror of the wisdom of

God, a pure chaste image without being, and yet in essence; though not manifest in the fire's essence, but in the source of the light.

7. This image God created into a being, and that from all the three Principles, that it might be a likeness according to the Deity and eternity, as a complete mirror of the ground and unground, of the spirit and also of the essence; and it was created from the Eternal, not for a fragile existence. But because the earthly and fragile was suspended to the Eternal, the earthly desire has introduced itself into the eternal heavenly desire and infected the heavenly property; for it wished to dwell in the eternal desire, and yet was corrupted in the wrath of God.

8. Thus the earthly quality corrupted the heavenly, and became the turba of the latter, as is to be recognized in earth and stones, which indeed have their origin from the Eternal, but have deteriorated in the wrath and in the source of fire: the fiat has made from the eternal Essence earth and stones. And on that account a day of separation is fixed, in which every individual thing shall enter again into its ether and be tried by fire.

9. So it is likewise with man. He was created in the Virginity in God's wisdom, but was laid hold of by the wrath and anger of God; hence he became at once corrupt and earthly. And as the earth passes and must be tried by fire, and enter again into that which it was, so also man: he must enter again into the virginity in which he was created. But as it was not possible to man to rise again from the fierce wrathful death and enter into a new birth (for his virginity was shut up with him in death, and for that reason God made for man a woman taken from him), the Deity had to put itself in motion, and disclose and make alive again what was shut up.

10. And this was done in Mary, the shut up virgin; that is, in the virginity which Adam inherited from God's wisdom; not from the earthly part of the third Principle, but from the heavenly holy part of the second Principle, which by earthly imagination and suggestion had been shut up in the earthly death in the wrath of God, and was as it were dead, as the earth appeared to be dead.

Therefore the heart of God has moved itself, has broken death on the cross and generated life again.

11. The birth and incarnation of Christ is for us a thing mighty in operation, in that the whole unfathomable heart of God has moved itself, and thus the heavenly essentiality, which was shut up in death, has become again alive, so that now it may be said with reason: God himself has resisted his wrath, since by the centre of his heart, which has filled the eternity without ground or limit, he has again revealed himself, has taken away the power of death and broken the sting of the anger and fierce wrath, seeing that love and gentleness have been revealed in the wrath and have extinguished the power of fire.

12. And still more is it for us men a great joy that God has in our dead and mort virginity revealed himself, and withal through everything. And that the Word, which is the power of the life of God, has given itself again to humanity, to the dead and as it were abandoned virginity, and has reopened the virgin life, at that we rejoice; and we enter by our imagination into the centre in which God has revealed himself in humanity, that is, into the incarnation of his Son, and become thus in our imagination, which we introduce into his incarnation, pregnant with his revealed Word and the power of the heavenly divine essentiality,-not indeed anything that is alien, but at the same time alien to what is earthly. The Word has revealed itself everywhere, and in every man's vital light; and there is nothing wanting but that the Spirit of the soul give itself up to it. And then the soul's spirit puts on again the eternal Virginity, not as a garment, but from its own essence God is born in it. For Mary along with all the daughters of Eve was born earthly, but the covenant of the love of God evinced in her essence that God would there in her open again the life.

13. And as regards Mary's virginity, according to the earthly life prior to the blessing, before the heart of God moved itself, we can by no means say that she was a completely perfect virgin in accordance with the first virgin before the fall; on the contrary, she was a natural daughter of Eve. But it may be said with reason, that in Mary, as well as in all Adam's children, the eternal

Virginity in the covenant of promise lay shut up just as if in death, and yet not amort in God. For the name Jesus, passing out of the centre or heart of God, has from eternity imprinted itself as a mirror in the Virgin of God's wisdom, and has opposed the centre of the Father, that is, the centre of fire and fierceness, not in fierceness in the fire, in the fire's essence, but in love in the light, in the light's essence. And man moreover was foreseen in this same essence in the name Jesus, before the foundation of the world was laid, when Adam still existed in the form of heavenly essence, without a natural or creaturely being. For the fall was known in wisdom before man became a creature, and that according to the property of fire, not in the property of light, but according to the first Principle.

14. And so then from our deep knowledge we say of Mary, that before the time of the angel's revelation and message she was a virgin like Eve, when she went out of Paradise, before Adam knew her. Eve was then indeed a virgin, but the true Virginity was hidden in her and infected with the earthly craving, and the animal property was manifest in her. For the earthly imagination broke the heavenly property, so that she was a woman and not a chaste virgin without spot; she was but a portion of the heavenly Virginity, the other portion was Adam. And hence from Eve was born no pure, true virgin, who would have to be undivided in nature,-the turba destroyed the Virginity in all,-till the champion in combat came: He was a masculine Virgin in God's wisdom according to the heavenly nature; the earthly element hung unto him, but the heavenly element ruled over the earthly; for thus was Adam to have been, who stood not firm.

15. We say, therefore, with good grounds that Mary was Joachim's daughter, born of Anna, and, by the earthly part, contained their essence essentially in her. And then, secondly, we say that she was the daughter of the covenant of God, that God set up in her the goal of the new birth, that the whole of the Old Testament has looked to this goal, and that all the prophets have prophesied of the same goal (to the effect that God would again reveal the eternal Virginity). And this goal was blessed; for, in

accordance with his mercy, God incorporated himself in this goal by the covenant of promise, and the Word of promise stood in the covenant, and confronted the wrath in the light of life. The first world, before and after the flood, was saved in that covenant which God set before himself as a mirror. For the eternal Virginity appeared in the covenant as in the mirror of God, and God had satisfaction therein. When Israel kept the covenant and did the works of the covenant, this was accepted by God as if humanity had been in the mirror of the wisdom of God. And though Israel was earthly and bad, yet God dwelt in Israel in his covenant, in wisdom, according to his love and mercy.

16. Thus the works of the law were before God in the mirror, till the life was born again from the covenant and the fulfilment came. Then the works in the mirror ceased, and the works of the fulfilment in flesh and blood, in the heavenly essentiality, began again; for in Mary was the beginning. When the angel brought her the message, and she said: Be it unto me as thou hast said (Luke i. 38), the centre of life in the Word of God, that is, the heart of God, forthwith moved in her dead heavenly seed, quickened it again, and gestation commenced. For all the three Principles of the Deity were stirred, and the divine tincture took hold in the dead heavenly essentiality. We are not to imagine that God has been without essence, but man was dead to heavenly essence. And now did the heart of God enter with living divine essentiality into death, and awaken the dead essentiality. This divine essentiality took not away the earthly nature, but entered into it as its master and vanquisher. For the true life had to be ushered in by death and God's wrath, which was accomplished on the cross, when death was broken to pieces and wrath taken captive, and overcome and extinguished by love.

17. Thus we understand now what Mary by the conception came to be, namely, a true pure virgin according to the heavenly part. For when the heart of God moved itself, and day dawned in her, the light of the clearness and pureness of God shone in her; for her dead Virginity or God's wisdom was disclosed and became living, for she was filled with the divine Virginity, that is, with

God's wisdom. And in this same wisdom and divine essentiality, as well as in the dead and now living essentiality, the Word became flesh in sulphur by the centrum naturae, by means of the Father's essences and the essences of Mary; from out of death a life, a fruit with the two tinctures in their perfection, since the two tinctures formed but one. And because Adam had become a man, Christ also became a man according to the outer world; for it was not Eve's image in the woman's tincture that was destined to remain, but Adam's image when he was man and woman. As then one of the signs must appear in consequence of the power of the external fiat, and that the champion in combat was to be established again in all the three Principles, the champion in combat got the masculine sign; for the man has the fire's tincture or the property of the Father. Thus, the Father is the strength and might of all things, and the Son is his love. Accordingly the Word became man in the feminine essence-but became, however, a manthat his love might extinguish the anger and wrath in the Father; for the tincture of Venus has the water-fountain, and the woman has the tincture of Venus. Consequently the fire had to be quenched by the water of eternal life, and the Father's burning essences in the fire again extinguished.

18. We know then Mary, the mother of Christ, in flesh, soul and spirit, by the blessing, to be a pure chaste virgin; for this constitutes her blessing, that God has revealed himself in her. She has carried in her body the Word of life, and it has moved within her. Mary has not moved the Word, but the Word has moved Mary, both the fruit which she bore, and also her soul along with the part of the dead essentiality, so that her soul was at once surrounded with divine living essentiality: not according to the earthly part or the third Principle, but according to the heavenly part or the second Principle, so that thus the earthly nature did but hang unto her. For her soul had also with the Word of life, which became man in her, to enter by death and the wrath of the Father into the heavenly divine quality. It was necessary that her outer man should die to the earthly quality, in order that such outer man might live to God. And because she was blessed and

has carried the goal in the covenant, her body has not evanished, for the heavenly nature has swallowed up the earthly and keeps it eternally a prisoner, to the honour and mirificence of God. It must never be forgotten that God has become man in her.

19. But that some say she has remained entirely in death and passed into corruption, these should envisage their Reason in another way, for what is highly blessed is incorruptible. Her heavenly part of the divine Essentiality, which has blessed her, is incorruptible; else God's essentiality in the blessing would once more have fallen and died, as happened in Adam; on account of which death, however, God became man, that He might bring back life again. She has, indeed, died as regards the outer life or earthly quality, but she lives as regards the blessing in God's essentiality and also in her own essentiality: not in the four elements, but in their root, that is, in one Element which keeps the four shut up in itself, in Paradise and the pure element, in the divine Essentiality, in the life of God.

20. Therefore we say that Mary is greater than any daughter of Adam, because God has placed the goal of the covenant in her and she alone among all the daughters of Eve has obtained the blessing, namely, the pure virgin chastity which was destroyed in all Eve's daughters. But in her case the Virginity lay in the covenant till the Word of life highly blessed her: then she became a true pure chaste Virgin, in whom God was born. For Christ said also to the Jews: I am from above, but ye are from beneath; I am not of this world, but ye are of this world (John viii. 23). If he had become man in an earthly vessel, and not in a pure, heavenly, chaste Virgin, he would have been of this world; whereas thus he became man in the heavenly Virgin, and the earthly quality did but hang unto him. For the essence of the soul had been infected in us poor children of men by the earthly quality, and he was to introduce our soul in the form of heavenly essence, in him, through the fire of God into the Holy Ternary. For the soul was of chief importance because it had been taken out of the Eternal, and hence it was God's will not to abandon it.

21. So then, if it be asked, what sort of matter it was to which the Word and heart of God has given itself and made for itself a body, whether it were a strange matter come from heaven, or whether it were the essence and seed of Mary: our answer is that God's heart was never without essence, for its dwelling is from eternity in the light, and the power in the light is the heart or Word which God has spoken from eternity. And the speaking is the Holy Spirit of God, which with the speaking goes out from the power of the light, from the spoken Word, into what is spoken forth. And what is spoken forth is God's wonder and wisdom; this contains in itself the divine mirror of wisdom, wherein the Spirit of God sees, and in which he reveals the wonders.

22. Therefore understand that the Word, from out of the heart of God the Father (surrounded with the heavenly and chaste Virgin of wisdom, dwelling in the heavenly essentiality), has revealed itself in Mary's essence and essentiality, in her own seed, that is, in the seed of man, and has taken into itself the seed of Mary, dead and blind as to God, and awakened it to life. The living essentiality came into the halfkilled essence of Mary, and took the half-killed essence as a body,-not as a corruptible body which would disappear, but as an eternal body which would remain eternally, for here the eternal life was reborn.

23. Thus the essentiality of the eternity in God in his whole ungrounded deep, and the essentiality of the dead Adam in humanity, became one essentiality, an entirely single being, so that the creature Christ with his essentiality filled at once the whole Father, who is without limit or ground. But the creaturely soul has remained, and is a creature. And according to the third Principle, as applying to the creature, this very Christ is a creature and a king of men, as well as also according to the second Principle, as being a child of the unfathomable Father. What the Father is in his unfathomable deep, that the Son is in his creature. For the power in the creature forms with the power out of the creature one power, one essentiality, in which dwell the angels and men. It gives Paradise and joyful delight, but in

humanity it gives also flesh and blood; therefore it is and remains also a creature, but uncreated, yet brought forth, on one part out of God from eternity, and on the other part out of humanity. God and man has become one person, one Christ, one God, one Lord, one Holy Trinity, in humanity, and also at the same time everywhere; so that when we see Christ, we see the Holy Trinity in one image. His creature is like an image, taken out of us men, our high-priest and king, our brother, our Emanuel; His power is our power if we be born again of God through faith in Him. He is not strange or terrible to us, but is our tincture of love. He is with His power the quickening of our souls, our life and the bliss of our souls. When we find Him, we find our helper, as Adam was to have found Him; but he allowed himself to be deceived, and ultimately found a woman, of whom he said This is flesh of my flesh, and bone of my bones, and he took her to him as an help, to bear him company (Gen. ii. 23).

24. Thus, when our soul finds Him, it says: This is my Virgin, whom I had lost in Adam, when she was changed into an earthly woman. Now I have found again my dear Virgin who sprang from my body, and I will no more let her go; she is mine, my flesh and blood, my strength and power, whom I lost in Adam: her I will retain. Oh, a friendly retaining! friendly inqualifying, beauty, fruit, power and virtue.

25. Accordingly the poor soul finds the tincture of its lost light, and its dear Virgin. In the woman is found the noble bridegroom, for which the matrix of Venus has always longed, but has found only an earthly masculine sulphur, and has been obliged to let itself be made pregnant with earthly seed. Here it gets the tincture of the right fire and right man, so that it becomes also a true masculine virgin, as Adam was in his innocence.

CHAPTER X

OF THE BIRTH OF JESUS CHRIST, THE SON OF GOD; AND HOW HE LAY NINE MONTHS SHUT UP IN THE WOMB, LIKE ALL THE CHILDREN OF MEN; AND WHAT PROPERLY HIS INCARNATION IS

1. THERE has been a great deal of dispute about the incarnation of Jesus Christ, but carried on almost blindly; and therefrom have been formed manifold opinions, so as to turn men about with these and leave untouched the true incarnation, in which lies our eternal salvation. The cause of all this was that it was sought for in outward understanding and art, and not in connection with the right goal. If they had entered into the incarnation of Christ and had been born of God, no dispute would have become requisite; for the Spirit of God reveals the incarnation of Christ to everyone in his own self, and without this Spirit there is no finding. For how shall we find in the reason of this world what is not in this world? We find in outward reason hardly a reflection thereof; but in God's Spirit is the true finding.

2. The incarnation of Christ is such a mystery that outward reason knows nothing of it; for it has been carried out in all the three Principles, and cannot be fathomed, unless we know fully the first man in his creation before the fall; for Adam was to beget from himself the second man in accordance with the character of the Holy Trinity, in which the name Jesus was incorporated, but this was not able to be. Therefore another Adam had to come, to whom this was possible; for Christ is the virgin image in accordance with the character of the Holy Trinity. Adam was conceived in God's love, and born into this world. He had divine essentiality, and his soul was from the first Principle, from the proprium of the Father. It was to be directed by the imagination to the Father's heart, that is, to the Word and spirit of love and purity, and was to eat of the essentiality of love; then it would have preserved in itself God's nature in the Word of life, and would have been made pregnant by the power springing from

the heart of God; whereby then it would of itself have imaginated into its essence, and would have itself made its essence pregnant, so that a complete likeness according to the first image would have arisen through imagination and the surrender of the soul's will, and would have been conceived in the power of the essence.

3. But because this could not be in Adam, on account of the earthliness attached to him, it was brought to pass in the second Adam, which is Christ. He was conceived in such a way through God's imaginating and entering into the image of the first Adam.

4. And we are able to recognize, that, as the first Adam put his imagination into earthliness and became earthly, and did this moreover contrary to the purpose of God, the purpose of God had nevertheless to stand. For now God established his purpose in Adam's child, and introduced his imagination into the corrupt image, and made it pregnant with his divine power and essentiality, and turned the soul's will round from earthliness to God; so that Mary became pregnant with such a child as Adam was to become pregnant with. This the individual's own power could not accomplish, but sank down into sleep as into the magia; whereupon out of Adam was made the woman, who should not have been made, but Adam should have made himself pregnant in the matrix of Venus, and brought forth magically. As, however, this could not be, Adam was divided, and his own will of great power was broken and shut up in death. As he would not place his imagination in the Spirit of God, his great power had to come to a standstill in death and suffer the Spirit of God to place His imagination in it, and do with him what He pleased.

5. Therefore the Spirit of God raised up to him life out of this death, and became the spirit of this life, in order that the image and likeness of God (which from eternity had been known in God's wisdom) might at last be born and endure. For it stood before the times of the world and even from eternity in the virgin mirror in the wisdom of God, and that in two forms: namely, according to the first Principle of the Father in fire, and in the second Principle of the Son in light, and yet was only manifest in the light, and in the fire just as if in a magia, that is, in a

possibility. As the astral heaven imprints by its power a figure in the mind of man, in his sleep so was represented the image in the centre of the nature of fire, quite invisibly; but in wisdom, in the mirror of the Deity, it has appeared as a figure, like a shadow, yet without material being, but has had being in the essence of the spirit. Which spirit, by beholding itself in the mirror of wisdom, has known and seen this image, and set its will to bring it into substance, in order that God might have an image or likeness in substantial being, and should no more need to behold himself as in a mirror, but find him self in substance. Therefore, when the first image imaginated into the severe might and in consequence became earthly and dead, the Spirit of God led its will and life into death, and retook from death the first life into himself, in order that the first life might stand in complete obedience before Him, and He alone be the willing and also the doing.

6. Thus, we know that God has entered into the half-dead image, that is, into Mary, and into the very same virgin form which was shut up in death, in which Adam was to become pregnant and bring forth an image according to himself in virgin chastity. In this shut up and half-dead virgin matrix, the Word or heart of God, viz. the centre of the Holy Trinity, has, without infringement of its being, become an image of man. And seeing the first living virgin matrix in Adam would not be obedient to God, it became thus, when raised again from death, obedient to him, and gave itself up humbly and willingly to God's will. Thus was again presented in figure the true virgin image in obedience to God; for the first

will had to remain in death, as one which imaginated contrary to God's will, and a pure obedient will was raised up, which remained in the heavenly gentleness and being, and no more suffered the image in the fire, in the sphere of the Father, to flame up in it, but remained in one source; as indeed the Deity lives only in one source, viz. in the light, in the Holy Spirit, and yet holds its sway over all the three Principles.

7. And so are we to understand regarding the incarnation of Christ. When God's Spirit raised up again in Mary the virgin life,

which in the earthly essence lay shut up in death and wrath, then this life turned itself only unto God's will and love, and gave itself up to the Spirit of God. Thus it became pregnant with a true virgin image, which was to have been in the case of Adam, but was not realized; for one imagination received the other. God's imagination received the imagination in death and brought it back to life; and this life imaginated again into God and became pregnant with God, and from the Deity and humanity sprang one Person. The Deity was suspended to the heavenly Essence, which from eternity had existed with kingdom, power, and glory, viz. as the kingdom of Paradise and the angelic world, as spirit and the seventh form in connection with the centrum naturae. And the humanity was suspended to the kingdom of this world. But seeing that the will of the humanity gave itself up to the Deity, this virgin image became in Christ Jesus only a guest in this world, and His deity was lord of this world; as it was to have been in Adam, so that the lesser and weaker might be subject to the greater and all-powerful. But because Adam's will went into what was feeble and impotent, he himself became impotent, and did sink down into sleep, and fall unto the Creator again. But with Christ this image persisted in the divine essentiality, and the earthly nature hung unto it in the office and manner of a servant; no longer as a master, as in Mary his mother before the high benediction and revelation of the Deity, but as a servant; for this image was now, in the Spirit and power of God, lord of the third Principle of this world.

8. Now says Reason: What then did take place in this incarnation? Was the life aroused immediately at the moment of conception in transcendence of the natural course, so that the part from Mary, that is, the woman's seed, did at once have life? No, for it was an essential seed, and was moved at its proper natural time, with soul and spirit, like all the children of Adam; but the part from the Deity, surrounded with divine essentiality and wisdom, has had life from eternity to eternity. Nothing went to nor from the Deity; what it was, that it remained, and what it was not, that it came to be. It gave itself with heavenly divine essence to the essence and

substance of Mary, and Mary's essence and God's essence became one person. But Mary's essence was mortal, and God's essence immortal. Therefore Mary's essences had to die on the cross and pass through death into life. To this God's essences contributed, else it would not have been possible. Thus God's essence helped us, and still helps us by the death of Christ into God's essence and life.

9. We understand, then, the incarnation of Christ in a natural way, like that of all the children of men. For the heavenly, divine essence has given itself with its life to the earthly half-killed essence. The master has submitted himself under the servant, in order that the servant might be made alive. Thus Christ in nine months became a perfect man and at the same time remained a true God, and was born into this world in the manner and mode of all Adam's children, by the same way as all men. And that, not that He needed it-He could have been born magically-but He desired and was destined to remedy our impure, animal birth and entrance into this life. He was to enter into this world by our entrance, and lead us out of this world into God's entrance, and bring us out of the earthly quality.

10. For if He had been born magically in a divine manner, then He would not by nature have been in this world. For the heavenly essence would necessarily have swallowed up the earthly quality; hence He would not have been like us. How then would He have willed to suffer death, and to enter into death and break death to pieces? But it is not so. He is truly the woman's seed, and He entered into this world the natural way, like all men; but went out by death the divine way, in the divine power and essentiality. It is His divine living essentiality which stood firm in death, which has broken down death and cast derision on it, and led the wounded halfdead humanity through death into the life eternal. For the earthly part, which He received from His mother Mary into Himself, into the divine nature, died on the cross to the earthly nature. The soul was thus in the essentiality of God, and descended as a conqueror into the hell of the devil, that is, into the fierce wrath of God, and quenched it with God's love and

gentleness that characterize the divine loveessentiality. For the fire of love entered into the fire of wrath and drowned the wrath, in which the devil desired to be God. Hence the devil was taken captive by the darkness and lost his dominion. The sting or sword of the Cherubin or destroying angel was here broken. And this was the reason that God became man, in order that He might lead us out of death into the life eternal, and quench with His love the wrath which burned within us.

11. Further, you must understand us rightly as to how the wrath of God was quenched. It was not quenched by the mortal blood of Christ, which he shed, and in regard to which the Jews mocked him, but by the blood of the eternal life from God's essence, which was immortal and had in it the fountain of the water of eternal life. This was shed on the cross along with the outer blood; and when the latter sank into death, the heavenly blood sank too, and yet it was immortal.

12. Thus the earth received the blood of Christ, whereby it trembled and quaked; for the wrath of God was now vanquished in it, and there entered into it now the living blood which had come from heaven, from God's essence. This heavenly blood opened the graves of the saints, and also opened death. It made a way through death, so that death was made an open show of. For when Christ's body rose from death, he made in his body an open show of death; for its power was broken.

CHAPTER XI

ON THE PRACTICAL APPLICATION: OF WHAT USE TO US POOR CHILDREN OF EVE IS THE INCARNATION AND BIRTH OF JESUS CHRIST, THE SON OF GOD?

The Gate fullest of loving-kindness

1. WE poor children of Eve were all dead in Adam; and even though we did live, yet we lived only to this world, and death waited for us, and swallowed up one after another. There was no remedy for us, if God had not begotten us again from his being; we should not have reappeared in body in eternity, and our soul would have abided eternally in God's source of wrath with all the devils. But the incarnation of Jesus Christ is become for us a thing mighty in operation; for God became man for our sakes, in order that he might bring our humanity back again out of death into himself, and deliver our souls from the fire of the wrath of God. For the soul is in itself a fire-source, and contains in itself the first Principle, the sour austereness, which in itself labours only unto fire. But if the gentleness and love of God be withdrawn from such soulic generation, or if it be mixed up with hard unyielding matter, then it remains a source in the darkness, an acerb stringent harshness, which devours itself, and yet at the same time is always generating in the will fresh hunger. For an existence which has no beginning nor ground, has likewise no end; but itself is its ground, it produces itself.

2. We do not, however, mean that the soul has not a beginning. It has a beginning, but only as regards the creature, not as regards the essence. Its essence is from eternity, for the divine fiat has grasped it in the centre of the Eternal Nature, and brought it into a substantial being, moreover with the entire + according to the character of the Holy Trinity, as a likeness of the threefold spirit of the Deity, in which God dwells. Now, let it be done either in love or wrath, that is, in light or fire, the one into which the soul

imaginates, with that does it become pregnant; for it is a magical spirit, a source in itself. It is the centre of eternity, a fire of the Deity in the Father, yet not in the freedom of the Father, but in the Eternal Nature. It is not prior to being, but in being; whereas the freedom of God is independent of being, but dwells in being. For in being is God made manifest. And there would be no God without being, but an eternal stillness without source. But in the source or fountain-principle fire is generated, and from fire light. Here then two beings separate and carry two kinds of quality, viz. a fierce, hungry, thirsty one in the fire, and a gentle, lovely, giving one in the light, for the light gives and the fire takes. The light gives gentleness, and from the gentleness arises substantiality, and this is the fire's food; else it were a fierce, dark hunger in itself, as indeed a spirit is if it have not the nature of the light; like unto a famished poison. But if it attain to the substance of the gentleness, it draws this into itself and dwells therein, and uses it as food and also as a body, for it becomes permeated and impregnated therewith; for its substantial being is its satisfying or appeasing, so that the hunger is stilled.

3. We have thus to consider the human soul It was taken out of the centrum naturae, not out of the mirror of the Eternal, as out of the source of this world, but out of the eternal essence of the Spirit of God, out of the first Principle, out of the Father's property in accordance with Nature. Not from substance or from something; but the Spirit of the Deity has itself breathed life unto him, understand into the image in Adam, from all the three Principles. It has breathed into him the centrum naturae, as the fire-source to life, and also the gentleness of love from the being of the Deity, that is, the second Principle with divine heavenly essentiality, as well as the spirit of this world, as the mirror and model of the wisdom of God with the wonders.

4. But the spirit of this world is corrupted by the enkindling of the devil and the poison which he has cast into it; for the devil dwells in this world, and is a constant infector of the outer nature and property, although he is powerful only in the wrath or the sour desiring. But he puts his imagination and his false tincture

even into the love, and poisons the soul's best jewel; and has infected Adam's soul with his imagination or craving, with his evil hunger-spirit, so that Adam's soul lusted after earthly quality, and by this desire it became impregnated with earthly quality, so that the outer kingdom was introduced into the inner, whereby the light in the fire of the first Principle was extinguished, and his divine essentiality, in which he was to live eternally, was shut up in earthly death.

5. Thus, for this image and human soul there was no longer any remedy unless the Deity put itself in motion according to the second Principle, that is, according to the light of eternal life in it, and kindled again with the brightness of love the essentiality that was shut up in death. This was done in the incarnation of Christ. And this is the greatest marvel which God has wrought, that He has put himself in motion in the woman's seed by means of the centre of the Holy Trinity. For not in fire, i.e. in the man's tincture, was God's heart to reveal itself, but in the spirit's tincture, in the love of the life; in order that the fire in the man's tincture should be laid hold of by the gentleness and love of God. For eternal life was and had to bud forth again from close shut up death: here has the root of Jesse and the true rod of Aaron budded, and borne fair fruit. For in Adam Paradise was shut up in death, when he became earthly; but in Christ it budded again from death.

6. From Adam we have all inherited death; from Christ we inherit eternal life. Christ is the virgin image, which Adam was to have generated from himself, with both tinctures. But as he could not, he was divided, and had to generate by two bodies, till Shiloh came, that is, the virgin's Son, who was born of God and man. He is the breaker through, of whom the prophets have spoken, growing up as a plant. He flourishes as a Laurel-tree in God's essence. He has broken down death by his entrance into the human half-slain essence, for he grew up at once in human and in divine essence. He brought with him into our humanity the virgin chastity of the wisdom of God; He surrounded the ground of our soul with heavenly essentiality; He became the champion in the

combat, in which the two kingdoms,-viz. God's wrath and love, were in conflict with each other; He gave himself voluntarily to the wrath and quenched it with his love, understand in the human essence. He came from God into this world, and took our soul into him, that he might lead us out of the earthliness of this world again into himself, into God. He begot us anew in himself, that we might be again qualified to live in God. Of his own will did he beget us, that we should put our will into him. In this way he brought us again into himself to the Father, into our former native land, that is, into Paradise, from which Adam went out. He has become our fountain, his water springs in us; he is the fountain, and we his drops in him. He has become the fulness of our nature, that we in him may live in God. For God has become man. He has introduced his unfathomable and immeasurable being into humanity; his being, which fills the heavens, he has manifested in humanity. Accordingly man's being and God's being have become one being, a fulness of God. Our being is his moving in his heaven. We are his children, his marvel, his moving in his unfathomable body. He is Father, and we his children in him. We live in him and he in us. We are his instrument, by which he seeks and does what he pleases. He is the fire and also the light with regard to every being, he is hidden, and the work makes him manifest.

7. Thus we know that God is a Spirit, and his eternal will is magical or desiring. He doth out of nothing continually make being, and that in a twofold source, viz. according to fire and light. From fire arises fierceness, elevation, pride, the refusing to be united to the light, a wrathful stern will, according to which he is not called God, but a fierce consuming fire. This fire is not manifest in the pure Deity, for the light has swallowed up the fire into itself, and gives to the fire its love, its essentiality, its water, so that in God's nature there is only love, joy and bliss, and no fire is known. But fire is only a cause of the desiring will and of love, as also of light and of majesty; else there would be no being.

8. We can now recognize wherein lies our new birth (seeing indeed we are covered in this world with the earthly tabernacle,

and subjected unto the earthly life), namely, in the imagination alone: that we enter with our will into God's will, and wholly unite and give up ourselves to him, which is called faith. For the word faith is not historical; but it is a taking out of God's nature, the eating of God's nature, the introducing of God's nature by the imagination into the fire of one's soul, to appease its hunger thereby, and thus putting on God's nature, not as a garment, but as a body of the soul. The soul must have God's nature in its fire; it must eat of God's bread, if it would be God's child.

9. It will in this way also be new-born in God's nature, who has grafted it from the field of the fierceness and wrath into the field of the love, gentleness and humility of God; and it blossoms forth with a new flower, which grows in God's love, in God's field. This flower, which grows in God's love, is the true real image of God, which God desired when he created Adam in his likeness; this then has Jesus Christ, Son of God and of man, generated again for us. For his new birth from God's and our nature is our new birth; his power, life and spirit is all ours; and we need do nothing more to effect this, except that solely with our will-spirit we enter by him into God's nature; then our will is newborn in God's will, and receives divine power and essence. Not strange essence, but our primal essence, with which we in Adam entered into death: it is awakened again to us by the firstborn from the dead, which is Christ. He is God, but was born from us, that he might revive us from death: not in the form of a strange life which we should not have had here in this world, but in the form of our own life. For God's purpose must stand, the fair flower and image must grow from the corrupt field; and not only that, but also from the pure field.

10. From the virgin we were to be reborn and not from the man of wrath, from the fire's tincture, but from the virgin of love, from the light's tincture. By our resignation or self-surrender we put on the virgin of Christ, and thereby become the virgin of modesty, chastity and purity in the Ternarius Sanctus, in the angelic world, in the mirror of the Holy Trinity, in which God beholds himself, and this virgin he has taken to himself for a

spouse. He is our husband, to whom we are in Christ espoused, betrothed and incorporated. We are thus Mary in the covenant of grace, from whom God and man is born. Mary was the first in the high benediction, for in her was the goal to which the covenant pointed; she was known in God in the precious name Jesus, before the foundation of the world was laid. Not that she is to be regarded as bringing life out of death, but God willed in her to bring life out of death. Therefore she was highly blessed, and the pure virgin, chastity was put on her. And from the same virginity from which Christ was born, we must all be born. For we must become virgins and follow the Lamb of God, else we shall not see God. For Christ saith: Ye must be born anew by water and the Holy Spirit, if ye will see the kingdom of God. The water is the virginity, for the virgin carries the light's and water's tincture, viz. love and gentleness. And the Spirit, from which we are to be born, is that which at the movement of the Deity gave itself up to the woman's seed, which broke death to pieces; which brings forth out of the water a light-flaming flower. For he is the spirit and life of the flower not according to the fire-source of the wrath, but according to the source of the light in meekness and humility.

CHAPTER XII

OF THE PURE VIRGINITY. HOW WE POOR CHILDREN OF EVE MUST, STARTING FROM THE PURE VIRGIN CHASTITY, BE CONCEIVED IN THE INCARNATION OF CHRIST, AND BE NEW-BORN IN GOD; OTHERWISE WE SHALL NOT SEE GOD

1. WE poor children of Eve find in ourselves no pure chaste virgin thought; for mother Eve, who was a woman, has made us all feminine and masculine. We have in Adam and Eve all become men and women, unless we enter with our desiring will into the heavenly virginity, in which God has begotten us from Christ to be virgins again. Not according to the earthly life, in which there is no chastity nor purity, but according to the life of the heavenly virgin, in which Christ became man, which was put on Mary by the overshadowing of the Holy Spirit, which is without ground, limit and end, which stands everywhere before the Deity, and is a mirror and image of the Deity. Into this virgin, in which the Holy Trinity. dwells, wherein we were seen before the times of the world by the Spirit of God, and were known in the name Jesus, we must enter with our willspirit. For our true image, in which we are the likeness of God, has through Adam and Eve faded for us and become earthly. This -came about by desire or imagination; and accordingly God's clear countenance was hidden to us, for we lost the heavenly chastity.

2. But seeing that God by his favour and love towards us has again disclosed to us his clear countenance in the incarnation of Christ, the matter lies solely in this, that as in Adam we have imagined into the earthly craving, and thereby have become earthly, we now put our desiring will again into the heavenly virgin, and bring our longing thereinto; then our image goes out from the earthly woman and receives virgin essence and property, in which God dwells, where the soul's image may again attain the countenance of God.

3. Outward Reason says: How can it happen that we should be born again of the virgin from which Christ was born? It understands Mary as such; but we understand not Mary who is a creaturely virgin, even as we become creaturely virgins in the immaterial virgin chastity. Now we enter into the incarnation of Christ, not according to the outer life in the four elements, but according to the inner life in the one element, where the fire of God swallows up the four elements into itself; and, again, in its light, viz. in the second Principle, in which the outer man and woman must enter by death into Christ's resurrection, we bud forth in the true virgin wisdom of God, a virgin in the one element, wherein all the four lie hidden. We must die to the man and the woman, and crucify the corrupt Adam. He must die with Christ and be cast into the Father's wrath. This swallows up the earthly man and woman, and gives to the soul through the incarnation of Christ a virgin image, in which the man and woman is but one image, with its own love. The man now places his love in the woman, and the woman in the man; but if the two loves be transformed into one, there is no longer any desire of commingling in the one image, but the image loves itself.

4. Now the image was created in the beginning in the virgin wisdom of God, from divine essence. Seeing then the essence has become earthly and fallen into death, the Word which became man awakens it again. Thus the earthly nature remains to death in the wrath, and what is awakened remains in the Word of life, in the virgin chastity. Accordingly here in this world we carry a twofold man in one person, viz. a virgin image born of the incarnation of Christ, and an earthly image, masculine or feminine, shut up in death and in the wrath of God. The earthly must bear the cross, suffer itself to be reviled, persecuted and tormented in the wrath, and is at length given to death; then the wrath swallows it up in the qualificative fire of God. And if the Word of life, which in Mary became man, is included in the earthly image, then Christ, who brought from God the Word of life, rises from death, and leads the essence of the qualificative fire, i.e. the human essence, out of death, for he has arisen from death and lives in

God; his life has become our life and his death our death; we are buried in his death, but we bud forth in his resurrection and conquest, in his life.

5. But understand the meaning correctly. Adam was the virgin image, he had love proper, for the Spirit of God had breathed it into him. For what else can the Spirit of God breathe from himself but what he himself is? Now he is all, and yet is not called God in respect of every, source; but in all sources there is one only Spirit which is God, viz. according to the second Principle in the light, and yet there is no light without fire. But in fire he is not the love-spirit or the Holy Spirit, but the wrath of nature and a cause of the Holy Spirit, an anger and consuming fire; for in fire the spirit of nature is liberated, and the essential fire indeed gives nature, and is itself nature.

6. We understand, however, but one Holy Spirit in the light. Though all is one being, yet we understand that the matter which is generated from the gentleness of the light is as if impotent and dark. This the fire draws into itself and swallows up, but gives from the material source, from the fire, a powerful spirit which is free from matter and also from fire. Though it is held by the fire, yet the fire does not reach its quality; as we see that light dwells in fire and yet has not the fire's quality, but a gentle love-quality, which however would not be if the matter had not died and been consumed in the fire.

7. Let us consider then the first Adam. He was composed from the essence and nature of the light; but because he was to enter into a creaturely existence and be a complete likeness of God in accord with the whole reality, with all the three Principles, he was grasped by the verbum fiat in the whole sphere of all the three Principles and brought into a creaturely being. All the three Principles were indeed free in him, and were one in another, each in its order, and he was a quite complete likeness of God, according to and derived from the Being of all beings. But we are to know that the third Principle or the source of this world had at the kindling of Lucifer become wrathful, thirsty and evil, and that this source at once in Adam thirsted after the second Principle,

viz. after the heavenly matter, whence craving arose in Adam. For the source of pure love springing from the Holy Spirit had rejected this. But when the love did enter into the earthly source in order to satisfy it in its enkindled thirst, the pure immaterial love received the desiring, earthly, corrupt craving. Here was extinguished the second Principle, not as a death, in such a sense that it had become a nothing, but it was caught in the raging thirst. And seeing then God is a Light, the pure love-source lay shut up in death out of the light of God. The image was thus corrupted-and taken captive in the wrath of God, and love proper lost its power, for it was shut up in the corrupt earthliness, and loved the earthliness.

8. From this image, then, a woman had to be made, and the two tinctures, viz. the fire's essence and the watery essence of the matrix, had to be divided into a man and woman, so that love should be moving in a twofold source, and that one tincture should love and desire the other, and they should commix, whereby this stock should be continued and preserved.

9. But this race of men, thus contained in the earthly source, could not know or see God, for the pure love without spot was shut up in the earthly thirsty source and imprisoned in the thirst of the wrath of the Eternal Nature, which Lucifer had kindled; for the wrath had drawn the love with the earthliness into itself. Now, in this imprisoned love lay the virgin chastity of the wisdom of God, which, with the second Principle, with the heavenly essentiality, was in Adam incorporated into his body, and still more the spirit of their gentle essentiality, by the insulation of the Holy Spirit, which was inbreathed into Adam.

10. Now there was no remedy unless the Deity should stir itself in the divine virgin according to the second Principle, in the virginity that was shut up in death, and another image should arise from the first. And we know and sufficiently understand that the first image had to be given to the wrath in order that it might quench its thirst, and had to enter into corruption, as into the essential fire, although the essence does not corrupt or die. And on this account God has decreed a day, in which he will

bring the essence of the old and first Adam through fire, when it shall be released from vanity, from the craving of the devil and from the wrath of the Eternal Nature.

11. We understand further how God has brought again into us the life of his holy Being by putting himself in motion with his own heart or Word and power of the divine life in the virginity that was shut up in death, viz. in the true pure love; and has rekindled this love and introduced his heavenly essentiality with the pure virginity into the virginity shut up in death, and has out of the heavenly virginity and that shut up in death and wrath generated a new image.

12. And thirdly we understand that this new image has had, through death and the fierceness of fire, to be introduced again into the heavenly divine essentiality, into the Ternarius Sanctus; for the earthly craving, which the devil had possessed, had to remain in the wrath-fire and was given to the devil for food; therein he was to be a prince in accordance with the wrath-source of the Eternal Nature; for the devil is the food of the fierce wrath, and the fierce wrath is the food of the devil.

13. Seeing then the Word of eternal life has again moved itself in our cold love and virginity that was shut up in death, and taken upon it our corrupt virginity, and become a man inwardly and outwardly, and has introduced the centre, viz. the fire of our soul, into his love: we acknowledge his love and virginity that has been introduced into us as our own virginity; for his love and virginity has espoused itself with our cold love and virginity, and given itself up to them, that God and man may be eternally one person.

14. Here Reason says: This has taken place in Mary, that is, only in one person, but what becomes of me? Christ has not been born also in me.

15. Oh, our great misery and blindness, that we will understand nothing! How entirely has the earthly material craving blinded us and the devil led us away by and through the abominable Antichrist in Babel, so that we refuse to have any understanding at all! Consider, thou wretched and miserable Reason, what thou art! Nothing but a whorish woman in reference to God. How else

shall I name thee, since thou art perjurious and perfidious to the pure virginity which is of God? Hast thou not Adam's flesh, soul and spirit, and art thou not come from Adam? Art thou not sprung from Adam's water and fire? Thou art in fact Adam's child. Do what thou mayest, thou must submit and be resigned; thou swimmest in Adam's mystery, both in life and in death.

16. The Word of God has indeed become man in Adam's virginity that was shut up in death. The heart of God has stirred itself in Adam's virginity, and from out of death through God's fire has introduced it into the divine source. Christ has become Adam, not indeed the divided Adam, but the virgin Adam, such as he was before his sleep. He has brought the corrupt Adam into death, into God's fire, and has brought the pure virgin Adam out of death through the fire. His son art thou, if thou remainest not in death like rotten wood which cannot

qualify, which in fire gives no essence, but takes the form of dark ashes.

17. Reason then says: How is it, seeing I am a member of Christ and the child of God, that I find not nor do I feel Him? Answer: Yes, there's the rub, dear soiled bit of wood! Smell in thy bosom, of what dost thou stink? Of devilish craving, viz. of temporal pleasure, of greed, honour and power. Hearken, that is the devil's dress. Strip off this pelt, and throw it away. Place thy desire in Christ's life, spirit, flesh and blood; imaginate thereinto, as thou hast imaginated into the earthly craving, then thou wilt put on Christ in thy body, in thy flesh and blood; thou wilt become Christ; his incarnation will forthwith begin to make itself felt in thee, and thou wilt be new-born in Christ.

18. For the Deity or the Word, which stirred itself in Mary and became man, at the same time also became man in all deceased men descended from Adam who had given up and committed their spirit to God or to the promised Messiah; and passed too upon all those who were yet to be born from the corrupt Adam and would suffer themselves to be awakened by this Word, for the first man comprehends also the last. Adam is the stem, we all are his branches; Christ, however, has become our sap, virtue and

life. If now a branch of the tree withers, what can the sap and virtue of the tree do to that? Is not the virtue given to all the branches? Why does the branch not draw the sap and virtue into it? The difficulty lies in the fact that man draws into himself devilish power and essence instead of divine essence, and allows himself to be led away by the devil into earthly craving and desire. For the devil knows the branch, which has grown up for him in his former domain, and still grows. Therefore, as he was a liar and murderer at the beginning, he is so still, and infects men, because he knows that they have fallen to the outer dominion of the stars, into his magical craving. Hence he is a constant poisoner of the complexion; and where he scents a spark which serves him, that he always sets before man; if a man imaginate thereinto, he will straightway infect him.

19. Therefore it is said: Watch, pray, be sober, lead a temperate life, for the devil, your adversary, walketh about as a roaring lion, seeking whom he may devour (1 Pet. v. 8). Follow not, then, after covetousness, money, goods, power and honour, for in Christ we are not of this world. For therefore it was that Christ went to the Father, viz. into the divine Being, in order that we should follow him with our hearts, minds and wills; and hence he says he will be with us all the days, even unto the end of the world (Matt. xxviii. 20); but not in the source of this world. We must force a way out of the source of this world, out of the earthly man, and give up our will to his will, and introduce our imagination and desire into him; then we become pregnant in his virginity, which he has quickened again in us, and we receive the Word, which stirred itself in him, into our virginity shut up in death, and we are new-born in Christ in ourselves. For as death passed upon us all by Adam, so the Word of life passes upon us all from Christ. For the motion of the Deity in the incarnation of Christ has remained active, and is open to all men; there is lacking only the power of entry, in that man allows himself to be kept back by the devil. Christ need not first leave his place and enter into us, when we are new-born in him; for the divine Being, in which he was born,

contains everywhere the second Principle. Wherever it may be said that God is present, there also it may be said that the incarnation of Christ is present too; for it has been revealed in Mary, and thus inqualifies backwards to Adam and forwards even to the last man.

20. Reason then says: It is only faith that attains it. Yes certainly, in the true faith the gestation begins; for faith is spirit and requires substance. The substance, moreover, exists in all men; there is nothing wanting but that the spirit of faith should lay hold of it. And if it be laid hold of, the fair lily grows and blossoms forth, not merely a spirit, but the virgin image is born out of death into life. The rod of Aaron, which is dry, buds forth from the dry death and takes its body from death, the fair new virgin life from the half-dead virginity. The rod of Aaron betokens this, and the same holds true of old Zacharias and of Abraham with his old Sarah, who were all according to the outer world just as if dead, and no longer fruitful. But the promise of the new birth was to accomplish it, life was to bud from death. Not the old Adam, who was earthly, was to be lord; nor Esau the first-born, to whom indeed the inheritance would have belonged if Adam had stood firm; but the second Adam, which is Christ, who buds forth from the first through death, is to remain lord. Not the man or the woman is destined to possess the kingdom of God, but the virgin which is born from the death of the man and woman is to be the queen of the heavens one sex, not two; one tree, not many. Christ was the stem, because he was the root of the new body which budded from death and brought the dead virgin again as a fair twig out of death; and we all are the branches and all rest upon one stem, which stem is Christ.

21. We are then Christ's branches, his twigs, his children, and God is the Father of us all, and also of Christ. In him we live and move and have our being. We bear Christ's flesh and blood in us, if we attain to the new birth; for in Christ's spirit are we reborn. He who in Mary, in the dead humanity, became a living man without involving contact with a man, he in like manner becomes in ourselves, in our dead virginity, a new man; and there is

nothing wanting but that we cast the old Adam or the husk into death, that the torment of the earthly life may pass from us, and we may thus go out from the domain of the devil.

22. And this not simpliciter, for the old Adam must not be wholly cast away, but only the husk or hull, in which the seed lies hidden. The new man must bud forth in the motion of God from the old essence, like a stalk from the grain, as Christ teaches us. Therefore the essence must be cast into God's wrath, be persecuted, tortured, mocked, and sink under the cross; for from God's wrath-fire must the new man bud forth; he must be tried and approved in fire. We had fallen into the power of the essence of the wrath, but the love of God presented itself in the wrath and quenched the wrath with the love in the blood of the heavenly essentiality in the death of Christ. Thus the wrath retained the husk or the corrupt man, understand the earthly nature, and the love retained the new man. Not by another man shall heavenly blood be shed, but only the earthly mortal blood. For Christ, who was conceived without the intervention of man and woman, could alone do that, for in his heavenly essentiality was no earthly blood. He shed, however, his heavenly blood 'mongst the earthly blood, in order that he might deliver us poor earthly men from the wrath. For his heavenly blood had in his blood-shedding to mingle with the earthly, that the turba in the earthliness in us, which kept us prisoner, might be drowned and the wrath extinguished with the love of the heavenly blood. He gave up his life to death for us, for us he descended into hell, into the fiery quality of the Father, and went out of hell again into God, in order that he might break death to pieces, drown the wrath and make a way for us. When Christ hung and died on the cross, we hung with and in him, and died in him, rose again also in him from death, and live eternally in him, as a member of his body. And thus the seed of the woman has bruised the serpent's head; Christ has done it in us and we in Christ: Divine and human essence has accomplished it.

23. Therefore the matter now lies in this, that we follow him. Christ has certainly broken down death and quenched the wrath. But if we wish to become like his image, we must follow him also

in his death, take his cross upon us, suffer ourselves to be persecuted, scorned, mocked and slain. For the old husk belongs to the wrath of God; it must be purged away, seeing it is not the old man that must live in us, but the new. The old is given up to the wrath. For from the wrath blossoms forth the new, as light shines from fire. The old Adam must thus be the wood for the fire, in order that the new may bud forth in the light of the fire; for he has to subsist in fire. Nothing is eternal that cannot subsist in fire, and that does not originally arise from fire.

24. Our soul comes from God's fire, and the body comes from the light's fire. But understand always by the body a dumb substantiality, which is not spirit, but an essential fire. The spirit is much higher, for its origin is the fire of the wrath, of the wrathful quality; and its true life or body, which it carries in itself, is the light of the gentleness; this dwells in the fire and gives to the fire its gentle nourishment or love; otherwise the fire would not subsist-; it will have something to feed upon. For God the Father says: I am an angry, jealous, wrathful God, a consuming fire (Deut. iv. 24); and yet is called also a compassionate, lovable God (I John iv. 8), in reference to his light, to his heart. Therefore He says: I am merciful, for in the light is born the water of eternal life, which extinguishes the fire and the wrath of the Father.

CHAPTER XIII

OF THE TWOFOLD MAN, THAT IS, OF THE OLD AND NEW ADAM, SHOWING HOW THE OLD EVIL ADAM BEHAVES TOWARDS THE NEW, WHAT SORT OF RELIGION, LIFE AND FAITH EACH PRACTISES, AND ALSO WHAT EACH OF THEM UNDERSTANDS

1. ALL that is taught, written, preached or spoken in the old Adam regarding Christ, whether it be as the result of art or no matter how, belongs to death, and has neither understanding nor life; for the old Adam is dead as to Christ. The new Adam only, who is born of the virgin, should do this; he alone understands the word of regeneration and enters by the door of Christ into the sheepfold. The old Adam aims at getting in by art and inquiry. He supposes that Christ may be grasped sufficiently in the letter. He holds that one who has learned arts and languages, who has read much, is appointed by God and called to teach; that the Spirit of God must speak through his preaching, even though he is but the old corrupt Adam. But Christ says: These are robbers and murderers, and have come only to rob and to steal. He that entereth not by the door into the sheepfold, but climbeth up some other way, the same is a thief and a murderer (John x. 1). And he says further I am the door of the sheep: by me if any man enter in, he shall find pasture, and the sheep will follow him (John x. 9). For he that is not with me is against me.

2. A teacher must necessarily be born of Christ, otherwise he is a thief and a murderer, and only stands forth to preach for the belly's sake. He does it for money and honour, he teaches his own word and not God's word. But if he be born again of Christ, he teaches Christ's word, for he lives in the tree of Christ, and gives his sound from the tree of Christ, in which he lives. Therefore is there such contrariety on the earth, because men heap to themselves teachers, to tell them what their ears itch after and what the old evil Adam readily listens to, what ministers to his

elevation and carnal pleasure, what is conducive to might and magnificence.

3. O ye devilish teachers, how will you stand before the wrath of God? Why do you teach, when you are not sent from God? You are sent from Babel, from the great whore, from the mother of the great spiritual whoredom on earth. Not of the virgin are ye born, but of the adulterous woman. For not only do ye teach human fictions, but also persecute the teachers that are sent, who are born of Christ. You contend about religion, and yet there is no contention in religion: there are diversity of gifts, but one and the same spirit speaketh. As a tree has manifold branches and the fruit has a manifold form, not being just like one another; or as the earth bears diverse herbs and flowers, the earth being the one mother so is it with those who speak by God's spirit; each of them speaks from the wonder of his gifts. But their tree or their field, upon which they rest, is Christ in God. And you, binders of the spirit, will not suffer this. You insist on stopping the mouth of your Christ, whom yet you yourselves teach unknown with the earthly tongue, and insist on binding him to your law. Oh, the true church of Christ has no law! Christ is the temple where we must enter. The heap of stones does not make a new man. But the temple of Christ, where God's spirit teaches, awakens the half-dead image, so that the image begins to bud. It is a matter of indifferency, God cares not for art or for eloquence, but he that cometh to Him He will in no wise cast out. Christ came into the world to call and save poor sinners; and Isaiah saith: Who is so simple as my servant? Therefore the wisdom of this world will not do, it only brings about pride and puffed up reason, it has high pretensions and wishes to lord it. But Christ says: He who forsakes not houses, lands, goods, money, wife and child, for my name's sake, is not worthy of me. All that is in this world should not be so dear as the precious name Jesus. For whatever this world has is earthly, but the name Jesus is heavenly, and out of the name Jesus we must be born again from the virgin.

4. Therefore the virgin's child is opposed to the old Adam. The latter shows himself by desires of temporal pleasure, honour,

power and authority, and is a fierce, horrible dragon, who seeks only to devour, as the Revelation of John represents him. The child of the virgin, however, stands upon the moon, and wears a crown of twelve stars; for it treads under foot what is terrestrial or the moon; it has grown forth from the terrestrial moon like a flower from the earth. Accordingly the virgin image stands upon the moon. Against it the fierce dragon casts out of his mouth water as a flood, and tries continually to drown the virgin image. But the earth comes to the aid of the virgin and swallows up the flood of water and brings the virgin into Egypt, where the virgin image must suffer itself to be put into servitude. But the earth, or the wrath of God, covers the virgin image and swallows up the torrent of the dragon. And though the dragon overwhelms with his abominations the virgin image, calumniates and reviles it, yet this does not do the child of the virgin any harm; for the wrath of God receives the reviling which is poured out upon the pure child, the earth always signifying the wrath of God. Thus the virgin child stands on the earth, that is, on the terrestrial moon, and must always flee from the earthly dragon into Egypt. There it must be in bondage to Pharaoh; but it stands upon the moon, not under. The prince Joshua or Jesus brings it through Jordan to Jerusalem. It must by death enter into Jerusalem and quit the moon. It is but a guest in this world, a stranger and pilgrim; it has to journey through the dragon's country. When the dragon shoots forth his torrent upon it, it must bow down and put itself under the cross; then the wrath of God receives the dragon's fire.

5. It is known to us that the old Adam knows and understands nothing of the new; he understands everything in an earthly way. He knows not where or what God is; he. acts the hypocrite to himself, ascribes to himself piety and thinks that he serves God, yet serves only the old dragon; he sacrifices, and his heart cleaves to the dragon; he will be genuinely devout and with what is earthly ascend into heaven, and yet mocks at the children of heaven. Thereby he shows that he is an alien in heaven; he is only a master on earth and a devil in hell.

6. Among such thorns and thistles must the children of God grow. They are not known in this world, for the wrath of God covers them. Even a child of God knows not himself aright; he sees only the old Adam who hangs unto him, who always strives to drown the child of the virgin. Unless indeed the virgin's child obtain a glimpse into the Ternarius Sanctus; then he knows himself, when the fair knightly garland is set upon him; in such case must the old Adam look on from behind, and knows not what happens to him. He is indeed joyful, but he dances as one who dances to the sound of stringed instruments: when the playing ceases, his joy has an end and he continues to be the old Adam; for he belongs to the earth and not to the angelic world.

7. As soon as a man gets to the point that the virgin image begins to bud forth from the old Adam, so that the man's soul and spirit gives itself up into the obedience of God, then in him does the combat begin, for the old Adam in the wrath of God fights against the new Adam in the love. The old Adam wishes to be lord in flesh and blood, and in this connection the devil can reach, infect and possess him. The virgin twig can the devil not endure, but he may not touch it. Because his own dwelling in the darkness of the abyss pleases him not, he willingly dwells in man; for he is an enemy of God and outside of man has no power. Therefore he possesses man, and leads man as he-pleases into the anger and wrath of God, so that he may mock at God's love and gentleness; for he still supposes, because he is a fierce fire-source, that he is higher than humility, seeing that he can sweep along in a terrible manner. But because he must not touch the virgin twig, he makes use of nothing but guile and villainy, and covers the twig, that it may not be known in this world; otherwise there might grow too many such twigs for him in his so-called country, for he is hostile to them. He brings his proud servants with mockery and molestation upon any such man, so that he is

persecuted, derided and accounted a fool. This he does by the reason-wise world, by those who call themselves shepherds of Christ, whom the world has regard to, in order that the lily-twig may not be known; otherwise men might observe it, and for him there might grow too many such twigs, and hence he might lose his dominion among men.

8. But the noble lily-twig grows in patience and meekness, and receives its essence, power and smell from the field of God, that is, from the incarnation of Christ. Christ's spirit is its power, God's essence is its body. Not from a foreign property, but from its own essence which is shut up in death and budding forth in Christ's spirit does the virgin lily-twig grow. It seeks not nor desires the beauty of this world, but of the angelic world; for it grows not in this world, in the third Principle, but in the second Principle, in the paradisaic world. Therefore there is great strife in flesh and blood, in the outer reason. The old Adam knows not the new and yet finds that he resists him: the new one wills not what the old Adam wills, he is always leading the latter to abstinence. This afflicts the old Adam, who desires only pleasure, possessions and temporal honour, and cannot suffer mockery and tribulation. But the new Adam is well pleased to bear the marks of Christ, that he may become like the image of Christ. Therefore the old Adam goes about often mournfully, for he sees that he must be regarded as a fool; nor knows what is happening to him, for he knows not God's will, he has only the will of this world: what shines there he will have, he would fain always be master, before whom people bow. But the new Adam bows himself before his God; he desires nothing, wills nothing, but only longs after his God as a child after its mother; he casts himself into the bosom of his mother and gives himself up to his heavenly mother in the spirit of Christ; he desires of his eternal mother food and drink, and eats in the bosom of the mother as a child in the womb eats of its mother. For as long as he is covered up in the old Adam, he is still in process of incarnation; but when the old Adam dies, the new Adam is born from the old he abandons the vessel, in which he lay and became a virgin child, to the earth and to the judgment of God; but he is born as a flower in God's kingdom. Then when the day of restoration shall come, all his works, which he has done in the old Adam, shall follow him; the iniquity of the old

Adam, however, shall be burnt away in the fire of God and given to the devil for food.

9. Here Reason says: Since then the new man in this world, in the old Adam, is only in process of incarnation, he is not perfect. Answer: This is no otherwise than as in a child, the seed being sown with two tinctures, masculine and feminine, united in each other, and from it a child grows. For as soon as a man turns round, and turns himself to God with his whole heart, mind and will, and goes out from the godless way and gives himself up in real earnest to God, then the gestation begins in the soul's fire, in the old corrupt image, and the soul seizes in itself the Word which put itself in motion in Mary in the centre of the Holy Trinity, which gave itself to Mary, to the half-dead virgin, with the chaste highly blessed heavenly Virgin of the wisdom of God, and became a true man. This Word, which moved or stirred itself in Mary in the centre of the Holy Trinity, which espoused itself with the halfdead shut-up virginity, is laid hold of by the soul's fire, and gestation begins immediately in the soul's image, that is, in the soul's light in the gentleness, in the shut-up virgin essence. For man's love-tincture seizes God's love-tincture, and the seed is sown in the Holy Spirit in the soul's image.

10. Now consider I When the virgin sign presents itself thus in God's love, such a twig may indeed be born, for in God all is perfect. But as long as it is covered up in the old Adam, and stands as it were in essence only as a seed, there is yet great danger in connection with it, for many a one attains this twig only at his latter end; and though he had brought it with him out of the womb, it yet becomes deteriorated and in the case of some is broken and terrestrialized.

11. So is it likewise with the poor sinner. When he repents, but afterwards becomes again a bad man, it fares with him as befell Adam, who was a beautiful, glorious image, created by God and highly enlightened; but when he let himself be overcome by desire, he became earthly and his beautiful image was imprisoned in the earthly source in the wrath of God: and so it happens still. But this we say, as having received illumination in the grace of God

and having striven a considerable time for this garland, that to him who continues steadfast in real earnest, until his twig becomes a tree, his twig in one or more storms will not easily be broken; for what is feeble has also a feeble life. We do not thus break in upon the Deity. On the contrary, the position is of a natural kind, and indeed all comes to pass naturally; for the Eternal itself has also its nature, and one merely proceeds out of another. If this world had not been poisoned by the malice and wrath of the devil, Adam would have remained in

this world in Paradise, nor would there have been any such wrath in the stars and elements; for the devil was a king and great lord in the place of this world: he has stirred up the wrath. God therefore created the heaven out of the midst of the waters in order that the fiery nature, viz. the fiery firmament, might be subject to the watery heaven, that its wrath might be extinguished. Otherwise, if the water were to disappear, we should certainly see what there would be in this world, namely, nothing but a mere cold, sour, fiery burning, and yet wholly dark, for there could be no light, because light exists only in the gentleness; hence also there can be no shining fire, unless it have gentle essentiality. And we can recognize that God has transmuted the heavenly essentiality into water, which was done naturally when God the Father put himself in motion and the devil fell, who wished to be a fire-lord over the gentleness; thus, such a bar was placed before his poisonous malignity that he is now God's ape and not lord, a rager and fulfiller in the wrathful source.

12. Seeing then we know that we are surrounded by the wrath, we ought to take heed to ourselves and not estimate ourselves lightly; for we have our being not only from this world, but also from the divine world, which lies hidden in this world and is near us. We may live and be at the same time in three worlds, if we bud forth again out of the evil life with the virgin image. For we live: (1) in the first Principle in the Father's world in fire, according to the essential soul, that is, according to the firesource in the centre of nature of eternity; and (2) with the true pure virgin image we live in the light-flaming paradisaic world, although it is not manifest

in the place of this world, but yet is known in the virgin image in the Holy Spirit, and in the Word which dwells in the virgin image; and (3) we live with the old Adam in this external corrupt distempered world, along with the devil in his enkindled desire: therefore it is necessary to be cautious. Christ says: Be simple as doves and wise as serpents (Matt. x. 16). Take heed to yourselves. In God's kingdom we need no guile, we are only children in the bosom of the mother; but in this world we should certainly be on our guard, we carry the noble treasure in an earthly vessel. It is soon done, losing God and the kingdom of heaven, which after this time can no longer be attained. Here, we are in the field and as seed, we are here in process of growth; though the stalk be broken, the root is still present, so that another stalk may grow.

13. In this life the door of grace stands open to man. However great the sinner, if he turn round and produce honest fruits of repentance, he may be new-born out of what is bad. But he who deliberately casts his root into the devil's fire (corruption) and despairs of his budding forth: who shall help him, who himself wills not? But if he turn his will to God, then God will have him. For he who wills into God's wrath, him will God's wrath have; but he who wills into the love, him will God's love have. Paul says: To whom ye yield yourselves servants to obey, his servants ye are to whom ye obey; whether of sin unto death, or of obedience unto righteousness (Rom. vi. 16). The wicked man is to God a sweet savour in the wrath, and the holy man is to God a sweet savour in His love (2 Cor. ii. 15, 16). A man can make of himself what he pleases: he has the two before him, viz. fire and light. If he will be an angel in the light, then the Spirit of God in Christ helps him to enter the angelic host; if he will be a devil in the fire, then God's anger and wrath help him, and draw him into the abyss to the devil. Further, he gets his ascendent, of which he has desire. But if he break the first desire and enter into another, then he gets another ascendent; but the first clings to him strongly, it strives continually to possess him again. Therefore the noble grain must frequently be in a great strait; it must suffer itself to be pricked by thorns, for the serpent always stings the woman's seed,

that is, the child of the virgin, in the heel. The sting of the serpent lies in the old Adam, it always stings the child of the virgin in the mother's womb, in the heel. Therefore life in this world is with us poor imprisoned men a vale of sorrow, full of anxiety, tribulation, misery and affliction. We are here strange guests, and are upon our pilgrim's path. We must traverse great waste, wild solitudes, and are surrounded with evil beasts, with adders and serpents, wolves and nothing but horrible beasts, and the most evil beast we carry in our bosom. In this evil villainous stable our fair virgin lodges.

14. But this we know and with good reason say, that when the noble twig grows and becomes strong, there in that man must the old Adam become servant, he must walk behind, and often do what he does not wish. Often, he must suffer tribulation, mockery and even death. This he does not do willingly, but the virgin image in Christ constrains him; for it would follow joyfully after Christ, who is its bridegroom, and become like Him in tribulation and affliction.

15. And certainly no one is crowned with the virgin's crown which the woman in the Revelation of John wears with twelve stars, viz. with six spirits of nature of a heavenly kind, and with six spirits of an earthly kind, unless he stand firm against the torrent of the dragon and flee into Egypt, that is, under the cross into the plagues of Egypt. He must carry the cross of Christ and put on Christ's crown of thorns, suffer himself to be mocked, fooled and scorned, if he would put on the crown of Christ and of the virgin. He must first wear the crown of thorns, if he. would put on the heavenly crown of pearls in the Ternarius Sanctus.

16. And we make known to the illuminates another great mystery, namely, that when the pearl is sown, the soul for the first time puts on the crown in the Ternarius Sanctus with great joy and honour before God's angels and all the holy virgins. And there is assuredly great joy there, for in that place God becomes man. But this crown conceals itself again. How should there not be joy there? The old Adam dances also, but as an ass to the sound of the lyre; but the crown is assigned to the incarnation.

17. Wouldest thou be a champion, then thou must in Christ's footsteps wage war with the old ass, as well as fight against the devil. If thou conquer and art acknowledged and accepted as a valiant child of God, the woman's crown with twelve stars will be put on thee. That shalt thou wear, till the virgin be born out of the woman from thy death or by thy death; she shall put on the triple crown of great honour in the Ternarius Sanctus. For as long as the virgin image is still shut up in the old Adam, it attains not the angelic crown, as it is still in danger. But when it is born at the death of the old Adam and emerges from the husk or shell, then it is an angel and can no longer perish, and the right crown as assigned, in which God became man, is put upon it. But the crown with the twelve stars it retains as an eternal sign; for it must never be forgotten that God has in the earthly woman again disclosed the virginity and become man. The Deity is spirit, and the holy pure Element is born out of the Word of eternity; and the master has passed into servant, at which all the angels in heaven marvel: and it is the greatest wonder which has been done from eternity, for it is against nature, and such may be described as love. The six earthly signs of the crown with twelve stars shall stand as an eternal wonder and be an eternal song of praise, in that God has redeemed us out of death and distress; and the six heavenly signs shall be our crown and glory, to show that we have overcome what is earthly by what is heavenly, that we were men and women, and thereafter are chaste virgins filled with love proper. Thus the signs of victory shall continue to eternity, whereby shall be recognized what God has had to do with humanity, and how man is the greatest wonder in heaven, at which the angels highly rejoice.

CHAPTER XIV

ON THE NEW BIRTH: IN WHAT SUBSTANCE, ESSENCE, BEING AND PROPERTY IS FOUND THE NEW BIRTH, THAT IS, THE CHILD OF THE VIRGIN, WHILE IT STILL LIES IN THE OLD ADAM

1. SINCE we swim in earthly flesh and blood in this sea of sorrow, and have become of an earthly nature, in which we are shut up in obscurity in the reflection, the noble mind ceases not to inquire regarding its true country, whither it is destined to go. It is always saying: Where then is God, or when will it be that I can see God's face? Where then is my noble pearl? Where is the child of the virgin? I see it not at all; how does it happen that I thus travail in desire after that which, nevertheless, I am unable to see? I find certainly great longing and desire for it, but can see nothing in which my heart might rest. I am always as a woman who would fain bring forth; how fain would I see my fruit, which is promised to me by my God I She yearns continually to bring forth; one day calls unto another, the morning unto the evening, and the night again unto the day; and in privation hopes for the moment when at last will arise the bright morningstar, which will bring rest to the soul; and it is with the soul as with a woman who labours to bring forth, who continually hopes for the sight of her fruit, and waits with longing and desire.

2. Thus does it fare with us, my dear children of God. We suppose that we are still far from it, and yet are thus in travail. We bring forth, accordingly, with great longing in anguish, and know not the seed which we bring forth, for it is hidden. We do not bring forth to this world; how then should we see the fruit with the eyes of this world? the fruit belongs not to this world.

3. But seeing that we have obtained the true knowledge of this thing, not according to the outer man, but according to the inner, we will portray it in a similitude, for the sake of the reader and for our own recreation and delight.

4. When we consider ourselves, as to how we are twofold, with twofold sense and will, we cannot better attain to knowledge than by considering creaturely existence. Lying in view is a rough stone, and in some we find the best gold. There it is seen how the gold glitters in the stone, but the stone is inert, and knows not that it contains in itself such a noble gold. This holds also of us: we are an earthly sulphur, but have a heavenly sulphur in the earthly, where each is its own possession. During this lifetime both are together, but inqualify not with each other; one is merely the container and tenement of the other, as we see in gold. The rough stone is not the gold, but only the receptacle of it. The roughness of the stone in no wise gives rise to the gold, but the tincture of the sun in the rough stone produces it. The rough stone is the mother and the sun the father; for the sun impregnates the rough stone, because it has the centrum naturae, to which the sun owes its origin.

5. So it is also with man: the earthly man is indicated by the rough stone, and the Word that became man is indicated by the sun, which makes the corrupt man pregnant. The cause is as follows The corrupt man is indeed earthly, but he contains in himself the centrum naturae eternally; he longs after God's sun, for at his creation God's sun was taken also into his being. The rough stone, however, has overgrown the sun and swallowed it up in itself, so that the sun is mixed up with the rough sulphur, and cannot escape the rough sulphur, unless it be purified in fire, so that what is rough is melted away, and the sun remains alone by itself. Understand this of death and corruption, in which the coarse earthly flesh is melted away, and the virgin spiritual flesh remains without the other.

6. Understand correctly what we mean; we speak solemnly and truly, as we know it. The new man is not a mere spirit; he lives in flesh and blood; just as the gold in the stone is not merely spirit, it has body, yet not such a body as the rough stone shows, but a body which in the centrum naturae subsists in fire. For the fire cannot consume its body, because the gold has another principle. But it justly remains dumb, for the earth is not worthy of the gold,

although it carries it and also produces it. So likewise the earthly man is not worthy of the jewel which he carries; and though he help to produce it, he is nevertheless a dark earth in comparison with the child of the virgin born of God.

7. And as the gold has a real body, which is hidden and imprisoned in the rough stone, so has the virgin tincture in the earthly man a real, heavenly, divine body in flesh and blood, but not in such flesh and blood as the earthly; it can resist fire, it passes through stone and wood and is not laid hold of. As the gold penetrates the rough stone and breaks it not, nor is itself broken, and the stone knows nothing of the gold, so is it also with the old earthly man: when he receives the Word of life which in Christ became man, he receives it in the corrupt sulphur of his flesh and blood, in the virgin centre that is shut up in death, in which centre Adam was a virgin image; and there the rough earth covered his gold of the clear divine essentiality, so that the heavenly nature had to remain in death, in the centre of fire. In the same centre the Word of life, which in Mary became man, moved itself; there the essence that was shut up in death obtained a living tincture. At this point the noble gold or the heavenly essence begins in death to bud, and has at once in itself, in the Word of life, the Holy Spirit, which proceeds from the Father and Son; and wisdom or the heavenly virgin, as a mirror and image of the Deity before itself, forms as it were a pure sulphur, a pure flesh and blood, in which the Holy Spirit dwells, not in the form of earthly essence, but in the form of divine essence, by means of heavenly essentiality. That is the true flesh and blood of Christ, for it grows in the spirit of Christ, in the Word of life which became man, which has broken down death so that the divine tincture budded again and produced being from itself, for all is born and has arisen out of God's desire. But as God is a fire and also a light, we know sufficiently from whence each individual thing has come. We cannot possibly say otherwise than that from what is good and loving good has arisen; for a good desiring will conceives in its imagination its like, it makes to itself its like by the hunger of its own desiring.

8. We recognize, then, that because the Deity desired to have a mirror, an image of itself, the Divine longing also in its self-impregnation will have generated in its desiring will what is good and most lovable, a true likeness according to the Good, according to the clear Deity. But the fact that the earthly element has become mixed up with it, that is the fault of the desiring wrath, of the fire, of the devil, who has kindled it by his longing.

9. So likewise it is highly recognizable by us that God would not abandon his own (viz. his best and dearest, which he created as his like to be a creaturely being); rather he became himself such a being as he had created, that he might generate again out of corruption what has been corrupted and turn it into what is best, in which he might dwell eternally. And we say with good ground that God dwells in the new man self-subsistingly, not by a reflection or extrinsic shine, but essentially, yet in his principle. The outer man touches or grasps him not. Further, the flesh and blood of the new man is not God, it is heavenly essentiality. God is Spirit, God does not decay and perish; though being decay and perish, yet God remains in himself. He has no need of any departing away, for he does not make use of any entering in; but he manifests himself in flesh and blood, it is his good pleasure to possess a likeness.

10. If then we know ourselves aright and follow this up, we find that man (i.e. the whole man) is a true likeness according to God. For by the earthly life and body he belongs to this world, and by the virgin life and body he belongs to heaven; for the virgin essence has a heavenly tincture, and makes heavenly flesh, in which God dwells. Just as the gold in the stone has a different tincture from the rough stone, and this tincture has another body; each body arises from its own tincture, as for instance we know that the earth has been generated from the fierceness springing from the centre of the sour or cold fire, from the sulphur of the austereness in the anguish for fire.

11. Thus also a good body is produced out of a good essence, for the essence makes the life, and yet is not itself life. Life has its origin in the Principle or in fire, whether it be in the cold or hot

fire, or in the fire of light; each of them is a special principle, and yet is not separated.

12. And now, on the basis of truth, we will speak of the incarnation or humanity, and say in clear, plain, unveiled language, not founded on conjecture or opinion, but on our own true knowledge, given to us by God in illumination

I. That the new regenerated man, who is hidden in the old like gold in the stone, has a heavenly tincture and divine heavenly flesh and blood in himself; and that the spirit of this flesh is no spirit of another, but his own spirit, generated from his own essence.

II. We acknowledge and say that the Word, which in Mary the Virgin became man, is the primal cause of the tincture that beginneth in the sulphur; and we acknowledge Christ's spirit, which fills the heavens everywhere, to be dwelling in this tincture.

III. We acknowledge this heavenly flesh as Christ's flesh, in which the Holy Trinity dwells undivided.

IV. We confess that it is possible that this same flesh and blood during the time of the old Adam may in turn be corrupted by imagination or desire, as took place in Adam.

V. We say that in the process of corruption nothing departs from the Deity, nor is it touched by anything that is evil; for what the love of God loses devolves to the wrath of God. Whatever falls away from the light is seized by the fire, and God's Spirit remains by itself uncorrupted.

VI. We say that in all men exists the possibility of the new birth, else God were divided, and not in one place as in another. And we acknowledge that man is drawn by fire and light: where he inclines with the balance [the will], there does he fall; and yet he may in the course of this time again lift up his hinge or balance. We say that the clear Deity wills no evil, and wills no devil either, nor has it willed any; much less does it will to have a man in hell in the wrath of God. But as there is no light without fire, we recognize how the devil has by desire set his imagination on the wrath-fire. In like manner all the men who are damned will not suffer themselves to be helped, but themselves fill up the rapacious fire-source. They allow themselves to be drawn, yet it would be possible for them to stand firm.

VII. We say that the true temple in which the Holy Spirit preaches is in the new birth; that all is dead, dumb, crooked, blind and lame, which is not or teaches not from God's Spirit; that the Holy Spirit does not mingle with the sound given by the godless mouth; that no godless man is Christ's pastor. For, though in the holy man the hour is struck by means of the voice of the godless man, this would also ensue from the cry of a beast, if its sound were intelligible or the precious name of God were mentioned. For as soon as the name of God is mentioned and gives a sound, then the other sound takes hold in the place where it is sounding, that is, in the holy soul. But no godless man awakens another godless man from death, for they are both in the wrath of God and are still shut up in death. Had we ourselves been able to rise from death and make ourselves alive, the heart of God would not have needed to become man. Therefore we say with good reason that that Word alone which became man awakens the poor sinner from his death and to repentance, and generates new life. Accordingly all ranters that are godless profit not the temple of Christ at all. But they who have the spirit of Christ, they are Christ's pastors.

VIII. We acknowledge and say that all teachers who profess to be servants and ministers of Christ, and are such in an unregenerated way, for the sake of the belly and honours, are Antichrist and the woman on the dragon in the Revelation of John (Rev. xvii. 3, 4).

IX. We say that all unjust tyranny and selfusurped power, whereby the wretched one is oppressed, sucked dry, crushed and tormented, whereby also he becomes fickle and loose, and is led and drawn to all kinds of excess and injustice, is the horrible abominable beast on which Antichrist rides.

X. We know and say that the time approaches and the day dawns in which this evil beast with the whore shall go into the abyss. Amen, Hallelujah,
Amen.

PART II

OF THE SUFFERING, DYING, DEATH AND RESURRECTION OF CHRIST

HOW WE MUST ENTER INTO CHRIST'S SUFFERING, DYING AND DEATH, AND OUT OF HIS DEATH RISE AGAIN WITH HIM AND THROUGH HIM, AND BECOME LIKE HIS IMAGE, AND LIVE ETERNALLY IN HIM

CHAPTER I

OF THE ORIGIN OF LIFE FROM FIRE. FURTHER, OF THE ETERNAL SPIRIT IN THE ETERNAL VIRGIN OF THE WISDOM OF GOD, AND WHAT THE ETERNAL BEGINNING AND THE ETERNAL END IS

1. OUTWARD Reason says: Would it not have been sufficient that God should become man in us; why had Christ to suffer and die? Could not God then introduce man thus into heaven by the new birth? Is God then not powerful enough to do what he wills? What pleasure has God in death and dying, that he has not only allowed his Son to die on the cross, but we must also all die? Since then God has redeemed us by the death of his Son, and he has paid for us, why must we also die and rot? Thus runs Reason.

2. Before this mirror we would have Antichrist invited, who calls himself Christ's minister and pastor, as well as all the universities of this world with their disputations and laws, as also all the children of Christ, who bear Christ's cross. They shall all see the real ground, not with the view to reviling someone in his ignorance, but of the true doctrine, that everyone ought to seek and find himself. For it will be a very serious matter, and touches man; it demands his body and soul, he must not jest with it at all, for he who has given this knowledge has prepared his trumpet; it concerns the human race, let everyone trim his lamp. A great king

of a twofold kind will come by two doors; he is one and yet two; he has fire and light; he makes his entry on earth and also in heaven: this we may leave to be a wonder.

3. Dear children of Christ, when we consider death, and how we must by death enter into life, we find quite a different life, which arises out of death. We soon find why Christ has been obliged to die, why we have also to die in Christ's death, rise again in him, and with and through him enter into God's kingdom.

4. If now we would find this, we must consider eternity in reference to the ground and unground, else there is no finding; we will find it only where it is. As we have our origin with God's image from the eternal ground, but with the soul and its image have been introduced into what is temporal and perishable, that is, into suffering (Qual), and eternity or the unground is a freedom out of or beyond suffering (Qual), therefore we must by dying enter again into freedom. It cannot, however, be said that there is no life there; it is the right life, which exists eternally without pain or suffering. And we give you this to consider of in a true similitude, which indeed is a likeness according to the kingdom of this world; but if we add to it the Divine world, it is the reality itself.

5. You know that our life is rooted in fire, for without heat we live not. Now fire has a special centre, its own maker in its circle, viz. the seven forms or spirits of nature. But only the first four forms are regarded as nature or the source in which fire is awakened and kindled, so that a principle or life-centre is present; the materia of the combustion being formed in the spirits or forms themselves, and always consumed in the fire. And the fire produces from the consumption something different, which is better than the first thing which the fire makes. For the fire mortifies and swallows up the nature which the fire itself makes (understand the essential fire, in the forms for fire); it consumes it, and produces from death something much nobler and better, which it cannot consume. This is shown in fire and light, which is not merely the veritable likeness, but the reality itself; only that

the principles have to be distinguished. All is indeed one fire, but it differentiates itself according to the source.

6. If now we would present this to be understood, it will be necessary to give information about the origin of fire. This, however, has been described at length in the book of the Three Principles and other works. Accordingly we give here only a brief abstract for the understanding, and refer the reader to the other writings, if he wish to investigate the seven forms of nature.

7. Fire has mainly three forms in itself as centre. The fourth form is fire itself and gives the Principle, i.e. life with spirit; for in the first three forms is no true spirit, there are essences only, viz. (1) Sour, that is the desiring will, the first and chiefest form; (2) Bitter, stinging, is the second form, a cause of the essences; (3) Anguish as the circle or centre of life, the turning wheel, which embraces in it the senses or the bitter essences, swallows them up as it were in death and gives (4) from the torture-chamber as from death, the mind, viz. another centre. Understand it thus

8. In eternity, i.e. in the Unground out of nature, there is nothing but a stillness without being; there is nothing either that can give anything; it is an eternal rest which has no parallel, a groundlessness without beginning and end. Nor is there any limit or place, nor any seeking or finding, or anything in which there were a possibility. This Unground is like an eye, for it is its own mirror. It has no essential principle, also neither light nor darkness, and is above all a magia and has a will, after which we should not strive and inquire, for it confuses us. By this will we understand the ground of the Deity, which has no origin, for it comprises itself in itself; whereat we are justly dumb, for it is out of nature.

9. Seeing then that we are in nature, we know not the will in eternity, for in the will the Deity itself is all, and the eternal origin of its own spirit and all beings. In the will the Deity is all-powerful and allknowing, and yet in this will is not called God or known as God, for there is in it neither good nor evil. We have here a desiring will, which is the beginning and also the end; for the end makes at the same time the beginning of this will, and the

beginning again the end. It is found thus that all beings are included in an eye, which is like a mirror wherein the will beholds itself and finds what it is; and in the beholding it becomes desireful of the entity which it is itself. And the desiring is a drawing-in, and yet there is nothing that can be drawn; but the will draws itself in its own desire, and in its desiring represents to itself what it is; and this representative image is the mirror in which the will sees what it is, for it is a likeness of the will. And we recognize this mirror (in which the will itself always beholds and has vision of itself) to be the eternal wisdom of God, for it is an eternal virgin without substantial being; and yet is the mirror of all beings, in which all things have been seen from eternity, whatever could or was to arise.

10. The mirror is not the seeing itself, but the will which is appetent; that is to say, the longing which goes out from the will is a spirit, and makes in the longing of desire the mirror. The spirit is the life, and the mirror is the manifestation of the life, without which the spirit would not know itself; for the mirror or wisdom is its ground and container; this is the discovery of the spirit, since the spirit finds itself in wisdom. Wisdom without the spirit is not a being, and the spirit without wisdom is not manifest to itself, each without the other were an ungrounded existence.

11. Thus wisdom, as the mirror of the spirit of the Deity, is of itself passive, and is the body of the Deity or of the spirit, in which the spirit dwells. It is a virgin matrix in which the spirit reveals itself, and is God's essence, that is, a holy divine sulphur formed in the imagination of the Spirit, of the Unground of eternity. And this mirror or sulphur is the eternal first beginning and the eternal first end, and everywhere resembles an eye, by which the Spirit sees what it is within, and what it has to disclose.

12. This mirror or eye is without ground and limit, so the spirit, too, has no ground, save in this eye. It is everywhere entire, undivided, as we know that the Unground cannot be divided, for there is nothing which can divide: there is no motion besides the

spirit. We are able, then, to recognize what is the eternal spirit in wisdom, and what is the eternal beginning and the eternal end.

CHAPTER II

THE TRUE AND HIGHLY PRECIOUS GATE OF THE HOLY TRINITY, THE EYE OF THE ETERNAL LIVING SHINE. OF THE DEITY OUT OF OR BEYOND NATURE

1. WE recognize that the eternal beginning in the Unground is in itself an eternal will, whose origin no creature shall know. But it has been given to us to know and to recognize in spirit its ground, which it makes in itself, in which it rests. For a will is thin like a nonentity; therefore it is desireful and wishes to be something, that it may be manifest in itself. For the nothing causalises* the will so that it becomes desireful, and the process of desire is a mode of imagination, as the will beholds itself in the mirror of wisdom. Accordingly it imaginates from the Unground into itself, and makes for itself in the imagination a ground in itself, and makes itself pregnant with imagination through wisdom, i.e. through the virgin mirror, which is a mother without bringing forth, without will.

2. The impregnation does not take place in the mirror, but in the will, in the imagination of the will. The mirror remains eternally a virgin without bringing forth, but the will becomes impregnate with the aspect of the mirror. For the will is Father, and the impregnation in the Father, i.e. in the will, is heart or Son, for it is the will's or Father's ground, as the spirit of the will lies in the ground, and proceeds from the will in the ground into virgin wisdom. Thus the will's imagination, viz. the Father, draws the mirror's vision or form, that is, the wonders of power, colours and virtue, into itself, and thus becomes pregnant with the splendour of wisdom, with power and virtue. This is the heart of the will or of the Father, as the unfathomable will obtains a ground in itself by and in the eternal unfathomable imagination.

3. We recognize, then, the impregnation of the Father to be the centre of the spirit of eternity, where the eternal spirit always seizes itself. For the will is the beginning, and motion or drawing-in for imagination, as for the mirror of wisdom, is the eternal

unfathomable spirit. This arises in the will and seizes itself in the centre of the heart, in the power of wisdom as drawn-in, and is the heart's life and spirit. Since then the eternal unfathomable will in itself were dumb, what is seized through [in] wisdom (which is called heart or centre) is the will's word, for it is the sound or power, and is the will's mouth which reveals the will. For the will, viz. the Father, with the movement of the spirit speaks forth power into the mirror of wisdom. And with the speaking forth the spirit proceeds from the will, from the word of the mouth of God, from the centre of the heart, into what is spoken forth, viz. into the virgin mirror, and reveals the Word of life in the mirror of wisdom, so that the threefold nature of the Deity becomes manifest in wisdom.

4. Thus, we recognize an eternal, unfathomable, divine Essence, and in its nature three persons, whereof one is not the other. The first person is the eternal Will which is a cause of all being. This will is not being itself, but the cause of all being, and is free from being, for it is the Unground. There is nothing before it which constitutes it, but it constitutes itself, of which we have no knowledge. It is all, yet at the same time one in itself; without the being it is a nothing. In this one will the eternal beginning arises from imagination or desire. And in the process of desire the will impregnates itself from the eye of wisdom, which exists in co-eternity with the will, without ground and beginning. This impregnation is the ground of the will and of the Being of all beings, and is the will's Son, for the will perpetually begets this Son from eternity to eternity; for he is its heart or its word, as a sound or revelation of the unground of the still eternity, and is the will's mouth or understanding. And he is justly called a person other than the Father, for he is the revelation of the Father, his ground and being; since a will is not a being, but the will's imagination makes being.

5. Thus, the other person is the being of the Deity (i.e. the being of the Holy Trinity), the mouth or revelation of the Being of all beings, and the power of the Life of all lives.

6. The third person is the Spirit, which proceeds out of the power of speech, from the grasp of the will by the imagination, out of the mouth of the Father into the eye, as into the mirror of wisdom; this is free from the will and also from the word. And though the will gives it through the word, yet it is free, as air is free from fire. We see that air is the fire's spirit and life, yet is something different from the fire, although it is given by the fire. And as we see that the air gives a living and moving sky, which is shining and mobile; so also is the Holy Spirit the life of the Deity, and a person other than the Father and Son. It has moreover a different office; it discloses the wisdom of God, so that the wonders appear, just as air initiates all the life of this world, so that everything lives and grows.

7. Such is then a short intimation regarding the Deity in the unground, indicating how God dwells in himself, and is himself his parturient centre. But the human mind does not rest satisfied with this; it inquires after nature, after that from which this world was born and all was created. Accordingly there follows further the text of the Principle, to which we have invited Reason as guest.

CHAPTER III

THE VERY EARNEST GATE. HOW, APART FROM THE PRINCIPLE OF FIRE, GOD IS NOT MANIFEST. ALSO, OF THE ETERNAL ESSENCE AND OF THE UNFATHOMABLE WILL

1. WE have by describing it shown what the Deity out of nature is. In this connection it is to be understood that the Deity, as regards the three persons, is, with the eternal wisdom, free from nature, and that the Deity has a still deeper ground than the Principle of fire. The Deity, again, without the Principle, would not be manifest. And understand the Deity apart from the Principle as an aspect of great wonders, where no one knows or can know what that is; where all colours, power and virtue shine forth in a terrible essence, which however resembles not any essence, but is like a terrible wonder-eye, where neither fire, light nor darkness is seen, but only an aspect of a corresponding spirit, in deep blue, green and mixed colour, in which lie all the colours, and yet not one is known from another, but resembles a terrible flash, whose aspect would confuse and consume all.

2. And so we are to know the eternal Essence, that is, the eternal Spirit beyond or out of fire and light; for it is a desiring will, which thus makes itself into a spirit. And this spirit is the eternal potence of the Unground, the Unground bringing itself into a ground from which all being arises. For every form in the spirit is a source of imagination, a desiring will, and desires to manifest itself. Every form impregnates its imagination, and every form also desires to manifest itself. Therefore the mirror of the aspect is a marvel of the Being of all beings; and of the wonders there is no number, origin nor end; it is pure wonder, of whose contents it is impossible to write. For the spirit of the soul, which springs from the said wonder, alone understands this.

3. And, secondly, we understand how this unfathomable will from eternity to eternity is ever desireful to manifest itself, to fathom

itself and find what it is, to bring the wonders into being and to reveal itself in the wonders. And the process of desire is a mode of imagination, as the will contracts into itself and makes itself pregnant, and overshadows itself with imagination, so that from the free will arises an opposing will to be liberated from the overshadowing or from the darkness. For what is drawnin forms the darkness of the free will, as apart from imagination it were free, and yet also in itself apart from the imagination were a nothing: thus there arises in the primal will, in the process of desire, an opposing will. For the desiring is intrahent, and the primal will is still and in itself without being, but impregnates itself with desire so that it becomes full of being, namely, of the wonders and power which overshadow it and make of it a darkness, whereby in the powers as drawn-in another will forms itself to go out from the dark power into freedom. This other will is the will of the heart or Word, for it is a cause of the Principle, a cause that the wheel of anguish kindles fire. It goes forth then through anguish, viz. through fire, with the shine of the light, viz. Majesty, in which the nature of the Holy Trinity is revealed, and receives here the dear name of GOD. Understand this further as follows

4. The primal will, i.e. God the Father, is and remains eternally free from the source of anguish as regards the will in itself. But its desiring becomes impregnate, and in the process of desire nature with the forms first takes its rise. Nature dwells in the will, in God, and the will in nature, and yet there is no commingling. For the will is thin like a nonentity, therefore it is not seizable, and is not laid hold of by nature. For if it could be laid hold of, there would be in the Deity but one person. It is indeed the cause of nature, but it is and remains nevertheless in eternity another world in itself, and nature remains likewise another world in itself. For nature exists in virtue of the essence from which the Principle arises; but the clear Deity in Majesty exists not in the essence or Principle, but in the freedom out of or beyond nature, and the shining light which proceeds from the Principle makes the unseizable and unfathomable Deity manifest. The Principle gives

the lustre of Majesty, and yet contains it not in itself, but takes it from the mirror of virgin wisdom, from the freedom of God. For if the mirror of wisdom were not, no fire or light could be generated: all has its origin from the mirror of the Deity. Further, it is to be understood in this way

5. God is in himself the unground, viz. the first world, of which no creature knows anything, for it lives with spirit and body solely in the ground. God also in the unground would not be manifest to himself, but from eternity his wisdom has become his ground, after which the eternal will of the unground of the Deity has longed, whereby the divine imagination arose, so that the unfathomable will of the Deity has thus from eternity in the imagination impregnated itself with the power of the vision or form of the mirror of wonders. Now, in this impregnation is to be understood the eternal origin of two principles, viz. (I) The eternal darkness, from which arises the world of fire; (2) the essence of wrath in the darkness, wherein we understand God's anger and the abyss of nature; thus, we recognize the world of fire as the great life.

6. We understand, secondly, how from fire light is generated, and how between the world of fire and of light death appears; how light shines out of death, and how the light-flaming world is in itself a principle and source other than the fire-world, and yet neither is separated from the other, nor can either lay hold of the other. And we understand, thirdly, how the light-world fills the eternal freedom, or the primal will which is called Father. Fourthly, we understand also here earnestly and fundamentally how the natural life that wishes to dwell in the light-flaming world must pass through death and be born out of death,understand the life which has its origin from the darkness, from the essence of the dark nature, that is to say, man's soul, which, in Adam, had turned itself away from the fire-world to the dark nature. Then, fifthly, we understand fundamentally and very exactly why God, i.e. the heart of God, became man, why he has had to die, enter into death and break his life in death, and then bring it through the world of fire into the light-flaming world;

and why we must follow him. Sixthly, why many souls remain in the world of fire, and cannot pass through death into the light-world; and what death is; also what the soul is. Now follows this point

7. When we consider what life is, we find that it consists mainly of three elements, viz. desire, the disposition and thinking. If we investigate further, what it is which gives this, we find the centre or the essential wheel, which contains within it the firesmith himself. If we reflect further, from whence the essential fire arises, we find that it has its origin in the desiring of the eternal unfathomable will, which by desire makes for itself a ground; for every desire is astringent, or attractive of that which the will desires, and yet there is nothing before it that it can desire, save only itself.

8. This is the great wonder-eye without limit and ground, in which lies everything, and yet also is a nothing, unless in the desiring will it be made into a something. This is effected by imagination, whereby it becomes a substance, although it is still a nothing, for it is but an overshadowing of the free will. This substance overshadows the freedom or the thin unfathomable will, so that two worlds arise: the first, which in itself is unseizable or imprehensible, an ungrounded existence and eternal freedom; the other, which seizes itself and makes itself into a darkness. And yet neither is separated from the other, with this difference only, that the darkness cannot lay hold of the freedom, because it is too thin and dwells also in itself, as indeed the darkness dwells also in itself.

The very earnest gate

9. Now, we understand here, (I) how the Father's other will, which he draws in the mirror of wisdom for his heart's centre, becomes impregnate in the Father's imagination with substance, and that this impregnation is a darkness in comparison with the freedom of the first will (which is called Father), and in this darkness or substance all power, colours and virtues lie involved

in the imagination, as also all wonders. And we understand (2) how the power, wonders and virtue must be made manifest through fire, that is, in the Principle, where all enters into its essence; for in the Principle essence first has its origin. And we understand (3) very earnestly that in the Principle before fire arises, a dying appears, viz. the great anguishful life, which in truth is not a death, but a sour, stern, dying source, from which the great and strong life arises, viz. the fire-life, and then from what has died the light-life, with the power of love. This light-life dwells with love in the eternal freedom, viz. in the primal will which is called Father; for the Father requires this in his own will, which he himself is, and requires nothing more.

10. Ye see and know that no light exists without fire, and no fire without severe pain, which pain is likened to a dying; and the substance from which the fire burns must thus die and be consumed. From the consuming process arise two principles of two great lives: the first, in pain (Qual), is called Fire; the other, derived from the subjugation or from death, is called Light, is non-material and without pain, yet contains in itself all source or quality (Qual), but not that of wrath, for wrath has remained in death. And the light-life buds out of death as a fair flower out of the earth, and is no longer reached by death. And indeed you see how the light dwells in fire and the fire cannot move it; nor is there anything than can move the light, for it is like the eternal freedom, and dwells in freedom.

11. Here it is understood how the Son is a person other than the Father, for he is the light-world, yet dwells in the Father, and the Father begets him in his will. He is truly the Father's love, as well as wonder, counsel and power, for the Father begets him in his imagination, in himself, and leads him forth through his own fire, through the Principle, through death, so that the Son makes and is in the Father another world or another Principle than the fire-world in the darkness.

12. And you understand also how the Father's eternal Spirit divides into three worlds: First, he is the issuing out of the imagination of the primal will of the unground which is called

Father, as by the issuing he reveals wisdom and dwells in wisdom, and wears this as his garment of great wonders.

13. Secondly, he is the cause of contraction for the entity of darkness, i.e. of the second world, and is the cause and spirit for the origin of the essential fire. He is, himself the source in the anguish of the Principle, and also the fiery world as the great life.

14. Thirdly, he is also himself the one who, in the dying of the Principle, brings the power out of the fire, where the power, emerging from the anguish, from the dying, separates from the dying and enters into freedom and dwells in freedom, and makes the light-world. Thus, he is the flame of love in the light-world. And here in this place the precious name of God the Father, Son and Holy Spirit has its origin. For in the world of fire he is not called the Holy Spirit or God, but God's anger, God's wrath, in reference to which God calls himself a consuming fire. But in the light-world, in the Son of God, he is the flame of love and the power of the holy divine life itself; there he is called God the Holy Spirit. And the light-world is called wonder, counsel and power of the Deity; it is the Holy Spirit who reveals it, for he is the life therein. And everything together, wherever our heart and mind can reach, is nothing but those three worlds: in them lies everything. First, the eternal freedom, and in it the light with the power in the mirror of wisdom, and it is called God the Father, Son and Holy Spirit. The second world is the dark nature in the imagination, in the sour desiring will, the impregnation of desire, where all is in darkness, in perpetual fearful and anguishful death. And the third world is the world of fire or the first Principle, which arises in the anguish and is the great, strong, all-powerful life, in which the light-world dwells, but unapprehended on the part of the fire.

CHAPTER IV

OF THE PRINCIPLE AND ORIGIN OF THE WORLD OF FIRE. ALSO OF THE CENTRE OF NATURE, AND HOW LIGHT SEPARATES FROM FIRE, SO THAT TWO WORLDS ARE CONTAINED IN ONE ANOTHER FROM ETERNITY TO ETERNITY

1. WE will not write dumbly but demonstratively. We recognize and know that every life has its origin in anguish, as in a poison which is a dying, and yet is also the life itself, as is to be seen in man and every creature. For without anguish or poison there is no life, as is evident in every creature, particularly in man, who lives in three Principles; namely, one in fire, wherein consists the great fire-life, to which belongs a dying poison, viz. the gall, which poison makes the torture chamber wherein the fire-life has its origin. And from out of the fire-life the second Principle or the light-life, whence arises the noble mind with the senses, in which we carry our noble image; and we understand how the fire-life in the heart springs from the death of the gall. And we understand the third Principle in the other torture chamber, i.e. the stomach, in which we stuff the four elements with the astrum, whereby the other torture chamber or the third centre constitutes, as the kingdom of this world, a stench and evil tormenthouse, in which the third life, viz. the astral and elemental life, is born, and through the outer body rules with the reason of the third Principle.

2. Now, we understand very well that in the heart, in the centre of fire, another world lies hidden, which is incomprehensible to the torment-house of stars and elements; for the heart longs after this world, and the spirit, which is born out of the death of the heart's poison and comes into being, possesses this other world, for it is free from the poison which kindles the fire, and yet dwells in the fire of the heart; but by its longing the spirit takes the other world of freedom into the imagination and dwells in freedom out of the torment of fire, in so far however as it has a desire of God.

3. Seeing then there is such a threefold dominion in man, this still more holds true outside of man; for if that were not, it could not have come into man. For where nothing exists, there also nothing arises; but if something arises, it is produced from that which is there. Every imagination fashions in itself only its like, and manifests itself in the likeness. Since then the Being of all beings is an eternal wonder in three Principles, it also brings forth only wonders, each Principle according to its property, and each property again by means of its imagination, whereby we know that the Eternal is a pure wonder. Now this wonder is to be meditated upon, and the nature and property of the eternal genetrix to be considered, for there can be no property unless it have a mother which gives it.

4. Now we understand in the great wonder of all wonders, which is God and eternity with nature, in particular seven mothers, from which the being of all beings arises. All seven are but a single existence, and none is first or last, they are all seven alike eternal, without beginning. Their beginning is the opening of the wonders of the one, eternal will, which is called God the Father; and the seven mothers could not be manifest if the one eternal will, which is called Father, were not desireful. But as he is desireful, he is an imaginating into himself, a longing to find himself. He finds himself also in the imagination, and finds particularly seven forms in himself, whereof not any is the other, nor is any without the other, but each brings forth the other. If one were not, neither would the other be; but the will would remain an eternal nothing, without being, shine and lustre.

5. Seeing then that the will is desireful, it is attractive of that which is in the imagination; but as however there is nothing, it draws itself, and becomes pregnant in the imagination, not in the will, for the will is thin like a nonentity.

6. Now every desire is astringent, for it is its property. That is the first mother, and the drawing of the will in the desire is the second mother, for these are two forms which are contrary to each other. For the will is still like a nothing, grim like a still death, and the drawing is its movement. This, the still will in the

astringency cannot suffer, and contracts much more violently into itself, and yet does but sharpen its own will in the drawing, and would enclose and hold the drawing by its stringent contraction, but only awakens it in this way. The harder the astringency gathers itself in with a view to holding the sting, the greater becomes the sting, the raging and breaking; for the sting will not allow itself to be kept down, and yet is held by its mother so rigorously that it cannot withdraw. It wishes to be above itself, and its mother wishes to be below itself; for the astringency contracts unto itself and makes itself heavy. and is a sinking below itself; it makes in sulphur the phur and in mercury the sul, and the sting makes in phur the bitter form, the pang, an enmity in the astringency, and is always wishing to break loose from the astringency, but cannot. Thus one ascends and the other descends. And if this is not possible, it becomes turning like a wheel, and turns continually on itself. That is the third form, from which arises essence and the wonder of plurality without number and ground. And in this wheel understand the wonder or power which the will, i.e. the primal unfathomable will, draws into itself from the mirror of the unground for its centre or heart; such is here the will of power and wonder. And in this wheel of the great anguish arises the other will, viz. the Son's will, to go out from the anguish into the still freedom of the primal unfathomable will, for the wheel causes nature to be. Accordingly nature first takes its origin thus; this forms the centre and a breaking of the still eternity; it kills nothing, but constitutes the great life.

7. And that we speak of killing, understand it in this way: It is not a killing, but the sensibility; for life prior to fire is dumb, without feeling; it is only a hunger after life, just as the material world is only a hunger after life, and in its hunger labours so hard, even unto the Principle, so that it attains fire, whereby the outer life of this world arises. And this cannot possibly be otherwise, unless the first matrix or the astringent desire break to pieces, that is, the wheel of the first three forms or the astringency; and the drawing of the astringency produces the sphere of anguish and torment. For it is a terror in itself, as the nothing must come into

sensibility; for what we have here is the poison-source whence wrath and all that is evil arises, and yet also is the true origin of the feeling life. For thus life finds itself, namely, in the pang of anguish. As is to be seen in all creatures, that life has its origin in stifled blood, in anguishment, both the creaturely and the essential life, as in a stinking dung in corruption, where in the death of the grain the greatest life springs; and yet in the essence no death is understood, but a pang of anguish, since the mother, which is a dumb entity, must burst asunder, as may be perceived in the grain, where the essential life buds forth from the disruption.

8. In like manner is it also with the centre of nature. The pang of anguish is the true centre and makes the triangle in nature, and the fire-flash, i.e. the fourth form of nature, makes of the triangle a cross; for there is the Principle, and is separated into two worlds of two Principles, as into a twofold source and life. The anguishful life or the fire is and remains one source, and the other source arises in the breaking of the anguish. Understand it thus The first form of the Essence, viz. astringency, in the desiring imprehensible will, must give itself up wholly to the source of anguish in the wheel of nature, for the sting becomes too strong. Accordingly the astringency sinks down like a death, and yet is not a death but a dying source; for the sting becomes master and transforms the astringency into its property, into a furious flash, into a pang of anguish which, coming from the sting and the astringency, is bitter, as is the nature of poison. For the poison or the dying has especially three forms, viz. astringent, bitter and anguish of fire; it creates itself thus in itself, and has no maker except the strong will for the great life in fire.

9. Understand us correctly The unground has no life, but thus in such a property the great eternal life is born. The unground has no movement or feeling, and thus is generated movement and feeling, and thus the nothing finds itself in the eternal will, whose ground we know not, nor should we make search, for this confuses us. The position thus indicated is, however, only an essential life without understanding, like the earth and death or

dying, where indeed there is a source in itself, but in darkness without understanding; for the astringent anguish contracts into itself, and what is drawn-in causes darkness, so that the anguishful life stands in darkness. For every being is in itself dark, unless it have the light's tincture in it; hence the tincture is a freedom from darkness, and is not laid hold of by the pang of anguish, for it is in the light-world. And though it is involved in essence, as in a dark body, it is nevertheless of the nature of the lightworld, where no circumscription exists.

10. An account has been given above, firstly, of the mirror of wisdom of the wonders of all being; and, secondly, of the trinity of the Being of all beings, showing how this trinity arises from a single eternal will which is called the Father of all beings, and how he draws in himself another will to manifest or to find himself in himself, or, as might be said, in order to be sensible of what and how he is. And further, how this other new-drawn magical will to feel itself is his heart or peculiar abode, and how the primal unfathomable will impregnates itself with imagination from the mirror of wonders, which in the light-world is called wisdom. And then we have set forth how that the same primal unfathomable will together with the impregnation and likewise the mirror of wonders or wisdom is not, in such a property, prior to the Principle of fire, rightly called a divine being, but rather a mystery of the wonders of all beings, which mystery receives in fire its severance into infinite parts or beings, and yet remains also but one being.

11. We give you now to understand with regard to the other will,-which the primal will draws in its imagination or impregnation, and which is the great mystery wherein the primal will, which is called Father, seeks, finds and feels itself, as a life in the heart,-that this other will is the parturient matrix in the impregnation as impressed or imprinted in the imagination. It is this will which is the cause of the seven forms of nature, and is the cause too of the wheel of anguish or the dying. It is this will also which, in anguish, goes out through death into freedom, breaks death to pieces and gives life; which kindles fire, and in fire

receives into itself the lustre of majesty, and in the light of majesty dwells in fire, being unapprehended on the part of the fire, like one who feels nothing, who is dead to the source, and has in himself another source, which feels not the former, to which he is dead.

12. And that we proceed to inform you briefly, at the same time fundamentally and exactly, of the origin of fire, we recognize in the deep that is revealed to us by God's grace, that fire in its origin depends on two causes: One cause is the will-spirit of the heart, understand the Father's other will or the Son's property; the second cause is the matter of the will, i.e. the wonder of the wheel of the essential life or the chamber of anguish. The anguish longs after the will of freedom, and the will longs after manifestation; for the will cannot in the still freedom, in itself, become manifest without the essential life, which in the anguish or in the dying attains to manifestation, that is, to the great life.

13. Thus the will is in the dark anguish, and the anguish is the darkness itself. Seeing then that the anguish longs so vehemently after the will of freedom, it receives in itself the will of freedom as a flash, as a great terror, as if water were poured into fire. And here takes place the true dying, for the fierce dark anguish is terrified at the flash, like darkness at the light, for the darkness is slain and vanquished, and the terror is a terror of great joy. There the fierce sour poison sinks down in itself into death and becomes powerless, for it loses the sting, and indeed is no death. On the contrary, in this way the true life of feeling and longing is kindled: it is just as if steel and flint were struck together, for they are two great hungers, of the will for essence, and of the essence for life. The will gives life, and the essence gives manifestation of the life. As a fire burns from a candle, so burns the will from the essential substance. The will is not the light itself, but the spirit of light or fire; the light arises from the essence, and the essence in turn from the will. The anguishful essential fire is the matter for the shining fire, and the will becomes kindled in the essential fire and gives the white lovely fire, which dwells in the hot fire without feeling. The will takes its feeling from the fierceness of the essential fire

in the fourth form, so that it is made manifest in itself, and yet remains free from the fierceness, for the source is changed in the kindling into a gentle source of love.

14. And here the other will receives its name which is Spirit. For by means of the essential fire it attains to the propria of all the wonders and also to the right life of power and might over the essential firelife, since from nature it takes power into itself, and has also in itself freedom. The freedom is a stillness without being, and the still freedom gives itself to the nature of the anguish, and the anguish receives this freedom that is void of pain, whereby it becomes so joyous that the anguish is changed into love (the fifth form of nature); for the will which had given itself up to the anguish is thus released from the death of the anguish: accordingly it finds itself in freedom, and goes out from the raging anguish. For here death is broken to pieces, and yet continues to be a death in itself; but the will-spirit, i.e. the true holy life, goes at the breaking to pieces out from the anguish and is now also a fire, but a fire in freedom, and burns in the source of love. As this may be seen in fire and light, how the essential fire is a burning pain, and the light a joyous delight, without sensible pain; and yet it contains in itself all the property of fire, but in another essence, as a gracious beneficent essence, a true aspect of the kingdom of joy, and fire an aspect of terror and anguish; and yet one dwells in the other, and one is not found without the other in the essential source.

15. Thus two worlds are contained in one another, whereof neither comprehends the other; and nothing can enter into the light-world except through death, and the imagination must have precedence over death. The anguishful will must long after the freedom of the power of the light, and wholly surrender itself, and by the desiring imagination take hold of the power of the freedom. Then the strong will passes through the death of the darkness, through the essential fire, breaks the darkness and falls into the light-world, and dwells in the fire that is void of pain, in the kingdom of joy. And this is the gate into Ternarius Sanctus, and faith in the Holy Spirit, dear children of men.

16. Here you understand the fall of the devil, who had turned the spirit of his will only to the essential fire, and willed to rule therewith over the light. And here understand also the fall of man, who turned his imagination to material essential substance, and has gone out from the light; on which account the will of love from the light-world has again entered into material essentiality, into humanity, and has again wedded itself and given itself up to the essential fire-spirit in man, i.e. to the soul, and has brought the same through death and fire into the light-world, into Ternarius Sanctus, into the will of the Holy Trinity.

17. Let this be a finding and knowing to you! Despise it not on account of the great depth, which will not be everyone's comprehension, the reason is the darkness into which man plunges himself. Otherwise, anyone might well find it, if the earthly way were broken through and the Adamic evil flesh were not too cherished, which is the hindrance.

CHAPTER V

OF THE PRINCIPLE IN ITSELF, WHAT IT IS

1. WE have to consider further the first four forms of nature, then we shall discover what a principle is. That is properly a principle when an existence becomes what it was not, when from nothing a source springs, and from the source a true life with understanding and senses. And again we recognize the right principle in the origin of fire, in the fire-source, which breaks the substantiality and also the darkness. Thus we acknowledge the fire's essence and property to be a principle, for it constitutes and gives the origin of life and of all movement, as well as the strong power of the fierce wrath.

2. And, secondly, we recognize that also as a principle which can dwell in the fire, being unapprehended on the part of the fire, which can deprive the fire of its power and transmute the fire's quality into a gentle love; which is omnipotent over all, which has understanding to break the root of the fire and make of the fire a darkness; and a dry hunger and thirst, without the finding of any refreshment, as is the torment of hell: that is the abyss, where essence is famished, where death exercises its sting like a fainting poison, where indeed there is an essential life, but at enmity with itself, where kindling of the right fire is not realized, but shines forth only as an unburning flash.

3. And we give you thus to understand that in the Eternal there are not more than two Principles (I) The burning fire, which is filled with the light; the light gives it its property, so that from the burning source springs a high kingdom of joy; for anguish attains freedom, and the burning fire thus remains but a cause of the finding of life and of the light of Majesty. The fire takes into itself the light's property, viz. gentleness, and the light takes into itself the fire's property, viz. life and self-discovery. And the second Principle is understood in the light; but the essential substantiality from which the fire burns remains eternally a darkness and a source of wrath wherein the devil dwells, as we see

that fire is a thing other than that from which the fire burns. Thus the Principle stands in fire, and not in the essential source of substantiality; the essential source is the centre of nature, the cause of the Principle, but it is dark and the fire is shining: here is shown rightly how the breaking of the wrath, viz. death, and also the eternal freedom out of nature, are both together the cause of the shining. For the wonderspirit of the unground is therefore desireful, in order that it may become shining; and hence it brings itself into qualification, that it may find and feel itself, that it may manifest its wonders in the qualification, for without qualification there can be no manifestation.

4. Understand us then further: The qualification as fierceness has no true substantiality, but the sour fierceness is the substantiality of the sting, wherein it pierces; nor does the anguish together with the fire form or make any true substantiality, but there is only a corresponding spirit; nevertheless, one must be thicker. than the other, else there were no finding, that is to say, the astringency causes it to be thick and dark. Thus the bitter sting finds the anguish in the sour dark property, as in a matter; for were there no matter, neither would there be any spirit or finding. The unground finds itself in the sour darkness, but it disperses the darkness and goes out from the sour darkness as a spirit which has found itself in the source of anguish; it abandons this sour matter of the darkness wherein it found itself, and enters into itself, again into freedom, into the unground, and dwells in itself. Thus the qualification must be its sharpness and finding, and is also for it a kindling of its freedom, of the light in which it sees itself and finds what it is.

5. Hence it no longer requires qualification for itself, for it is now itself a qualifying principle; but it modelizes itself and sees itself according to all the forms, and every form is desireful to find itself and to manifest itself; every form thus also finds itself in itself, but with the desiring passes out of itself, and manifests itself as a figure or spirit; and that is the eternal wisdom in colours, wonders and virtues, and yet exists not in particularity, but the whole universally, though in infinite form. These forms

have by the motion of the primal will which is called Father embodied themselves in spirits, that is, in angels, so that the hidden nature might see, feel and find itself in creatures, and that there might be an eternal play in the wonders of the wisdom of God.

6. Further, let us understand the substantiality of the light-world, that it veritably is a true substantiality, for no real substance can subsist in fire, but only the spirit of substance. Fire is, however, the cause of substance, for it is a hunger, an earnest desiring; it must have substance or it goes out.

Understand it in this way: The gentleness gives and the fire takes. The gentleness is emanant from itself, and gives a substance that is like itself, every form from its own self, and the fire swallows this up, but out of it produces light. It gives something nobler than it has swallowed up, gives spirit for substance; for it swallows up the gentle beneficence, that is, the water of eternal life, but at the same time gives the spirit of eternal life: as you see that wind arises from fire, so also air or the true spirit arises from the fire-life.

7. Understand our meaning aright: God the Father is in himself the freedom out of nature, but makes himself manifest by fire in nature. The nature of fire is his property, though he is in himself the unground, where there is no feeling of any pain. But he brings his desiring will into pain (Qual), and draws for himself in the pain another will to go out from the pain again into the freedom beyond pain. This other will is his Son, which he begets out of his eternal one will from eternity, which he leads forth through fire, through the breaking of the source of death, as out of his fierce ferventness. It is this other will, viz. the Son of God the Father, which breaks down death as the stern, dark source, which kindles fire and proceeds through the fire as a shine or lustre of the fire, and fills the primal will which is called Father; for the lustre is also as thin as a nonentity, or as the will which is called Father. Therefore it can dwell in freedom, that is, in the Father's will, and makes the Father bright, clear, gracious and friendly, for it is the heart of the Father or mercifulness; it is the Father's

substantiality, it fills the Father everywhere, although in him is no place, no beginning nor end.

8. The Father's fire swallows up the gentle substance, viz. the water-fountain of eternal life into itself, into the fire's own essence, and meekens and sweetens itself therewith. Here must the substantiality die as it were in the fire, for the fire swallows it up into itself and consumes it, and gives from the consumption a living joyous spirit. This is the Holy Spirit; it proceeds thus from the Father and Son into the great wonders of the holy Essence, and reveals them ever and eternally.

9. The Deity is accordingly an eternal bond which cannot dissolve. Hence it brings forth itself from eternity to eternity, and the first is also always the last, and the last again the first. Understand, then, the Father as the world of fire, the Son as the world of light and power, the Holy Spirit as the life of the Deity, that is, as the emanating guiding power; all is nevertheless but one God, just as fire and light and air are but one single existence, yet it divides into three parts, and neither can subsist without the other. For fire is not light, nor the wind that arises from fire; each has its own office, and each is a specific nature in itself, yet each is the other's life and a cause of the other's life. For the wind blows up the fire, else it would stifle in its wrath, so that it would fall into dark death; and indeed the stifling is real death, as the fire of nature is extinguished and no longer draws substance into itself.

10. Of all this you have a good similitude in the outer world, in all the creatures, showing how every life, namely the essential fire-life, draws substance, which is its food, into itself; further, the fire of its life consumes the substance, and gives from what is consumed the spirit of power, which is the life of the creatures. Here may certainly be seen how life takes its origin from death. No life comes into being
unless it break through that out of which life must arise. All must enter into the torture-chamber, into the centre, and attain in the anguish the fire-flash, else no kindling results. Fire, however, is manifold, so also life; but from the greatest anguish arises also the greatest life, as from a true fire.

11. Thus, dear children of God in Christ, we give you our knowledge and purpose to ponder over. At the outset we made mention we would show you the death of Christ, why Christ was obliged to die, and why we also must die and rise again in Christ. This you see now in this description clearly, and understand our great misery, that it was needful for us that the Word or life of the holy Light-world became man and generated us anew in himself. He who here understands nothing is not born of God. Consider into what lodging Adam has introduced us. He was an extract of all the three Principles, a complete likeness according to all the three worlds, and in his soul and spirit had angelic quality in him. He was introduced into the holy power and essentiality, viz. into Paradise, that is, divine essentiality. He was to eat of divine essentiality and drink the water of eternal life in an angelic manner. But he lost the divine essentiality and the angelic quality, and imaginated into the extern birth, into the kingdom of the earthly quality, which the devil had kindled in his fall. He turned his eyes away from God to the spiritus mundi or earthly god, away from the divine light to the light of this world hence he was taken captive and remained in the earthly quality. Thus he fell into the earthly fragile quality, which rules in him and fills him. It puts a body on him, breaks this up again and consumes it in its own essence, in its essential fire.

12. But because the soul was inbreathed into man from the Spirit of God, namely, from the Eternal, so that the soul is an angel, therefore God has shown interest in it again; and the power of the holy lightworld, viz. God's heart, has entered into the human essence which lay shut up in death, into the torturechamber of our misery, has from our essence drawn a soul into himself, has taken on himself our mortal life, and brought the soul through death, through the severe fire of God the Father, into the light-world, has broken down death which held us captive and disclosed the true life.

13. Now, this may not and cannot be otherwise. He who would possess the light-world must enter by the same way that Christ has made. He must enter into the death of Christ, and in Christ's

resurrection he enters into the light-world. Just as we know that the eternal Word of the Father, which is the Father's heart, is begotten from eternity to eternity out of the wrath of the death of darkness through the Father's fire, and is in itself the true centre of the Holy Trinity, and out of itself with the processional Holy Spirit is the light-flaming Majesty or lightworld: so also in like manner and capacity must we with our heart, mind and soul go out from the harsh stringent and evil earthliness, out of ourselves, out of the corrupt Adamic man, break him and slay him by our earnest will and doing. We must take upon us the cross of the old Adam, who cleaves to us as long as we live, and must upon and in the cross enter into the centrum naturae, into the Triangle, and be new-born out of the wheel of anguish, if we would become angels and live eternally in God.

14. But because we were not able to do this, Christ gave himself to this centre of wrath, broke down the fierce wrath and extinguished it with his love. For he brought heavenly divine substantiality into this wrath, into the centre of the torture-chamber, and put out the soul's anguish-fire, viz. the fierce wrath of the Father of the fiery world in the soul, so that we no longer fall unto the fierce wrath; but if we give ourselves up to the death of Christ, and go out from the evil Adam, then we fall into Christ's death, into the way which he has made for us, we fall into the bosom of Abraham, that is, into Christ's arms; he receives us into himself. For the bosom of Abraham is the light-world that is opened in the death of Christ, it is the Paradise in which God created us. And the matter now lies in this, not that we be lip-Christians, picture to ourselves Christ's death and remain in heart, soul and spirit hypocrites, but that we seriously and earnestly with mind and heart, will and doing, go out from the evil inclinations, and fight against them. Though they cling unto us, we must nevertheless daily and hourly mortify this evil Adam's will and doing. We must do what we would not willingly do, we must deny our earthly evil life itself, and draw Christ's life into us; then the kingdom of heaven suffers violence, and they who force it draw it to themselves, as Christ says.

15. Thus we become pregnant with the kingdom of heaven and enter thus whilst alive into Christ's death, and receive the body of Christ or the divine essentiality; we carry the kingdom of heaven within us. Accordingly we are Christ's children, members and heirs in God's kingdom, and the image of the holy divine world, which is God the Father, Son, Holy Spirit, and the substantiality of this same holy Threefoldness. All that is born and disclosed out of wisdom is our Paradise; and nothing dies in us save the dead Adam, the earthly evil one, whose will we have moreover broken here, to whom we have become the enemy. Our enemy retreats from us, he must go into the fire, understand into the essential fire, into the four elements and into the mystery, and must at the end of this time be proved by the fire of God, and must present to us again our wonders and works. Whatever the earthly mystery has swallowed up into itself, that it must furnish again in the fire of God, and not a corresponding evil. On the contrary, the fire of God swallows up the evil, and gives us in return for it such a thing as we have sought after here in our anxious searching. As fire swallows up substance, but gives spirit for substance, so will our works in spirit and heavenly joy from out of the fire of God be presented to us as a clear mirror, like the wonder of the wisdom of God.

16. Let this be revealed to you, dear children, for it is highly known; and suffer not yourselves to be tickled or flattered with the death of Christ and to picture it as a work which suffices us if we do but know and believe that it was accomplished for us. What does it avail me to know a treasure lies hid, and I dig it not up? It is not enough to take comfort, play the hypocrite and give fair words with the tongue, and yet retain the impostor in the soul. Christ says: Ye must be born anew, or ye shall not see the kingdom of God. We must turn round and become as a child in the womb, and be born of Divine essence. We must put a new garment on our souls, viz. the coat of Christ, the humanity of Christ; else no glistering appearances will avail. All is lies that verbal lip-labour tells, which pourtrays Christ as if he had done this for us in order that we should only comfort ourselves

therewith, and at the same time live in the old Adam, in covetousness, pride and falsehood, in the lusts of wickedness. It is the Antichristian deceit of the false clergy, of whom the Revelation warns us. It all avails nothing that we play the hypocrite to ourselves, that we tickle ourselves with Christ's sufferings and death; we must enter into them, become like his image, then Christ's sufferings and death are of use to us. We must take his cross upon us, follow after him, suppress and slay the evil desires, and always exercise good-willing then we shall assuredly see what the foot-steps of Christ are, when we shall fight against the devil, the old Adam and the wicked world, against earthly reason which desires only temporal pleasure. Then is Christ's cross truly laid upon us, for what we have here is the devil, the world and our own evil Adam all these are our enemies, here must the new man stand as a champion and fight in the footsteps of Christ. O how many numberless enemies will he here awaken, who will all fall upon him! Here the chief thing is to fight as a champion for the knightly garland of thorns of Christ, and yet always only be despised as one that is not worthy of the earth. Here war and faith must be the watchwords. Where external reason doth flatly gainsay it, there 'tis well to set Christ's sufferings and death in the forefront, and put them before the devil, the world and death, and earthly reason, and not to despair; for here an angelic crown is at stake, to be either an angel or devil. We must in tribulation be new-born, and it costs much to wrestle with God's wrath and vanquish the devil. If we had not here Christ with us, nay in us, we should lose the fight. Of no avail is a handful of knowledge, to the effect that we know this and flatter ourselves with God's grace and make God a cloak for our sins, so that thus we conceal and subtly cover up the impostor and devil's monster under the sufferings of Christ. O no I the impostor must be destroyed in Christ's sufferings and death; he must not be an impostor if he wishes to be a child; he must become an obedient son; he must labour in the sufferings of Christ, tread in the footsteps of truth, righteousness and love; he must do, not merely know. The devil is also well aware of this, what is he profited? Practice must follow, else there is falsehood and deceit.

17. Hypocritical Reason says: Christ has done it, we cannot do it. Yes indeed, he has done what we could not do; he has broken down death and restored life. What does it profit me, if I enter not into him? He is in heaven and I in this world; by his path that he has made for us must I enter into him, otherwise I remain outside. For he says: Come unto me all ye that are weary and heavy laden, and I will refresh you. Take my yoke upon you, and learn of me, for I am meek and lowly of heart, and ye shall find rest unto your souls. It is upon his path that we must enter into him; we must do good for evil, and love one another, as he did us, and gave his life for us.

18. If we do this, we extinguish the wrath of God also in our neighbour. We must give a good example, not in guile and artifice, but in simplicity, with good will and heart. Not like a glistering hypocritical strumpet who says: I am a virgin, and makes a fine show in outward modesty, but is at heart a whore. Entire and downright earnestness is required. Better have no money nor goods, also lose temporal honour and power, than God's kingdom. He who finds God has found all, and he who loses Him has lost all; he has lost himself. O how difficult it is to break the earthly will! Do but enter the lists, thou wilt no longer need to inquire after the footsteps of Christ, thou wilt see them well. Thou wilt certainly feel the cross of Christ, likewise the wrath of God, which in general rests and sleeps finely in the old Adam until thou fattenest it plumply, and then it gives thee thy kingdom of heaven which thou hast sought here, in which thou must sweat eternally.

CHAPTER VI

OF OUR DEATH. WHY WE MUST DIE, SEEING THAT CHRIST HAS DIED FOR US

Citatio prima

1. COME hither as guest, dear showy specious Reason, hither have we invited you all, knowers and ignorant, all ye who wish to see God. There is a solemn seal and hard lock to be opened. Meditate thereon, it concerns you all.

2. Reason says: Was God then not sufficiently powerful to forgive Adam his sin, that He had first to become man, suffer and allow himself to be put to death? What pleasure has God in death? Or again, since He willed then to save us in this way, why, as Christ has redeemed us, must we also die? Yes, dance, dear Reason, guess till thou hittest upon it; here thou art a doctor and knowest nothing, art learned and also dumb. If thou wouldest not, then certainly thou must, unless thou comest to this school, i.e. the school of the Holy Spirit. Who is here that can open? Is not this the closed book of him that sits on the throne in the Revelation of Jesus Christ? Then says the hypocrite: We know it well. Accordingly I say that I have never heard it from their lips, nor read it in their writings; they have forbidden me this quest, and interdicted it, and accounted it as sin to one who should inquire after or desire to know the closed book referred to; thus the fair woman has remained subtly covered up. O how Antichrist has been able to play under such covering! But this shall be revealed, against the will of the devil and of hell; for the time is born, the day of restoration dawns, so that it will be found what Adam has lost.

3. The Scripture says: We are dust and ashes (Gen. xviii. 27). That is correct, we are dust and earth. But it may be asked whether God made man out of earth. Reason insists on maintaining it, and authenticates it by Moses, whom Reason however understands not. Nor does investigation give this

position, but indicates rather that man is a limus, that is, an extract of all the three Principles. If he was destined to be a likeness according to God's nature, he must have come from God's nature; for whatever issues not from the Eternal is unabiding. All that begins belongs to that from which it arose. But if we have come merely from the earth, we are of the earth: what should then accuse us that we do just as the earth's property works and wills? But if there be a law within us which accuses us of living in an earthly way, this law is not earthly, but it is from that to which it directs and draws us, namely, from the Eternal; and our own conscience accuses us before the Eternal of doing what is contrary to the Eternal. But if we commit ourselves to that which draws us into the Eternal, then must the other, which draws us into what is earthly, break and enter into that towards which it wills, viz. into the earth, whither it draws us; but the will which we give up to the Eternal, that the Eternal receives.

4. And if God has created man in a being, to be therein eternally as flesh and blood, then must the will which gives itself up to the Eternal be clothed with flesh and blood such as these were when God had created them for Paradise, for the Eternal. Thereby we recognize clearly that God has not created us in flesh and blood such as we now carry, but in such a flesh as the will is clothed with in the new birth; else it would have been earthly and perishable even before the fall. Why then should my conscience blame me for that in which God had created me? Or, why should it desire anything but what it- were in its own nature? Thus we find plainly that there is in our flesh another nature, which longs after that which it now is not. But if it yearn after that which it now is not, then this must in the beginning have belonged to its own nature, for which it yearns; else no yearning nor desire for another would be in it. For we know that every entity longs after that from which it has its primal origin.

5. Thus our will longs after such a flesh as God created, which may subsist in God, not after an earthly perishable flesh in pain, but after a durable flesh without pain: whereby we clearly understand that we have gone out from the Eternal into what is

perishable; that we have attracted matter into the limos and have become earth, from which however God has extracted us as a mass, and thereinto introduced his Spirit with the Eternal. For Adam's imagination has drawn the earthly source of the stars and four elements into the limos, and the stars and elements have absorbed the earth's craving. Thus the heavenly matter of the heavenly flesh became earthly; for the Spirit of God, which by the verbum fiat was breathed into the limos out of God's heart, had heavenly essentiality or heavenly flesh and blood in itself: this Spirit was to rule Adam in accordance with the heavenly divine property. But as the devil had infected the limus when he was in heaven, he now also did Adam this villainy, and infected him with his imagination, so that he began to imaginate according to the corrupt craving of the earthly source, whereby he was caught by the kingdom of this perverted world, which entered into the limus as a master. Thus the image of God was spoiled and fell into the earthly source.

6. But seeing that the heavenly spirit was in the corrupt earthly sulphur, the heavenly brightness and the divine fire could not therefore subsist in the burning, for the light of the eternal fire has its subsistence in freedom out of the source. And again, the water of freedom, which was the food of the eternal fire, had become earthly, that is, filled with earthliness, and the gentle love was infected with the earthly evil craving: thus the eternal fire could not burn nor give light, but sprang accordingly in the corrupt flesh as a choked fire that cannot burn for moisture. This fire gnaws us now and always accuses us; it would fain burn again and be capable of heavenly essence. It has to devour into itself earthly quality, i.e. earthly imagination, with which the devil's craving becomes intermingled: therefore it also becomes bad, and draws us continually towards the abyss, into the centre of nature, into the torture chamber, from which in the beginning it arose.

hou seest, then, O man, what thou art; and what thou further makest of thyself, that thou wilt be to eternity. And thou seest why thou must break up and die, for the kingdom of this world passes. Accordingly thou art in thy external being not master of this kingdom, to continue unto its ether (perpetuity), but thou art powerless therein and only existest in a constellation which the astrum had when thou begannest to grow in the womb in flesh and blood of the earthly nature. Thou art by the external life so powerless that thou canst not defend thyself from thy constellation; thou must enter into the breaking up of thy body when the constellation abandons thee. Thou seest then what thou art, namely, a dust of earth, an earth full of stench, a dead carcass while thou yet livest. Thou livest unto the stars and elements; these rule and urge thee according to their property, they give thee practical rules and art. But when their saeculum and their constellation, under which thou wert conceived and born into this world, is completed, they let thee fall. Then thy body is given up unto the four elements, and thy spirit, which led thee, unto the Mystery from which the astrum was produced, and is kept for the judgment of God, when God will prove all by the fire of his might. Thus, thou must rot and become earth and a nothingness, except the spirit, which has proceeded out of the Eternal which God introduced into the limos. Consider then what thou art, a handful of earth and a torment-house of the stars and elements. If in this world, in this time, thou hast not enkindled again in God's light thy soul and eternal spirit, which was given thee by the highest Good, so that it has been reborn in the light of the divine Essence, then it falls in the Mystery unto the centrum naturae again, as unto the first mother, and enters into the torture chamber of the first four forms of nature. There it must be a spirit in the dark source of anguish along with all the devils, and devour that which it has in this time introduced into itself; that will be its food and life.

8. But seeing that God has not willed such with regard to man, who is his likeness and image, He has himself become what poor man became after he had fallen away from the divine essentiality, from Paradise, so that He might help him back again; that man might thus have in himself the gate of regeneration, that he might in the soul's fire be born again in God, and that this same soul's fire might again draw into itself divine essentiality and be filled

with the divine love-source, whereby the divine kingdom of joy would again be generated and the soul's fire again bring forth the Holy Spirit; which Spirit would proceed out of the soul's fire and wrest the ungodly will from the Adamic flesh, so that the poor soul would not again be filled with the earthly and devilish craving.

The gate of the new man

9. This is to be understood thus: God has become man and has introduced our human soul into the divine essentiality again in Christ; it eats again of divine essentiality, viz. of love and gentleness, and drinks of the water-spirit of eternal life, springing from the eternal wisdom, which is the fountain of divine essentiality. The same soul of Christ received into itself divine heavenly flesh and blood by the Word which is the centre of the light-world, which Word longed after the poor imprisoned -soul. This Word dwelt in the divine essentiality and in the virgin of wisdom, but came into Mary, took our own flesh and blood into the divine essentiality, and broke through the power which held us captive in the wrath of death and fierceness, on the cross, i.e. in the centre of nature of the origin, in the Father's eternal will to nature, out of which our soul was taken, and kindled again in this essence, in the soul's dark fire, the burning light-fire, and brought the other will of the soul through the fire of God, that is, out of the origin into the burning white clear light. When nature felt this in the soul, it became joyous, broke death to pieces and budded forth by God's power in the light-world, and made of the fire a love-desire, so that in eternity no longer any fire is known, but a great and strong will in love towards its twigs and branches, namely, towards our soul.

10. And this is what we say: God thirsted after our soul. He has become our stem, we are his twigs and branches. As a stem always gives its sap to the branches, so that they live and bear fruit, to the glory of the whole tree, so does also to us our stem. The tree Jesus Christ in the light-world, who has revealed himself in our soul,

will have our souls as his branches. He has come in Adam's place, who caused us to decay and perish; he has become Adam in the new birth. Adam brought our soul into this world, into the death of fierce wrathfulness; and He brought our soul out of death, through the fire of God, and rekindled it in fire, so that it obtained again the shining light, as otherwise it would necessarily have had to emain in the dark death in the source of anguish.

11. Now, it depends only on our own acceptance that we follow the same path that Christ has made. We need only introduce into Him our imagination and entire will, which is called faith, and resist the old earthly will: then we receive out of the new birth the spirit of Christ, and it draws into our souls heavenly essentiality, i.e. Christ's heavenly flesh and blood. And when the soul tastes this, it breaks up the dark death within it and kindles in itself the fire of eternity, from which the shining light of gentleness burns. This gentleness the soul draws again into itself, into its soulic fire, and swallows it up into itself, and gives from death the life and spirit of Christ. Thus, this spirit, which proceeds out of the eternal fire, dwells in the light-world with God, and is the true image of the Holy Trinity. It dwells not in this world, the body comprehends it not, but the noble mind, in which the soul is a fire, comprehends it, though not in a graspable way. Certainly the noble image dwells in the soulic fire of the mind, but it only hovers therein, as light in fire. For so long as the earthly man lives, the soul is always in danger, for the devil has enmity with it, and is ever shooting his rays with false desire into the astral and elemental spirit, and reaches therewith after the fire of the soul, and aims at continually infecting it with earthly devilish craving. Here the noble image is compelled to defend itself against the fire of the soul; here fighting is required for the angelic garland; here rises frequently in the old Adam fear, doubt and unbelief, when the devil makes an onset upon the soul. Ah, cross of Christ, how heavy art thou oftentimes! O, how heaven conceals itself! But thus the noble grain is sown; and when it springs up, it brings forth many fair fruits in patience.

12. Thus every twig in the soul grows up out of divine wisdom. All must put forth out of the torture chamber, and grow as a branch from the root of the tree: all is generated in anguish. If a man wish to obtain divine knowledge, he must repeatedly enter into the torture chamber, into the centre. For every spark of divine knowledge which proceeds from God's wisdom must be born out of the centre of nature, else it is not lasting nor eternal. It must rest upon the eternal foundation, upon the eternal root. In this way it is a twig in God's kingdom springing from Christ's tree.

13. Thus we understand the dying, what it is, and why Christ has had to die, and why we must all die in Christ's death, if we would possess his glory. The old Adam cannot do this; he must go again into that out of which he went, he must be proved by the fire of God and restore the wonders which he has swallowed up. They must return to man, and appear to man in his will, in so far as he has done them here in God's will; but if conducive to God's dishonour, they belong to the devil in the abyss.

14. Therefore let everyone take heed what he does and brings about in this world, with that inward disposition and conscience he speaks, acts and lives all must be tried by fire. And whatever shall be susceptible of this fire, that it will swallow up and give to the abyss, to the anguish. Of that shall man suffer loss and be without it in the other world, by which he might and should have had joy, if he had been a worker in God's vineyard; but thus he will be found to be an idle servant. Therefore also the power, might and clearness in the wonders of divine wisdom will be unequal in the other world. Many a one is here a king, and in the other world a swineherd shall be preferred to him in the clearness and wisdom: the reason is, his wonders will be given to" the abyss, because they were evil.

15. Ye dear men, behold, I show you a similitude of the angelic world: Look upon the flowering earth or the stars, see how one star or herb excels another in the vigour, beauty and gracefulness of its form so is also the angelic world; for we shall be embodied in a spiritual flesh and blood, not in such a form as here. The

spiritual body can pass through earthly stones, so subtle is it; otherwise it would not be susceptible of the Deity; for God dwells out of or beyond the palpable source, in the still freedom, and his own being is the light and power of Majesty. So must we also get a power-body, but truly in flesh and blood, in which however is a brightness of the tincture. Spirit is so thin that it is imprehensible by the body, yet is prehensible in freedom, else it were a nonentity. And body is much thicker than spirit, so that spirit can lay hold of it and eat it, whereby it preserves the spirit-life in fire, and produces from spirit the light of Majesty, and from light again gentleness in flesh and blood, so that thus there is an eternal being.

16. If we then find and know ourselves, we see and know what God is and is able to do, and what the Being of all beings is. And we find that we are being led erroneously and blindly, as much is told us regarding God's will, and the Deity is represented always as a strange nature that is remote from us, as if God were a strange existence and bore only a will inclining towards us; as one who forgives sin by favour, like a king grants one his life who has forfeited it. But no, hearken, it is not a question of playing the hypocrite and remaining an impostor; it is necessary to be born of God or to be lost eternally from God. The right faith and will must accomplish it; this will must enter earnestly into God and become one Spirit with God; it must acquire heavenly essence, else neither singing, ringing, nor glistering show, will avail. God requires no service; we ought to serve and love one another, and give thanks to the great God, that is, elevate ourselves in one mind into God and proclaim his wonders, invoke his name and praise him. That is the joy in Ternarius Sanctus, where wonders, power and growth are realized out of the praise by the eternal wisdom. And hence the devil's kingdom is destroyed, and God's kingdom comes to us, and his will is done. Apart from this, all is human conceits and works, in the sight of God a useless thing, an hypocrisy, and brings about no reconciliation, but only leads man away from God.

17. God's kingdom must come in us and his will be done in us, then we serve him aright. If we love him with all our heart, with all our soul and with all our strength and our neighbour as ourselves, that is all the worship which he accepts of us. Why should we play the hypocrite to ourselves? If we are righteous, we are ourselves gods in the great God; what we do then, God does it in us and through us. If his Spirit is in us, why are we so much concerned about divine worship? If he would do something, we ought to be servants and willing; he must be the masterworker, if a work is to please him. Whatever is outside of that, is built in an earthly way, in the spirit of this world; we build the same unto the outward heavens, unto the stars and elements, which have their fulfilment and wonders in us, and we serve the dark devil by works outside of God's Spirit.

18. Let this be declared to you, it is highly known No work is pleasing to God, unless it arise from faith in God. Play the hypocrite as thou wilt, thou labourest only in this world, thou sowest in an earthly field. But if thou wouldest reap heavenly fruit, thou must sow heavenly seed. If it shall refuse to strike root in the field of another, thy seed comes to thee again and grows in thy field, and thou wilt enjoy the fruit thyself.

CHAPTER VII

OF SPIRITUAL SEEING; HOW A MAN MAY IN THIS WORLD HAVE DIVINE AND HEAVENLY KNOWLEDGE, SO THAT HE CAN SPEAK CORRECTLY REGARDING GOD; AND HOW HIS SEEING IS

The second citation or summons of the outward Reason of this world in flesh and blood

1. EXTERNAL Reason says: How can a man in this world see into God, as into another world, and say what God is? That cannot possibly be; it must be a mere fancy, with which man tickles and deludes himself.

2. Answer: So far external Reason reacheth; and further it cannot explore, so that it might rest. And if I were still involved in that art, I should also speak in like manner. For he who sees nothing, says there is nothing there. What he sees, that he knows; he is cognisant of nothing more than what is before his eyes. But I would have the scoffer and earthly man asked, whether heaven is blind, as well as hell and God himself? Whether in the divine world there is also a seeing? Whether the Spirit of God can see, both in the world of love and light, and also in the fierceness in the world of wrath, in the centre? If he says that there is a seeing therein-and, indeed, this is true let him look to it carefully that he do not often see with the devil's eyes in his purposed wickedness, when long beforehand he fashions to himself a thing in his imagination, to bring it about in guileful malice, and sees beforehand how he may and will accomplish his wickedness. And if he can here see beforehand what is bad, why does he not also see beforehand his reward? O no: the devil sees with his eyes and covers up the penalty, so that he may accomplish the wickedness. If he would expel the devil, he would see his great folly, which the devil had assigned to him. He shows him the bad and lends him eyes for this purpose, so that he sees what is distant, what is yet to

happen; and he is thus blinded and knows not that he sees with the devil's eyes.

3. So too in like manner he that is holy sees with God's eyes what God has in view, and that the Spirit of God sees in the new birth by true human eyes, by the image of God. This Spirit is to the wise man a seeing and also a doing; not to the old Adam, he must be a servant to it, he must practically work out what the new man sees in God. Christ has said The Son of man doeth nothing but what he sees the Father do, that he doeth also. Now the Son of man has become our habitation into which we have entered; he has become our body, and his spirit is our spirit. If we live in Christ, shall we then be blind in God? The spirit of Christ sees through and in us what he wills; and what he wills, that we see and know in him, and out of him we know nothing of God. He does divine works and sees what and when he pleases, not when Adam pleases, when Adam would willingly (with pride of showing himself) pour out his malignity. O no, there he conceals himself and sees not in us in the light of joy in God, but in the cross, in tribulation, in Christ's sufferings and death, persecution and reproach, in great sorrowfulness; in these does he see and leaves the old ass to struggle and to carry Christ's cross, that is its office. But by this way through the death of Christ the new man sees into the angelic world; it is to him easier and clearer to understand than the earthly world. This comes about naturally, not by illusion, but by seeing eyes, by those eyes which are destined to possess the angelic world, by the eyes of the soul's image, by the spirit which proceeds from the soul's fire. The same spirit sees into heaven, it looks upon God and eternity, and no other can, and it is also the noble image according to God's likeness.

4. As the result of such seeing has this pen written, not under guidance of other masters or out of conjecture as to whether it be true. Though a creature is a part and not a whole, so that we see only in part, yet such fragmentary knowledge is sound. But the wisdom of God cannot be written, it is infinite, without number and circumscription; we know this only in part. Even though we

know much more, the earthly tongue cannot extol and declare such: it speaks only language of this world, and retains the meaning in the hidden man. Therefore one always understands differently from another; according as each is endowed with wisdom, so does he seize it and so does he interpret it.

5. Everyone will not understand my writings in my sense,-nay, not even anyone. But everyone receives according to his endowment, for his amendment, one more than another, according as the Spirit has its property in him. For the Spirit of God is often subject to the spirits of men, if they exercise good-willing, and sees what man wills, that his good be not hindered, but that God's will be everywhere done. For the spirit which is born out of the soul's fire, out of God's gentleness and essence, is also the Holy Spirit. It dwells in divine quality and takes its seeing from divine quality.

6. What is there that is alien in us that we cannot see God? This world and the devil in God's wrath is the cause that we see not with God's eyes; otherwise no impediment exists.

7. If then anyone says: I see nothing divine; let him consider that flesh and blood along with the subtlety of the devil is a hindrance and veil to him frequently by the fact that he wishes in his pride to see God for his own honour, and frequently by the fact that he is filled and blinded with earthly malignity. If he would look into the footsteps of Christ and would go into a new life, submit himself under the cross of Christ and desire only the entering of Christ by the aid of Christ's death, descent into hell and ascent to the Father: how in sooth should he not see the Father, his Saviour Christ and the Holy Spirit?

8. Is then the Holy Spirit to be supposed blind when he dwells in man? Or do I write this for my glorification? Not so, but for the reader's guidance, that he may desist from his error, proceed from the path of reviling and blasphemy into a holy divine existence, that he also may see with divine eyes the wonders of God, so that God's will may be done. To which end this pen has written much, and not for our own honour and the pleasure of this life, as the oppressor is always reproaching and reviling us, and yet only

remains the oppressor in the wrath of God, to whom we would fain wish the kingdom of heaven, if he might be released from the devil and the earthly craze for pride, which make him blind.

9. Therefore, dear children of God, ye who seek with many tears, only put your serious earnestness into it. Our seeing and knowing is in God. He reveals to everyone in this world as much as He pleases, as much as He knows is profitable and good for him. For he who sees with the eyes of God has to work the work of God; he must work, teach, speak and do what he sees, else the seeing is taken away from him. For this world is not worthy of God's seeing; but for the sake of the wonders and manifestation of God it is given to some to see, in order that the name of God may be made manifest to the world, which also will be a witness unto every godless being of those who pervert the truth into lies and despise the Holy Spirit. For we are not our own, but his whom we serve in his light. We know nothing of God; he himself is our knowing and seeing. We are a nothingness, that he may be all in us. We should be blind, deaf and dumb and know no life in ourselves, in order that he may be our life and soul, and our work be his. Our tongue ought not to say if we have done something that is good: this have we done, but rather: this has the Lord done in us; his name be highly praised! But what doth this wicked world now? If any say This has God done in me if it be good, then the world says: Thou fool, thou hast done it; God is not in thee, thou liest. Thus the Spirit of God must be their fool and liar. What is it then, or who speaks out of the blasphemous mouth? The devil, who is an enemy of God, that he may cover up the work of God, in order that God's Spirit may not become known, and that he may continue to be prince of this world till the judgment.

10. If then you see that the world fights against you, persecutes you, reviles and calumniates you on account of the knowledge and name of God, then consider that you have the black devil before you. Accordingly bless, so that God's kingdom may come to us and destroy the devil's sting; so that the man may by your blessing and prayer be released from the devil. Thus you will labour

rightly in God's vineyard and hinder the devil's kingdom, and produce fruit for God's table; for in love and gentleness we are new-born out of the wrath of God. We must in love-and gentleness bathe among the devil's thorns, and in this world fight against him; for love is his poison, it is to him a fire of terror in which he cannot remain. If he were cognisant of a spark of love in himself, he would cast it away, or would burst asunder that he might be rid of it. Therefore love and gentleness is our sword, with which we can, under Christ's crown of thorns, fight with the devil and the world for the noble garland. For love is the fire of the second Principle; it is God's fire, to which the devil and the world are hostile. Love has God's eyes and sees in God, and wrath has the eye of fierceness in the anger of God, it sees in hell, torment and death.

11. The world simply supposes that one must see God with the earthly and stellar eyes; it knows not that God dwells not in the outer life but in the inner. If then it sees nothing strange in God's children, it says: Oh I he is a fool, he was born foolish, he is melancholy. So much it knows. Listen, Master Hans, I know well what melancholy is, I also know well what is of God; I know both of these, and also thee in thy blindness. But such knowledge requires not a state of melancholy, but a knightly wrestling; for to none is it given without wrestling (except he be a goal chosen by God), unless he strive for the garland. Many a one indeed is chosen thereto in the womb, as John the Baptist (Luke i. 15), and others, laid hold of in God's covenant of the promise, which is always a goal of a saeculum, which is born at the time of the great year, and is chosen by God to disclose the wonders which he has before him. But not all as springing from the goal, but many of them from zealous seeking; for Christ said: Seek and ye shall find, knock and it shall be opened unto you (Matt. vii. 7). Further: Him that cometh to me I will in no wise cast out (John vi. 37). Also: Father, I will that they whom thou hast given me be where I am (John xvii. 24), that is, with the new man born of Christ in God his Father. Further: Father, I will that they see my glory which I had before the foundation of the world. Here we have

seeing out of Christ's spirit, out of God's kingdom, in the power of the Word, of the essence of the Deity, with God's eyes, and not with the eyes of this world and of the outer flesh.

12. Therefore, thou blind world, know with what we see when we speak and write of God, and give over thy false judging. See thou with thy eyes and let God's children see with their eyes. See thou by means of thy gifts and let God's children, or another person, see by means of his gifts. As everyone is called, so let him see, and so let him walk; for we do not all pursue one and the same walk and coversation, but everyone according to his gift and calling unto the honour and wonders of God. The Spirit of God suffers not itself to be bound, as outward Reason with its laws and Councils supposes, whereby always a chain of Antichrist is formed, so that men undertake to judge God's Spirit, and hold their conceits and reasonings for God's covenant, as if God were not at home in this world or as if they were gods upon earth; they confirm also by oath what they choose to believe. Is it not a fool's work to bind to an oath the Holy Spirit in his wonderful gifts? He is to believe what they wish, and they know him not, nor are born of him, yet make laws as to what he shall do.

13. I say that all such compacts are Antichrist and want of faith, whatever devout show of holiness there may be, God's Spirit is unbound, he enters not into compact, but freely appears to the seeking humble mind according to its gift, according as it is constituted. He is even subject to it, if it desire him wholly with earnestness. What then is the purpose of the compact in human wisdom of this world if it relate to the honour of God? Are not all compacts born of personal pride? Friendly conversation is certainly good and necessary, so that one may exhibit his gift to another, but compacts are a false chain contrary to God. God has once made a covenant with us in Christ, this suffices to all eternity; he will make no more. He has taken the human race once for all into the covenant, and formed a permanent testament by death and blood. That is sufficient, we content ourselves justly with that, and we cleave to this covenant. We ought not to dance

boldly around the cup of Christ, as is done at present, else it will be taken away, as happened to the Turks.

14. There is a very great earnest severity at hand, such as never was seen from the time of the world. Let this be told you: It is known that Antichrist shall stand naked. But look to it that thus you become not worse! For the axe is put to the tree the bad tree shall be hewn down and cast into the fire. The time is near; let no one ensconce himself in carnal pleasure. For it avails nothing that any-one know how he may be new-born, and yet remains in the old skin, in the sensuality of the old Adam, in greed, pride and unrighteousness, in licentiousness and a scandalous life: such a one is dead while he lives, and lies in the jaws of the wrath of God; his knowledge will accuse and condemn him at the judgment. If he receive and accept the word which God gives him to know, that it is the right way to life, he must at once become a doer of the word and go out from what is bad, else he will have a severe judgment pronounced regarding him. What is he better than the devil? The devil also knows God's will, but does his own evil will. No one is good till he becomes a doer of the word: then he walks in God's ways, and is in the vineyard engaged in God's work.

15. Hypocritical Babel teaches now that our works merit nothing, that Christ has redeemed us from death and hell, that we have only to believe this, and so we shall be righteous. Hearken Babel! The servant who knows his master's will and does it not, shall suffer many stripes. A knowing without doing is just like a fire which glimmers, and cannot burn on account of moisture. If thou wouldest that thy divine fire of faith should burn, thou must blow up the fire, and extract from it the moisture of the devil and of the world; thou must enter into the life of Christ. Wouldest thou become his child, thou must enter into his house and do his work, else thou art outside and a hypocrite, who utters the name of God uselessly. Thou teachest one thing and doest another, and thus testifiest that God's judgment is right regarding thee. Or again, what pleasure has God in thy knowledge, since thou remainest an impostor? Thinkest thou that he accepts thy hypocrisy when thou criest to him: Lord, give me a strong faith in

the merits of thy Son Christ, that I may believe with all my heart that he has done satisfaction for my sins? Thinkest thou that that is enough? O no! Thou must enter into Christ's sufferings and death, and be born again out of his death; thou must become a member with and in him; thou must continually crucify the old Adam, and always hang on Christ's cross, and must become an obedient child that always gives ear to what the father* says, and would always fain do that. Thou must enter upon action, else thou art a monstrous shape without life; thou must with God work good works of love towards thy neighbour, constantly practise thy faith, and always be ready at the voice of the Lord when he bids thee go home from out of the old skin into the pure vesture. Mark! Though thou walkest in this path, thou wilt nevertheless have weakness enough and be sensible of too much in thee. Thou wilt still work too much evil, for we have an evil guest lodging within us. It is not a question merely of taking comfort, but of fighting and warring against him, of continually slaying and vanquishing him; he is in any case always too strong, and will have the upper hand. Christ has indeed broken down death for us and in us, and made a way unto God; but what does it profit me that I comfort myself with this and learn to know it as such, yet continue shut up in dark wrath and imprisoned in the chains of the devil? I must enter into this way and walk in this path, as a pilgrim who wends out of death into life.

CHAPTER VIII

THE PILGRIM'S PATH FROM DEATH UNTO LIFE

1. DEAR children, let us discourse together deeply concerning the ground of things. Our true life, with which we are to see God, is as a choked fire; in some even as the fire shut up in a stone; we must kindle it by right and earnest turning to God. Consider God's care: He has regenerated us in Christ by the water of eternal life, and has in the covenant of baptism left us the same water as a key of refreshment by which we may unlock and sprinkle therewith the fire of our souls, so that it may become capable of the divine fire. He has given us his body for food and his blood for drink, that we may appropriate these, enter into his covenant and feed our soul therewith, that it may be quickened and wake up from death, so that it may kindle the divine fire., Dear children, it must burn and not remain shut up in the stone, or as tinder that fain would glimmer and cannot for the devil's moisture. Historical faith is tinder which glimmers as a small spark; it must be enkindled; we must give it matter in which the spark may inflame itself. The soul must penetrate out of the reason of this world into the life of Christ, into Christ's flesh and blood, then it receives matter for its enkindling. There must be earnestness; for history reaches not Christ's flesh and blood. Death must be broken to pieces; according as Christ has broken it to pieces, the earnest desire must now just follow along, and do that gladly and always labour to that result, as a pilgrim or messenger, having to go a long dangerous journey, runs on continually towards the term or goal, and is indefatigable: though misfortune and calamity befall him, he still hopes for the term or goal and approaches ever nearer, where then he is expectant of his reward and delight, and rejoices that his hard journeying will come to an end.

2. Thus, a man who would journey to God must set out upon the pilgrim's path. He must depart always more and more from the earthly reason, from the will of the flesh, of the devil and of the

world. Frequently pain and woe befall him when he has to abandon that which he might have, and by which he might sweep along in temporal honours. But if he will walk in the true narrow path, he must only put on the coat of righteousness, and put off the coat of covetousness and of the specious hypocritical life. He must part his bread with the hungry and give his garment for a covering, not be an oppressor of the wretched and wish only to fill his own pocket, wring his sweat from the miserable and simple man, and give him laws merely for his own pride and pleasure. He is not a Christian who does this, but he walks in the path of this world, just as the stars and elements with the devil's infection and desire impel him. And though he know the form of faith, as relating to God's mercy, to the atonement of Christ, this will be of no avail to him. For not all they that say, Lord, Lord, shall enter into the kingdom of heaven; but he that doeth the will of my Father which is in heaven. And that will is: Love thy neighbour as thyself; Whatsoever ye would that men should do unto you, even so do ye also unto them.

3. Say not in thy heart: I sit in this office and lordship with good right; I have bought or inherited it; what my vassals do for me, they owe me. See and inquire where this right originates, whether it be ordained by God or whether it arise from fraud and personal pride, and from greed. If thou findest that it is God's ordering, then observe, and walk therein according to the commandment of love and righteousness. Think that in this position thou art a servant, and not a lord over Christ's children, and not only sittest there to draw their sweat to thee, but that thou art their judge and pastor, that thou must give an account of thy charge: to thee have been given five talents, thou hast to deliver them to thy lord with interest. Thou shouldest lead thy inferiors on the right path, and give them a good example in connection with doctrine and the punishment of the wicked. It will be required of thee, if thou punish not the wicked and protect not the oppressed. Thou art not a ruler only in order that thou mayest be their lord; not thou, but God is their lord; thou shouldest be their judge and decide between them, not for thy greed's sake but for the sake of their

conscience. Thou shouldest teach, guide and direct the simple not merely through pressure of his toil, but through gentleness. Thou hast a heavy charge upon thee; thou must therefore furnish a serious reckoning. When the wretched man groans with reference to thee in his misery, he accuses thee before his and thy lord: in such case thou shalt and must stand with him before the judgment; for sentence is pronounced regarding souls, no hypocrisy is of any avail.

4. All that is sown in tears, in true real earnest, that becomes a substance and belongs to the judgment of God; unless indeed the man turn round and become reconciled by benefits to the oppressed person, so that he should bless him: in this way the substance is dissolved. Therefore ye who are in authority have a heavy charge upon you. You may well study your rank or position, wherever it may originate, the root will be closely sought after; everyone shall give an account of his rank or position. Take heed, however, that by it ye ride not in hellish fire, as the fierce devil himself does, and ye be found his servants; as the spirit of wonders shows us, that ye have come to be the filling up of the eternal anger and wrath. Say not in thy heart: Thus have my parents and forefathers lived; I have inherited such mode of life. Thou knowest not into what abode they have entered. If thou wouldest be a Christian and a child of God, thou must not give attention to the way of predecessors, as to how they have careered in lust, but to God's word: that must be a lamp unto thy feet. For many who have done ill have gone into the abyss, and thou wilt also follow them if thou walk in their footsteps. Suffer not the devil to pourtray to thee the specious hypocritical path; its colour shines on the outside and in the essence it is poison.

5. O how very dangerous a path we have to walk in through this world! and it were to be wished that there were in the wicked nothing that is eternal, then they would not suffer eternal torment and be in eternal reproach. As in this life they are enemies of the children of God, so likewise they remain eternal enemies of God and of his children. Therefore the children of God must take the cross upon them, and here sweat in the bath of thistles and thorns,

and be new-born in anguish; they must walk in the narrow way, where Reason is always saying: Thou art a fool, thou mightest live in joy and still be saved. O how external Reason often strikes the noble image, which grows up out of the thorny bath of tribulation! How many a twig is torn away from the tree of pearl by doubt and unbelief, which bring the individual into the false path! The wretched man sighs after temporal nourishment and curses the coercer who wrings from him his sweat, and thinks he does right in this; whereas he does but bring destruction on himself thereby, he acts just as wickedly as his oppressor. If he would take patience in himself and remember that he walks in the pilgrim's path, and if he would put his hope in his goal, and consider that thus under tribulation and misery, under oppression, he labours in the vineyard of Christ: O how blessedly would he journey! he would thus have reason to seek another and better life, seeing that here he must be in anguish and misery. If he would but understand aright how well God is inclined towards him, that thus He allures him and endeavours that he should not build upon the earthly life. Since he sees that it is but a vale of sorrow and a state of affliction, that he must spend his days here in hard constraint, in misery, in mere toil, he ought indeed to consider that God lets not things take their course thus in vain, but that thus He gives him occasion at the same time to seek the true rest, which is not in this world. Besides, he is under the necessity at all hours of awaiting death and leaving his work to others. Why is it then that a man builds his hope upon this world, in which he is but a guest and pilgrim who has to walk in the paths of his constellation? If he would adopt the inner constellation, O how blessedly would he work in God's work and let the outer life go as it can.

6. A man in this world who looks to possess God's kingdom has no better way and he can have no better help than constantly to remember and set before himself that he is in the vineyard of God with all his doing and being, in order that he may do it for God. His soul should be directed to God in a constant hope that he shall obtain from Him his reward for his labour, and that he may

work in God's mirificence. Therefore he ought to be diligent in his work which he performs; even though he is compelled often to serve his oppressor by toil without pay, let him but consider that he works for God only, and be patient in hope that God assuredly will give him his reward in due season. For the master of the vineyard pays not his labourers in the day, but in the evening when the day's work has been done. When we go home to our Lord out of the vale of this tabernacle, then everyone will receive his pay. He who for a long time has laboured much has much pay to expect; but he who has been a blusterer, grumbler, sluggard and bad worker by want of patience, has earned little, and will even have to expect punishment from his Lord; for he has only led away other workers, and has been a useless worker, has done nothing but false work in order to defraud his Lord, and he will receive justly punishment instead of reward.

The gate in the centre of nature

The third citation

7. Reason says: Why does God permit things to go in such a way that there is nothing but misery and hardship in this world, moreover only coercion and oppression, so that one torments and afflicts another? And though many a one possess much and does not want, yet he has no rest; he strives only after turmoil and unrest, and his heart is never quiet.

8. See! thou shut-up cognition. The foundation of the world is such, the origin of life also is such. It cannot be otherwise in this world unless a man be new-born. He exists differently in the new man, and yet this impulse in the old man always cleaves to him. It is the struggle of the spirit against the flesh, in which the flesh lusts against the spirit and the spirit against the flesh. Reason now says: Where then does it first take its rise?

9. Answer: Mark! in the centrum naturae there is such a mode of being. Do but reflect. The eternal will, which is called God, is free, for he contains in himself nothing but the light of Majesty, and

dwells in the eternal nothing, hence also nothing can move him. But his desiring, which makes the centrum naturae, has only one such a property. For there astringency is found, viz. the first form of nature. It is always drawing to itself, and takes where there is nothing; where it has made nothing, there does it take, and gathers this in, and yet cannot eat it, nor is it of any advantage to it; it creates for itself thus anguish, torture and unrest, in the same way as greed and covetousness does in man. The second form is its attraction or sting, that is, its servant, who gathers in what the desiring wishes; he is the worker and signifies the underman; he is angry, wrathful, furious, he stings and rages in the astringency. This can the astringency not suffer from the servant, and draws him only more vehemently; hence the servant becomes more angry and frantic, and storms the master's house, Accordingly the master tries to bind and hold the servant, and the servant breaks loose with rage beyond measure. If then his master, viz. the astringency, cannot reduce him to subjection, they fall together into great anguish, enmity and opposition, and begin to make a revolving wheel, to kill, murder and slay one another. Such is the third form of nature, from which arises war, conflict, devastation of country and cities, envy and terrible malice, -where each would have the other dead, and would devour and draw into itself everything. It desires alone to possess it, yet to it alone by itself it is of no use, but only hurtful. It acts as the wrath of nature acts: this devours itself in like manner in itself, consumes and destroys itself, yet in like manner generates itself. Therefrom comes all evil, the devil and every evil thing comes from thence. It is thus that it first takes its rise.

10. As nature in the centre acts, understand apart from the light, so also does the devil act, who possesses not the light; similarly the evil man and beast, as well as herbs, grass and all that is hostile. For what we have here is the poison-wheel, from which life has its origin; this revolves thus in great anguish, in stinging, raging and breaking, till it draw for itself another will to go out from the anguish, and sinks into death, and freely gives itself up to freedom. In this way the stinging and breaking is shattered in

death, and falls into the freedom of the primal will, which kindles the anguish of death with the still freedom, whereby the anguish is terrified, breaks death to pieces, and out of the anguish flames up as a life of joy.

11. Thus is it also with man. When he is in the anguish of enmity and the sting of death and anger rages within him, so that he is anguishful, covetous, envious, angry and hostile, he ought not to remain in this evil nature; otherwise he is in the forms of death, anger, wrath and hell-fire. If the water-fountain were not in him in connection with flesh and blood, he would be already an enkindled devil and nothing else. But he must reflect and in his evil anguish draw another will to go out from the covetous malice into the freedom of God, where there is always rest and peace enough. He must sink down into death, into patience, willingly give himself up to the wheel of anguish, and draw a thirst for the refreshment of God, which is freedom; in this way he sinks down through the anguishful death into freedom. When then his anguish tastes freedom, that it is such a still gentle life, the anguish-source is terrified; and in the terror the hostile grim death is broken to pieces, for this terror is a terror of great joy and a kindling of the life of God. And so the branch of pearls is born; it is found now in trembling joy, but in great danger, for death and the anguishsource is its root; and it is encompassed therewith, as a fair green branch that grows up out of a stinking dunghill, out of the fetid source, and acquires an essence, smell and quality other than its mother has, out of which it was born; and indeed the source in nature has such a property, so that out of evil, i.e. out of anguish, is produced the great life.

12. And as we know further that nature in the terror divides into two kingdoms into the kingdom of joy, and (2) into a sinking down of death into a darkness-so also does the nature of man, if the lily-twig as requisite for the kingdom of joy be generated accordingly, divide into two wills. The first arises in the lily and grows up in God's kingdom; the other sinks down into dark death, and longs after the earth as its mother. The latter will is always fighting against the lily, and the lily flees from the

roughness. As a twig grows out of the earth, and the essence flees from the earth, and is drawn up by the sun till a stalk or tree is produced out of it: so also does God's sun in his, power always draw man's lily, i.e. the new man, from the evil essence, and at length draws up a tree therefrom in God's kingdom. Then he lets the old evil tree, or the bark beneath which the new has grown, fall into the earth, into its mother after which it longs, and go out from the earth again into the centrum naturae at the end of the day of separation, when all must enter again into its ether. Then the lily also enters into its ether, into the will of freedom, into the light of Majesty.

13. Understand it further in this way: When in the terror of nature two kingdoms thus separate, the terror is in itself a flash of lightning and a cause of fire, or of the enkindling of life. Thus the prima materia, which the astringency made by its contraction, wherein enmity has originated, separates into two parts. Namely, one below itself into death, which is the essential life with the substantiality of this world, such as earth and stones; and, secondly, the other part separates out of the terror of fire into the light of freedom, for the fire-terror inflames freedom so that it also becomes desireful and in its desiring draws into itself the kingdom of joy, i.e. the gentle beneficence, and makes it also a materia. This is then the heavenly divine essentiality; it draws the fire again into itself and swallows it up it its terror, which is the source of the fire. There the source consumes the gentle essentiality and is brought into great joyfulness, so that anguish is changed into love and fire into a love-burning, and gives from the burning the joyous spirit of eternal life that is called God's Spirit, which originally arises in the primal will that is called Father. For it is the desiring of nature, and in the fire is a fire-source, and in the anguish of death a sting of death, of wrath and enmity in the essence of nature, i.e. in the centre. And in the light it is the divine kingdom of joy, revealing in the divine Essence or in wisdom (as being the colours of virtue) the noble tincture, which forms the lustre of the heavenly Essence; and in the Essence it produces the Element of the angelic world, of which this world is an extern

birth, but kindled in wrath by the devil, who is a cause that the wrath of nature has been kindled, whereby in the Essence earth and stones have arisen, as is evident, and this has the mightiest source separated in the verbum fiat into a Principle)

14. Understand, then, the fire-flash as the fourth form of nature, and the love-birth of the kingdom of joy as the fifth form; and the swallowing up of the essentiality out of the gentleness into the firesource, where fire also attains the kingdom of joy, i.e. the sound or manifestation of colours, wonders and virtues, from whence arise the five senses, viz. seeing, hearing, smelling, tasting and feeling, understand as the sixth form of nature; and the essentiality of the light, in which is comprised the divine Element wherefrom budding or Paradise originates, understand as the seventh form, or, again, as the mother of all the forms, giving essence, power and gentleness to all the forms, so that there is an eternal life and rapture of life. For the seventh form contains in itself the angelic world as well as Paradise or the true kingdom of heaven, in which the nature of the Deity is made manifest and all that the light-world includes.

CHAPTER IX

SEVERAL FURTHER PARTICULARS REGARDING THIS THIRD CITATION, HIGHLY TO BE CONSIDERED

1. THUS, ye children of men, be now seeing and not, blind. Pray observe what is revealed to you, it does not take place in vain; there is something behind it. Sleep not, the time is come. Do but see what the Being of all beings is. This world is progenerated from the Eternal; the centre of nature has existed from eternity, but it has not been manifest. Through this world and through the devil's fierce wrath it has come into substantial being. Understand though what the devil is. He is a spirit of his legions which proceeds from the centre of nature. He was created unto divine essentiality, yet he was to be tried in fire and was to place his desire in love. He put his desire back into the centre of fierceness, into the fourth form of anguish, and wished in fire to rule over God's gentleness, as an enemy of the kingdom of joy; and he despised love because he saw that fire gave strength and might: therefore he was thrust out of the fire of God into the anguish of darkness, into the centre of the four forms. He has no longer anything of fire but the terrible flash, that is his true life; but the will of God, which in angels and men longs after the life, which comes to the aid of the life with freedom, i.e. gentleness, has abandoned him. Hence he cannot attain the light in eternity, nor can he draw any desire for it, for God's Will-spirit torments him in the torture chamber, in the first four forms of nature; the fifth form he cannot reach. And though he has all the forms of nature, yet all is hostile and adverse; for the Holy Spirit has abandoned him, and now wrath or the fierce quality is in him. God, who is all, has opened His fierceness or the centre of the origin in him, so that it also became creaturely, for it has also longed *to manifest itself. And when God put himself in motion for the creation of the angels, all that was hidden from eternity in the

wonders of wisdom, in the centre, both in love and wrath, was revealed.

2. Seeing that we know what we are, and that God enables us to know it, let us take heed and produce from ourselves something that is good. For we have the centre of nature in us. If we make of ourselves an angel, then we are that; if we make of ourselves a devil, then in like manner we are that. We are in this world in the source of making and creating, we are in the field. God's will in love is presented to us in the centre of life. God has become man and wishes to have us; his wrath also wishes to have us into the kingdom of fierceness. The devil wishes to have us into his company and God's angels into theirs: the one towards which we aspire, into that do we go. If we place our desire in the light of God and enter with earnestness, then we come in, and are also with earnestness drawn in. If we will place our will in the glory of this world and let the Eternal go, we have to expect that we will necessarily enter with this world's fierceness into the first Mystery. If we shall then not have in us divine imagination [formative power] or faith, the divine love will abandon us and not admit us at her door. In truth, if God break not open [our dark prison], we come to misery. If thou bringest not God's Spirit with thee, thou wilt never reach it: therefore it is well to come to full growth here in this life. Christ has become our field, we may realize this without too great anguish and distress. The object in view is only this, that we break the will; this is painful, for Adam will not, nor will the wrath nor the devil.

3. Behold, O man, thou art thine own enemy. What thou regardest as friend, that is thine enemy. If thou wilt be saved and see God, thou must become the worst enemy of thy best friend, i.e. of the outer life. Not that thou shouldest break it, but only its will. Thou must do what thou wouldest not, thou must become thine own enemy or thou canst not see God. He whom now thou holdest for thy friend has arisen from the torture chamber, and still has the anguish-life in himself; he has the craving of the wrath-source and of the devil in him. Thou must draw a will in God, from thy soul must thou draw a will, and with it go out

from wickedness into God; in this way thou wilt be introduced into the fire of God, that is, the Will-spirit will kindle thy soul. Thereupon reach after the life and spirit of Christ, and thou wilt receive it. It will regenerate thee with a new will which will remain to thee. This will is the flower of thy soul, wherein lies the new child in the image of God: to it God gives Christ's flesh and blood to feed upon, and not to the Adamic ass, as Babel hoaxes strangely, as if the godless man could become participative of Christ's body. O no! he receives the four elements and in them the wrath of God, because he discerns not the Lord's body, which is present in heaven, and is eaten by the soul that attains heaven. Not as a sign, as the other phantasy hoaxes, not spirit without essentiality, but the essentiality of the spirit along with it, enclosed in God's wisdom, Christ's flesh which fills the light-world everywhere, which the Word that became man brought with it into Mary. This essentiality, although it was revealed in Mary in her flesh and blood, and took human essence unto itself, was nevertheless during the time that Christ lay in Mary's womb, in heaven, in the Element, everywhere. It passed not over many miles from any place into Mary: no; but the shut up centre, which Adam had shut up in the wrath of God, in death, that did the Word of the Deity open, and introduced divine essentiality into the virgin centre that was shut up in death. This took place in the womb of Mary, in the goal of the covenant, not by way of absence nor entrance, but disclosingly, ingeneratingly, and in this world progeneratingly, God and Man, one Person, heavenly as well as in death shut up essentiality and virginity, one Substance, one Man in heaven and in this world. And such must we also be, for the Word that became man is stirring in the soul and stands in vital sound in all souls; it draws all souls and the wrath likewise draws all souls. Now, go whither thou wilt, thou hast in thyself the centre of the Deity in sound and in motion, and also the centre of wrath; into which thou goest and which thou awakenest, in that is rooted thy life. Do what is pleasing to thee, thou art free and God enables thee to know it. He calleth to thee; if thou comest, thou wilt be his child; if thou goest into the wrath, thou wilt also be received.

CHAPTER X

OF THE IMAGE OF GOD WHICH IS MAN, OR OF THE LIKENESS OF GOD AND MAN

1. WE cannot in this world behold our essentiality or new body, because we are in the earthly life. The outer man knows it not, but the spirit, which is generated and proceeds from the new man, this knows its body.

2. As however we have knowledge of it, and wish to know whether we are in the new birth, there is no better test than by the likeness of God, which we understand to be desire, sense and mind. These three things contain the centre of the spirit, from which is generated the strong will wherein lies the true real likeness and image of God in flesh and blood, which the outer man knows not. For this image is not in this world, it has another principle in the angelic world, and during this lifetime remains in the mystery, in hiddenness, like the gold in the stone, where the gold has another tincture, essence and lustre, and the roughness of the stone cannot lay hold of it; nor does the gold lay hold upon the roughness, and yet the roughness, as the anguishcentre, is a cause of the gold, for it is mother and the sun father. So likewise is our old Adam a cause of the new body, for it is the mother: from the old entity springs the new body, and God's Spirit in Christ is the father. As the sun is father of the gold, so also is God's heart the father of the new man.

3. Now, we know not the new man better than in the centre, viz. in desire, sense and mind. If we find that our desire stands wholly in accordance with and directed towards God, that our senses constantly run in the will of God, that the mind gives itself up entirely in obedience to God's will, and that the imagination seizes something of God's power: then we may know certainly that the noble lily-twig is born, that the image of God exists in essential being, that God has become man in the likeness. Here it is highly necessary to safeguard the noble image and give not room to the old Adam with his lusts, but to kill him continually,

so that the new man may grow, increase, and be adorned with the wonders of wisdom.

4. Reason, however, now asks: How is then God's likeness? Behold, God is a Spirit, and the mind with the senses and desires is also spirit. The mind is the wheel of nature, desire is the centre as the first thing for the realization of nature, and the senses are the essences. For the senses arise from the essences, they have their origin from the sting of desire, from the sourness; they are the bitterness and run always in the mind, i.e. the wheel of anguish, and seek rest, to see whether they may attain the freedom of God. It is they who, in the anguish-wheel or mind, kindle fire, and in the kindling, in the terror, willingly give themselves up to death, and thus sink down through the torment of fire into freedom, into God's arms; they proceed into freedom as a life which proceeds out of death. They are the roots of the new taste, which penetrate into God's wisdom and wonders; they bring desire out of the pangs of death; they fill their mother the mind, and give her power from God's essence.

5. Thus the mind (das Gemüth)1 is the wheel or the true chamber of life, the proper habitation of the soul, of which itself is a part if the essence (understand the essence of the tincture) be reckoned thereamong, and is the fire-life, for from the fire-life arises the mind, and the fire-life dwells in the mind. But mind is nobler than fire, for it is the mobility of the fire-life; it makes the understanding. The senses are the mind's servants and are the subtlest messengers; they go into God, and again out of God into evils, and wherever they become kindled, either in God or in evils, as in falseness, that do they bring home to the mind. And hence the noble mind must often attack what is bad and stifle it in its anguish when the senses have admitted false imagination into the desire.

6. Understand it, then, lastly in this way: God is himself all and in all; but he goes out from fierceness and finds the world of light and power in himself. He himself constitutes it, so that fierceness with all the forms is but a cause of life (and the finding of himself in great wonders). He is the ground and unground, freedom and

also nature, in light and darkness. And man too is all that, if he do but thus seek and find himself like God.

7. Our whole writing and teaching comes only to this, as to how we must seek, make and ultimately find ourselves; how we must bring forth, so that we are one spirit with God, that God may be in us and we in God, that God's love-spirit may be in us the will and also the doing, and that we may escape from the source of anguish; that we may dispose ourselves into the true likeness in three worlds, where each stands in its order, and that the light-world may be lord in us, as that which bears rule; that thus the anguish-world may remain hidden in the light-world as it remains hidden in God, and so only be a cause of life and of the wonders of God. Otherwise, if we attain not the light-world, the anguish-world in us is the dominant influence, and we shall live eternally in hostile pain. This struggle goes on as long as the earthly life lasts; after that, such life passes into the eternal ether, into light or darkness, from which there is no longer any deliverance, and of which God's Spirit warns us and instructs us in the right way. Amen.

Conclusion

8. Thus, God-loving reader, know that a man is the true likeness of God, which God highly loves and reveals himself in this likeness as in his own being. God is in man the middle, the middlemost, but he dwells only in himself, unless the spirit of man become one spirit with him, when he manifests himself in humanity as in the mind, senses and desire, so that the mind feels him; otherwise he is in this world much too subtle for us to behold. But the senses behold him in spirit, understand in the will's spirit, for the will sends the senses into God and God gives himself up to the senses and becomes one being with them. Then the senses bring the power of God to the will, which receives it with joy, but at the same time with trembling; for it knows itself unworthy, because it comes from a rude lodging, from the wavering mind; therefore it receives the power in sinking down

before God. Accordingly its triumph is changed into gentle humility, which is and embraces God's true nature; and this same nature as embraced is in the will the heavenly body and is called the true and right faith, which the will has received in the power of God; it sinks into the mind and dwells in the fire of the soul.

9. Thus the image of God is complete, and God sees or finds himself in such a likeness. And we are by no means to think with regard to God that he is a strange being. To the godless he is a strange being, for the godless man does not lay hold of him. God is certainly in him, but not manifest according to his love-light in the will and mind of the godless man. His wrath only is revealed in him; the light he cannot attain, it is in him, but it is of no use to him; his essence seizes it not, he shrinks from it; it is his torture and pain, he does but show enmity towards it, as the devil is hostile to the sun and also to the light of God. The devil would be better satisfied if he could live eternally in the darkness and knew that God were far from him, then he would find no shame and reproach in himself. As, however, he knows that God is so near him and yet he cannot lay hold of him, this is his great torment, so that he has an enmity against himself and makes for himself an eternal contra-will, fear and despair, in that he knows that he cannot reach the countenance and gracious favour of God; his own falseness torments him, but he can draw no consolation that he may attain to grace. For he reaches not God, but only the centre in anguish, in wrath; he remains in death and in the dying source; he cannot break through, for nothing comes to his aid by which he might maintain himself so that he might be established in God's kingdom. Though he carry on for a thousand years in the abyss, in the deep, yet he is in the darkness out of God, and nevertheless God is in him, and it profits him nothing; nor does he know him, but he is aware of him and is sensible of his fierce wrath only.

10. Understand it thus: As fire exists in a stone, and the stone knows it not, feels it not, but feels the fierce cause of the fire which keeps the hard stone imprisoned in a body: so likewise the devil feels only the cause of the light. This cause is the fierce

centre and keeps him a prisoner, and hence, too, he hates it, nor has he anything that were better. Accordingly he is nothing but a poisonous fierce malignity, a dying pang, yet there is no dying, but a famished poison, a hunger and thirst but no refreshment. All that is bad, envious, hard and bitter, whatever flees from humility as he did, that is his strength and his hostile desire. Whatever shows enmity to God and flees from or curses God is serviceable to him. Whatever turns truth into lies, that is his will upon which he rides and in which he willingly dwells. So also is the godless man: when he loses God, he is in the anguish-source and has the devil's will. But know this

11. God has in the human soul broken through the hardness of death and has entered into the limit where death is broken to pieces. He has burst the limit in the centre of the soul and has set his light over against man's light of life; the light is vouchsafed to man so long as he lives in the virtue of the sun. If he choose to turn round and enter into God's light, he will be received: no election is concluded regarding him. But when he loses the sun's life and also has nothing of God's life, it is all over with him, he is and remains a devil. But God knows his own and knows who will turn themselves to him; upon those is set the election of which the Scripture speaks. And upon those who will not hardening is set or withdrawal of the light. Man has both centres in himself: if accordingly he wish only to be a devil, is God then to cast pearls on the path of the devil? Is he to pour his spirit into the godless will? Further, out of man's will must God's spirit be born, man must himself become God in the spirit of the will, otherwise he attains not divine essentiality or wisdom.

12. Therefore reflect, dear children, and enter in at the right door. It is necessary not merely to be forgiven, but to be born. Then we are to be regarded as forgiven, that is, sin is then but a husk. The new man grows out of this husk, and throws the husk away; that constitutes God's forgiveness. God clears off evil from the new man, he gets rid of it from him. It is not carried off from the body, but sin is given to the centre as if for fuel, and must thus be a cause of the Principle of fire, from which the light shines, and

so must serve for the best unto the holy man, as St. Paul says: All things must serve for the best unto them that love God, even sin (Rom. viii. 28).

13. What shall we say then? Shall we then sin in order that our salvation may be generated? God forbid. How should I wish to enter again into that to which I am dead? Am I to go out of the light again into the darkness?

14. It must, then, be that the saints of God lose nothing; all must be of service to them. That which to sinners is a sting unto death, is to the saints a power unto life.

15. Outward reason says: Accordingly I must sin, that my salvation may increase. We know that whoever goes out from the light goes into the darkness. Let him look to it that he remain not in the darkness, for he sins deliberately against the Holy Spirit. Be not deceived; God is not mocked. As the result of his love we have, after our fall, again become righteous by his entering into our flesh. But he who enters deliberately into sin, despises and does dishonour to the incarnation of Christ, and receives into himself a heavy burden. Let him look carefully to it: he will have more difficulty in departing again from deliberate sin, than one to whom the way of God has not yet been revealed.

16. Therefore it is well to avoid and flee from evil, to turn away one's eyes from what is false, so that the senses do not enter thereinto and bring this to the heart, whence lust and desire arise in the mind whereby the noble image is destroyed and becomes an abomination in the sight of God.

17. We would have the God-loving reader and hearer faithfully warned from out of our gift and deep knowledge: we have earnestly and faithfully expounded to you the way of truth and light, and we Christianly exhort you all to meditate on it and to read it diligently; it has its fruit in itself. Hallelujah, Amen.

PART III
THE TREE OF CHRISTIAN FAITH

A TRUE INSTRUCTION, SHOWING HOW MAN MAY BECOME ONE SPIRIT WITH GOD, AND WHAT HE HAS TO DO TO WORK THE WORKS OF GOD; IN WHICH THE WHOLE CHRISTIAN DOCTRINE AND FAITH IS SUMMARIZED. ITEM, WHAT FAITH AND DOCTRINE ARE. AN OPEN GATE OF THE GREAT MYSTERY OF GOD, AS ARISING OUT OF THE DIVINE MAGIA ON THE BASIS OF THE THREE PRINCIPLES OF THE DIVINE NATURE

CHAPTER I

WHAT FAITH IS, AND HOW IT IS ONE SPIRIT WITH GOD

1. CHRIST says: Seek ye first the kingdom of God and his righteousness, and all these things shall be added unto you (Matt. vi. 33). Item: My Father will give the Holy Spirit to them that ask him (Luke xi. 13); and when he is come, he will guide you into all truth; he will put you in mind of all that I have told you of; for he shall take of mine, and shall declare it unto you (John xvi. 13-15). Item: I will give you a mouth and wisdom what ye should speak (Luke xxi. 15). And St. Paul says: We know not what we should pray and speak; but the Spirit of God intercedes powerfully for us, according to the pleasure of God (Rom. viii. 26).

2. Now, faith is not an historical knowledge, that a man should frame articles to himself and -depend on them alone, and force his mind into the works of his reason; but faith is one Spirit with God, for the Holy Spirit moves in the spirit of faith.

3. True faith is a power of God, one Spirit with God. It works in and with God. It is free and bound to no article, save only to true love, in which it gathers the power and strength of its life; human delusion and conjecture are of no consequence.

4. For as God is free from all inclination, in such a sense that he does whatever he wills, and needs to give no account about it: so also is the true right faith free in the Spirit of God. It has no more than one inclination, viz. to the love and mercy of God, so that it casts its will into God's will and goes out from the sidereal and elemental Reason; it seeks not itself in carnal Reason, but in God's love. And when in this way it finds itself, it finds itself in God, and works with God; not in acting according to Reason, whatever the latter will have, but in God, whatever God's Spirit will have. For it regards the earthly life as nothing, in order that it may live in God, and that God's Spirit in it may be the will and the doing. It gives itself up in humility to the will of God, and sinks down through reason into death, but springs up with God's Spirit in the life of God. It is as if it were a nothing, and yet in God is all; it is an ornament and crown of the Deity, a wonder in the divine magia. It makes where there is nothing, and takes where nothing is made. It is operative, and no one sees its being; it uplifts itself, and yet needs no elevation. It is mighty, and yet is the lowliest humility. It possesses all, and yet embraces nothing more than gentleness. It is thus free from all iniquity and has no law, for the fierce wrath of nature has no influence upon it. It exists in eternity, for it is comprehended in no ground; it is impent in nothing, just as the unground of eternity is free and "rests in nothing save in itself only, where there is an eternal gentleness [tranquillity].

5. So is it also with the right true faith in the unground. It is in itself essential being. It has life, and yet seeks not its life, but it seeks the life of the eternal calm tranquillity. It goes out from the spirit of its life, and possesses itself: it is thus free from pain (Qual) as God is free from pain, and dwells thus in eternal freedom in God. It is with regard to the eternal freedom of God as a nothing, and yet is in everything. All that God and eternity is and is able to do serves it in some stead. It is laid hold of by nothing, and yet is a fair indwelling in the great might of God. It is a being, and yet is grasped by no being. It is a playmate and friend of the divine Virgin which is the wisdom of God; in it lie

the great wonders of God. It is free from all things, just as light is free from fire, and though it is always generated by fire, yet the torment of fire cannot seize or reach it.

6. So in like manner we give you to understand that faith is begotten out of the spirit of life, as out of an ever-burning fire, and shines in that fire; it fills the fire of life and yet is never laid hold of. But if it be laid hold of, then itself has entered into reason as into a prison, and is no longer in God, in his freedom, but has entered into torment; it torments itself, though assuredly it may become free. In reason it works wonders in the fire of nature, and in freedom it works the wonders of God in love.

CHAPTER II

OF THE ORIGIN OF FAITH, AND WHY FAITH AND DOUBT DWELL TOGETHER

1. SEEING then that faith is thus one Spirit with God, we are to consider its origin, for we cannot say that it is a figure or image of Reason. On the contrary, it is God's image, God's likeness, an eternal figure, and yet may be destroyed during the time of the body, or be transformed into source of anguish. For it is in its own nature, in the original state, merely a will, and the same will is a seed: this seed must the firespirit or soul sow in the freedom of God. In this way there grows from that seed a tree, of which the soul eats and appeases its fire-life, so that it becomes strong and gives its power to the root of the tree, whereby the tree grows up in the Spirit of God even unto the wonders of the Majesty of God, and buds in the Paradise of God.

2. And though by describing it we might be regarded as dumb and obscure, for Reason wants to see and to touch everything, we will reveal quite clearly why faith and doubt keep company and are as it were connected with a chain, so that there is a violent conflict in man all the time he is a guest in this tabernacle of the earthly life, unless he sink down so much in himself that he is able to introduce the fire of life into the freedom of God: then he is in the life of Reason as dead. Though he lives, he lives unto God, which indeed is a highly precious life of a man, and is seldom found in any, for it resembles the first image which God created. Although what is mortal still clings to him, yet it is as it were dead, as if a dead image did cling to him which pertains to dissolution wherein the true man lives not. For the true life stands reversed, and is in another world, in another Principle, and lives in another source.

3. Understand us now in this way: You see and know the origin of human life, how it arises in the womb; and then you see in what it qualifies and moves, viz. in four forms,-in fire, air, water and flesh. And though it lives thus therein, yet in such life it is no

more than an animal life, for its reason comes to it from the stars, and it is found that the sun and stars make in the four elements a tincture, whence comes reason and qualifying-power, as well as pleasure and pain. But it is far from being the true human life, for natural reason seeks nothing higher than itself in its wonders. There is nevertheless in man a desire and a great yearning for a higher, better and eternal life, in which no such torment exists. And though reason grasps not nor sees this desire, yet in reason is a mysterium which tastes and knows that from which the craving springs. Thereby we recognize that this mysterium was implanted at the first creation and is man's own possession, as a desiring and yearning, a magical craving. Further, we find that with this mysterium we are in a strange lodging, and that the mysterium is not found in the spirit of this world, for the latter comprehends it not nor does it find it. By this we recognize the heavy fall of Adam. Then we find that this mysterium in the will of the soul is a hidden fountain which is revealed in another Principle. We understand moreover that this mysterium lies hidden in fire, in the source of anguish, and is disclosed through the anguish of the will. Thirdly, we find how the same mysterium is kept imprisoned by the spirit of this world and how the reason of the outer life has power to enter into it and frustrate it, so that the mysterium does not attain to light but covers it up so that the genetrix [divine love] cannot bring forth, and so remains hidden in the mysterium. And when the body breaks, the will has not another which might reveal the mysterium; consequently the spirit of the soul, or fire spirit, remains in darkness, and the mysterium is eternally hidden in it as in another Principle.

4. We recognize, then, the mysterium as God's kingdom, which is hidden in the soul and gives to the soul a longing and desire, so that it imaginates into this mysterium, whereby it is impregnated magically in the same mysterium. Therefrom arises to it the will to go out from the fire-life into the mysterium of God. And if it uplift the will and cast it from it into the mysterium, the will is impregnated in the mysterium, for it has longing and acquires the body and essence of the mysterium, i.e. God's essence, which is

incomprehensible to nature. Thus the will draws God's likeness or image to itself.

5. Seeing then that the will is begotten out of the soul's fire, it is indeed rooted in the soul, and there is no separation between the will and the soul. But the will becomes thus a spirit in God and becomes the soul's garment, so that the soul in the will is hidden in God, though it dwells in the body. It is thus in the will, which is the right earnest faith, a child of God, and dwells in another world.

6. This is not to be understood as an historical will, where Reason knows there is in it a desire for God, but keeps this desire imprisoned in wickedness, so that the will cannot go out from the soul and enter into the life or mysterium of God. This Reason forms opinions and involves the will in delusion, whereby the will cannot attain the mysterium of God. It remains thus in delusion, or quite hidden in the soul, for it is directed towards something future, as Reason keeps the will a prisoner in the itch of the flesh, in the sidereal magia, and is always saying: To-morrow thou shalt go forth and seek after the mysterium of God. In truth, there is no individual faculty of finding: this opinion deludes. In like manner freedom exists in no delusion where the will is able to enter and see God, in such a manner that Reason may imagine to itself to do something and so to be pleasing to God.

7. For there is no other way which can be more perfect than to go out with the will from Reason, and not will to seek oneself; but to cast oneself wholly into God's love and into God's will, and to let be all that Reason throws in the way. And though these were great sins and perpetrated vices, into which the body had entered, we should by the will only pass above them, and value God's love more highly than the filth of sin. For God is not a receiver of sins, but a receiver of obedience and of freewill. He suffers not sin within him, but a humble will which goes from the house of sin and wills no more sin, but sinks out of or beyond reason into His love, as an obedient humble child this child He receives, for it is pure. But if it still remain in delusion, it is encircled also with delusion, and is not free. Seeing then that God is in himself free

from what is bad, the will also must be free, for thus it is God's likeness, image and own possession; for whatever cometh unto Him, into His freedom, He will not cast out, as Christ teaches us (John vi. 37).

CHAPTER III

OF THE PROPERTY OF FAITH, HOW IT GOES OUT FROM THE WILL OF THE NATURAL CRAVING INTO THE FREEWILL OF GOD

1. UNDERSTAND US further in this way: We know and recognize it in the Holy Scripture as well as by the light of nature that all comes from the eternal Being, viz. good and evil, love and wrath, life and death, joy and sorrow. We cannot on this account say that evil and death come from God, for in God is no evil nor any death, and to all eternity nothing that is bad enters into Him. Fierceness comes solely from the fire of nature, where life is found as in a magia, where each form of craving desires and awakens another. Therefrom arise the essences of plurality, from which wonders are generated wherein eternity manifests itself in similitudes. And yet we must say that in God's will is a desiring which gives rise to the magia wherefrom plurality springs. The plurality however is not God's will itself, which is free from all being; but in the craving of the will is brought forth nature with all the forms, so that all arises from the process of desire or from the eternal magia.

2. And we are further to know that all that which attains to life, which imaginates into the craving and places its will in nature, is the child of nature and one life with nature. But whatever with its will goes out from the craving of nature into the freewill of God is received and known of the Freewill, and is a spirit in God. And though it be in nature, just as nature has been generated from eternity in God's will, its spirit-life is nevertheless out of nature in the Freewill, and so the wonders of nature stand revealed in God, and yet are not God himself. And if the spirit of the soul's will (the image) go out from the reason of nature into the freewill of God, then the spirit of the will is God's child and the nature-spirit God's wonder, and the creature is introverted on itself like God himself. Then the sidereal or reasonspirit seeks in its magia, in its centre of reason, the wonders of eternity, to which end God

has created the soul in the body of the outer nature, though it is apprehended in the inner life alone. And the spirit of the will goes into the freedom of God, where then the Holy Spirit in the free divine mysterium leads it, so that the Deity is revealed in the spirit of the will, and in the reason-spirit is revealed the magia of nature with its wonders.

3. Seeing then the soul is the centre where the true spirit of the will, as distinguished from the freedom of God, proceeds into the freedom of God, as into the divine mysterium, it has also the sidereal spirit through connection. And if it tame this spirit, so that it work not wickedness, then it is able to introduce the sidereal wonders, which in the elemental mirror were made a substance, before the Majesty of God, into the freewill of God, so that the wonders appear in the freedom of divine Majesty as a likeness of the will of God. This is not to be understood as though the freedom of God co-mingles with the wonders of Nature and with the likeness so as to be One. No; God remains eternally free, he dwells in the wonders as the soul in the body. As little as the body lays hold of the soul, or the fire of the light, so little does Nature lay hold of the Deity. Yet it is a being and has from all eternity separated into two, even as fire and light, seeing that in fire we understand the source of nature, and in light the mysterium of the spirit-life without a source, albeit fire also is a mysterium.

4. Thus, understand us, it is also with regard to man. The soul is the fire of the true human life which God breathed out in Adam with his spirit out of the eternal nature as out of the centre of God. And the spirit which was generated out of the soul fire, and was formed by God's spirit in his own image, this spirit has the divine mysterium from which the will to the love of God is generated, whence arises the divine magia or craving so that the will spirit craves for God. Now when it arises, that is, goes forth from the hidden mysterium into the freedom of God, it is a branch or growth in God's kingdom. It has grown out of God's mysterium, and works in God's will, and continually reveals the wonders in God's wisdom. Not in such a way as though in God

something new were generated that was not from everlasting in God's wisdom, which has neither ground nor number, but alone in the spirit of the soul, in itself, does this eternal and infinite mysterium become revealed to God's honour and mirificence, and to its own, that is, the creature's, everlasting joy.

5. Since then the earthly and corrupt craving mingles with the sidereal source and the soul in the grievous fall of Adam has with its will imaginated into the stars as well as in the earthly craving and has introduced into itself the alien magia, therefore the will has been broken and the divine image destroyed. And the heavenly divine image of man became earthly, so that the right will is as it were turned about, that is in the spirit of this world, namely in the reason which is generated out of the stars. It is now needful for the true image of God which has thus been destroyed and has become earthly, that it should become other and be born again. And there would have been found no remedy for this image had not the Word out of the centre of God, that is God's own life, become man and had given a new birth in himself to the poor soul whose image was now corrupted. Then was succour again given to the true image, else it would have been eternally robbed of the freedom and majesty of God.

6. And since all souls have proceeded from one, they have all been generated out of the corrupt root; but since new regenerated life in Christ has come into a soul again, it is needful for us all to cast our will into the regeneration through Christ. For in Christ we have been born again with our souls in God, and have attained again to the image. For after the Fall the mysterium in our soul stood only in the magia of nature which in its centre is a fire. And the image was turned out of the freedom of God into the outer magia, that is the external principle. Now when that breaks in pieces in the being the poor corrupt image of the soul stands bare, like a lost child; it can awaken in its own centre nothing but the fierce fire source. For it has gone out of the Word of God, that is God's mysterium, and has entered into a destructible mirror, that is the Spirit of this world, which has a beginning and an end.

Wherefore also the soul's body has become wholly earthly and a prey to destructibility and death.

7. Now seeing that God has through grace turned his love to us and has in Christ turned the soul to himself into freedom, and has quickened the divine mysterium in the image so that the image can again dwell in God, that is in the wonders of paradise, it is needful for us to break off our will from the outer centre, that is from the transitory life, and to introduce it into the freewill of God. And for this is required not only a history or science, so that a man may say I believe that is, I know it or desire it, and nonetheless remains standing with his will in the external principle, that is in the outer craving. No, Scripture says, you must be born again through water and the Holy Spirit, else you will not see the kingdom of God (John iii. 5). There must be earnestness, the will of the reason must be broken, there must be a living movement of the will which breaks through reason and fights against reason. And though it is hardly possible for the soul, seeing it is very corrupt, yet there is no other and better remedy for it than to make itself as it were dead with all its reason and mind, and only to enter into and surrender itself to God's mercy that no room be left any more for reason, but that reason be mastered. And when the will thus beats down reason, reason appears as dead, though it still lives. But it becomes the servant of the right will, though out of it it would be master. For God's will must be master over reason if reason is to do any good that may subsist before God. For nothing subsists before God unless it be generated in God's will. But when the will turns towards God the will spirit becomes a child of God; then too the wonders which are done with the reason-spirit subsist before God, for they are done in God's will and are removed from that which has a beginning to the eternal.

8. And though we cannot well say that our works or achievements abide for ever, yet there abides their shadow or image, although they remain truly in being. But that is in the mysterium, namely the divine magia before the wisdom of God against which only the outer principle breaks itself. For in the human image no more

is broken than the outer dominion in the four elements, and the four are again set into one. Then also all colours and forms of the four elements are recognized with all which is generated therein. Therefore a final day of separation has been appointed by God in Nature when everything shall be tried by fire, whether it be generated in God's will or no, and when each principle shall reap its wonders. Then shall much of many a man's works remain in the fire because they were not generated in God's will, for in God there enters nothing impure (Rev. xxi. 27; xxii. 15). But what has been generated out of another magia is not pure.

9. We have an example of this in the earth which is corrupt. If thou ask: Why? the answer is The devil with his legions in his creation (though he was created an angel) sat in the Sulphur, or the centre of Nature, from which the earth was afterwards created. It is the devil who has excited the wrath in Nature so that the earth has an evil, impure craving, although it is shut up in death and reserved for putrefaction. Then it will be tried in the everlasting fire, and come again into that state in which it was before the creation, namely into the eternal magia of the eternal nature.

CHAPTER IV

WHAT THE WORK OF FAITH IS AND HOW THE WILL MAY WALK THEREIN AND CONCERNING ITS GUIDE

1. SINCE then all that is generated out of nature is comprehended in God's will and we thus understand that nothing can enter God's will unless it be generated or made in God's will, we understand clearly that it is needful for us that we should with all our reason and mind give ourselves into God's will, and labour with our hands in the world and seek food for the belly, but not set our will therein at all, nor wish to account an earthly thing our treasure for where our will and heart are there also is our treasure. If our will is in God's will we have the great mysterium of God out of which this world was generated as a similitude of it. Thus we have both, the eternal and the perishable and yet more. We bring the wonders of our works into the eternal mysterium for they cleave to the will-spirit. But when we turn aside our will from the eternal to the earthly mysterium and consider money our treasure, and the beauty of the body our glory, and honour or power as our fairest jewel, then our will is taken prisoner in it and thus we cling only to the mirror and do not attain to the freedom of God. For the mirror, which is the outer kingdom, shall be tried by fire and the wrath separated from the pure, for the wrath will be an everlasting burning.

2. Now when reason introduces the soul's mind together with the soul's will-spirit in which is the image of God and the true man into the external mirror, that is into a hypocritical craving, then indeed the image and the true man are made prisoner by it and infected with the outer magia, that is that same craving. For the image puts on the outer substantiality, not merely as a garment, but it is an infection and complete intermingling. For though the soul's fire does not mingle with the external kingdom, yet the soul's will-spirit which is of the magia is mingled with it and the image of God is destroyed and transformed into an earthly one,

whereby the soul's fire life remains fierce and has an earthly image in The will-spirit.

C3. Now when the body breaks up and dies the soul retains its image, that is its will-spirit. Now it is disjoined from the bodily image, for in death there is separation. Then the image appears together with and in those things which it has here taken into itself, with which it has been tainted, for it has the same source within itself. What it has loved here and what has been its treasure and what the willspirit has entered into, according to this will the soul's image also be fashioned. If during his life a man has applied his heart and mind to pride, that same source will ever gush forth in the soul fire in the image and pass out over the love and gentleness, that is God's freedom, and can neither lay hold of nor possess the freedom. But it gushes up in itself with such an anguishful torment and continuously fashions the will-spirit according to earthly things into which its will has entered. Thus it glitters therewith in the soul's fire and ever raises itself in pride and wishes to pass in the fire over God's gentleness, for it can create no other will. For it cannot enter into the freedom of God, into the holy mysterium wherein it might obtain another will, it lives only in itself alone. It has nothing, nor can it attain to anything but just that which it has in its outer life laid hold of in itself. So also it happens to the covetous man who has in his will and image the magia of the covetous craving. He always wants to have much and fashions to himself in the willspirit that with which he has associated in the life of the body. But because the latter has forsaken him and his being is no longer earthly, he yet bears about with him the earthly will and plagues and torments himself with it, for he can attain to nothing else..,

4. Far worse does it go with Falseness at "which the wretched have cried out and have cursed the false man for his oppression. For whatever has been wrought in wickedness has been caused by him, it follows him, for it has been wrought in the mysterium of the wrath. Therefore the corrupt soul after the death of the body falls into it and must bathe in those same abominations. And if it were possible with the will to enter into the love of God, yet these

same abominations and wickednesses hold it back, for they produce an everlasting despair, so that finally the soul becomes reckless, renounces God and desires only to rise up and to live in those abominations. And that is its joy: to blaspheme God and his saints, and but to exalt itself in the abominations above God and the kingdom of heaven, and yet neither to lay hold of nor to see either.

5. Thus we give you to consider what are the will and confidence, viz. the master and guide, which introduce man's image both into God's love and God's wrath. For in the will is generated the right true faith in which stands the noble image of God; for in faith we are through Christ born again in God, and obtain again the noble image which Adam had lost and which Christ has again brought among mankind with the life of God.

6. A false will moreover destroys the image, for the will is the root of the image, it draws the mysterium of God into itself. And the spirit of that mysterium reveals that beautiful picture and clothes it with the divine mysterium which is God's substantiality, understand by this Christ's heavenly body which was born out of God in the dear and fair virgin of his wisdom, and which fills the heaven. If then our mind and will are set on that and the will desires it, then the will becomes magical and enters in. And if it hunger it may eat of the bread of God; now the new body grows upon it which is the blessed tree of the Christian faith, for every body loves itself. Now when the soul receives the body of God, which is so sweet and fair, how should it not love that which is given it for its own, in which it dwells and lives and of whose power it eats and by which it grows strong.

7. Thus no man should deceive himself and remain fixed in his falseness and unrighteousness, and take comfort in an historic faith by thinking: surely God is good, he will doubtless forgive me; I will gather treasure and enjoy it well and will leave to my children much wealth and honour, and later I will repent. But all this is pure deception. Thou gatherest for them falseness and drawest into thyself unrighteousness. And though it still be done in the best way, yet it is earthly, for thou hast sunk thy heart and

will in an earthly vessel, thou hast clothed thy noble image and infected it wholly therewith. Moreover thou leavest as an heritage to thy children only pride, so that they also set their will-spirit on that alone. Thou thinkest to do good to thyself and thy children and thou doest thyself and them the very worst.

8. It is true the outer life must have sustenance and he does foolishly who voluntarily gives his goods to the wicked. But far more foolishly does he who makes himself a wicked man with his goods, by setting his heart on them, and holding the temporal, transitory pleasure more in honour than the eternal abiding good which has no end. But that man brings blessing upon himself who comes to the help of the wretched, for they wish him all good and pray to God that He would bless him in body and soul. Thus their wish and blessing enter with the giver into the mysterium and surround him and follow him as a good work born in God. For this same treasure he takes with him, and not the earthly one. For when the body dies the image enters the mysterium, that is, it is revealed in the mysterium of God, for during the time of the earthly life the external principle has been a covering before it. Now this falls away with the dying of the body and then there appears the divine mysterium in the image and within it all the good deeds and works which have been generated by love in the will of God.

9. The wish and prayer of all good children of God are set in the mysterium and join themselves to the image, for the children of the wretched whom he has helped in their necessity and tribulations have sent their will in their prayer into God's mysterium and have therewith joined themselves to their deliverer and consoler and have given him that straightway in the divine mysterium. So when that benefactor enters the mysterium and his earthly life falls away, then all things are revealed and each joins itself to its own to which the will has directed it.

10. All this will be reserved for the judgment of God the Holy Spirit in the mysterium, when each man shall reap what he has sown in his field here. Then it will all bud forth, grow and flower in a new heavenly earth, in which man will clothe his divine image

with the body of the perfect mysterium of God; and before him, viz. before his bodily image, he will see standing his righteousness, and understand why he is so fair. He will know the cause of it and eternally rejoice thereat and frame his song of praise therein, to God's honour and mirificence. On the other hand the godless crowd will have scorn, envy, pride, malice and cursing of the wretched in their mysterium gathered together in the wrath, and these will follow them. Thus they will ever know the cause of their torment and therefore be eternal enemies of God and His children.

CHAPTER V

WHY THE UNGODLY ARE NOT CONVERTED; WHICH IS THE MOST PAINFUL PART OF CONVERSION; OF THE FALSE SHEPHERDS; HOW WE MUST ENTER INTO GOD'S KINGDOM; OF THE DESTRUCTION OF THE DEVIL'S KINGDOM; OF THE THREE FORMS AND WHAT WE HAVE INHERITED FROM ADAM AND CHRIST

1. THE ungodly crowd cannot now lay hold of all this, and the cause of it is that there is not the will in them which desires to lay hold on it, for the earthly being holds them bound so that they cannot obtain a will in God's mysterium. They are before God as the dead, there is no breath of the divine life in them. Nor do they desire it, they are locked up in God's wrath mysterium, so that they do not know themselves. It is not God who has done this to them, but they have gone into it with their will-spirit and have sunk themselves into it thus; therefore they runn like crazy men. Whereas the noble treasure is hidden within them in the centre, in the divine principle, and they might very well with their will pass out of the earthly being and wickedness into the will of God. They wilfully allow the wrath to hold them, for the proud and self-honouring life pleases them too well, and it is that which holds them.

2. But after this life there is no remedy for them any more. When the soul fire is bare and fierce it can be quenched by nothing but God's gentleness, that is with the water of eternal life in the mysterium of God. But they do not attain to this for there is a great gulf between them, namely an entire principle. But in this life, while the soul as yet swims and burns in blood, it may well be, for the Spirit of God flies on the wings of the wind. God has become man, the Spirit of God enters the soul with the will, he desires the soul, he places his magia towards the soul; the soul need only open the door and he will enter voluntarily and open up the noble grain of the tree of Christian faith. But that is the

most painful part, and the one which enters into man most hardly (if the tree of faith is to be generated in him), that he must lead the spirit of his will out of his earthly treasure, that is out of pride, covetousness, envy, wrath and falseness towards the Spirit of God. His mouth must not be a dissembler nor his heart and will remain fixed in the earthly mysterium: he must be in earnest from the ground of his heart and soul; the will must turn about into the divine mysterium, namely God's love, that the Spirit of God may have space and room in him to blow up the small divine spark. There is no other remedy, and dissembling avails not.

3. Though a man should learn by heart all the Scripture, and sit all his life in church, but remain in his soul image an earthly and bestial man who is set only on falseness in his heart, his dissembling will avail him nothing. A preacher who acts outwardly according to God's mysterium, but has not God's image within, and is set only on honour and covetousness, is as close to the devil as the very meanest, for he is only a juggler with God's mysterium, and a dissembler without power. He himself has not God's mysterium, how then will he give it to others? He is a false shepherd, and a wolf among the sheep. For every man who bears God's mysterium, that is who has awakened it and has surrendered to it, so that God's Spirit drives him, he is God's priest, for he teaches from God. No man can teach aright unless he teach out of God's mysterium. But how will he teach who is outside it? Will he not teach from art and earthly reason? And what does that concern God's mysterium? Albeit reason is a noble thing, yet without God's Spirit it is blind. For Christ says: Without me ye can do nothing (John xv. 5). Those whom God's spirit leads they are the children of God (Rom. viii. 14). He who climbs into the sheepfold by another way and not through Christ's spirit he is a thief and a murderer and comes only to rob and to steal (John x. 1) and to seek his own profit. He is not a feeder of the sheep, but a devourer of them, as a wolf does.

4. This is how we must understand concerning the tree of the Christian faith. It must be living and not a dead history or science. The word of life must be born a man in the image, so that the

soul may bear God's image, else it is not God's child. It is of no use to be a hypocrite or to put off repentance upon hope, for so long as a man still bears the earthly image on his soul he is outside God's mysterium. Nor mayest thou think: I will indeed turn sometime, but I will previously gather enough for myself, so that I may not want and that earthly business may not afterwards lie in my way. No, that is the devil's trick. But it is through persecution, the cross, tribulation, scorn, contempt that we must enter into God's kingdom. For the devil holds sway in the earthly image and he mocks the children of God in his proud seat when they would escape from him. Therefore the wicked crowd serves the devil and helps him carry on his work.

5. The man who wishes to get to God must account all this as nothing. He must consider that he is in a strange country among murderers and that he is a pilgrim on the way to his true native land. He falls among murderers who torment and rob him, but so long as he carries off only so much that he preserve his noble image he has possessions enough, for in return for it he receives the heavenly mysterium within which lies everything and outside of which this world is but a mirror of it. Hence he is indeed most foolish who takes the reflection in a mirror for a substantial being, for the mirror breaks and its lover is bereft of it. He is like one who builds his house by a great water upon sand where the water carries away his house. So it is also with earthly hope.

6. O child of man, thou noble creature, do not yield it the power. It will cost thee thine eternal kingdom. Seek thyself and find thyself, but not in the earthly kingdom. How well does it truly befall him who finds himself in God's kingdom, who clothes himself in the heavenly and divine mysterium and enters into it! All the bravery of this world is filth in comparison with the heavenly, and is not worth that a man should fix his love upon it, although it be that it must be brought to a wonder to which end God has also created it.

7. Understand me: the outer man is to manifest the wonders of external nature, that is in the outer mysterium, both out of the earth and above the earth. All that the stars can do and the earth

has in itself, all this man is to express in wonders, forms and being according to the eternal figure as has been seen in God's wisdom before the times of the world. But his will he is not to place therein, nor to consider it his treasure, but he may use it only for his ornament and delight. With his inner man he is to work in God's mysterium, then God's spirit will also help him seek and find that which is without.

8. Since then through the grievous fall we have been so corrupted that our mind has been turned from the heavenly mysterium into the earthly, that is the mirror, so that we are found to be as it were half dead, it is therefore most necessary for us that we go forth with our mind and will from the earthly glitter and seek ourselves first before we seek the earthly adornment, and that we first learn to know where we are at home and not make our mind earthly.

9. For man, though he be in God's image, is yet in a threefold life. But when he loses God's image, he is only in a twofold life, for the first life is that of the soul and arises in the fire of the eternal nature. And it stands chiefly in seven forms, all according to the spirit of nature. The second life stands in the image which proceeds from the fountain of the eternal nature, namely the soul's fire, the which image stands in the light in another source and has its living spirit as has been found with regard to fire and light. For the source of light is not the same as the source of fire and yet light proceeds from fire; and by the source of light we understand the gentle, pure and pleasant spirit, and by the source of the fire the causes of it. Thus it is seen that from the fire air arises which is the spirit, and the air is also understood to be in four forms, viz. a dry one according to the fierceness of the fire, and a moist one as water from the astringent attraction. Thirdly a gentle one from light and fourthly an upthrusting one from the fierce fire terror. Thus we understand that light in all forms is master, for it has gentleness and it is a life which is generated through the bitter death, that is through the anguish source in the sinking down, that is another principle which exists in fire without feeling, and yet it has its feeling in itself, namely a

pleasant taste. Thus we understand that water is generated through death, through the sinking down through the fire anguish. And we must further understand that it yet is no death, though it is a death. But the light causes it to bud forth so that there is life in it, which life stands in the power of light, seeing that life grows out of death, namely the substantiality, which is the comprehensibility, just as water which in itself is dead, but the fire life and the power of light is its life. Thus the substantiality is considered as dead, for the life within it is its own and possesses and generates itself within itself. And the death of the substantiality must give the body thereto. So we must by the light-life and the water of death understand two forms and according to the anguish in the fire the third. That is, first, in the anguish of the mortifying in the wrath of the fire we understand a fierce water, which with regard to the first four forms to nature, namely astringent, bitter, anguish and fire is like poison, and is indeed a poison, a hellish substantiality in the wrath according to the origin of the first principle, in which God's wrath springs up.

10. Secondly we understand the other water in the light-terror, in which the source sinks through the mortifying and in death becomes as it were a nothing, for in the nothing the eternal freedom, that is the eternal abyss of eternity, is attained. Now when the imnahable light in that very sinking looks into eternity and always continues in the sinking down, the power of the light buds forth in the light and that is life coming forth from the sunk down death, for the wrath of the fire remains in the fiery source of the fierce water and does not go also into death. Nor can this be, for the fierceness is the strong almighty life that cannot die and cannot reach the eternal freedom, for it is called and remains for ever the nature life. Although there is also a nature found in the light life, yet it is not painful or hostile as in the origin of nature in respect of which God calls himself a jealous wrathful God. For in the light source the water which through death has sunk into freedom becomes a source and water of the eternal life of joy, in which love and gentleness eternally flow upwards, and then it is no longer a sinking, but a budding forth which is called

paradise. And the moving out from the source of the water is called Element, and that is the pure element in the angelic world. And the cause of the fire in light is the eternal firmament in which the eternal knowledge of God is manifested in wisdom, of which we have a similitude in the outer firmament and the stars.

11. Thus we understand two worlds one within 6e other, of which neither comprehends the other, namely one in the wrath of the fiery nature, in the water of poison and the anguish source wherein dwell the devils, and then one in the light in which the water of light has sunk down out of the anguish into the eternal freedom, and this the poison water cannot attain or lay hold of, and yet it is not separated except by death only, where it divides into two principles and falls into two lives: the one in the wrath and the other in the love, which life is known to be the true life in God. And in this lies the reason why, when with Adam we went out from this (light) life into the outer (world) life, God became man. Thus he had through this death to bring us back through and out of the fierce source, out of the fiery anguish life, through death, into the light and love life. Though the gate of death was indeed locked in the wrath in the human soul, so that the soul was in the anguish source in the inner nature, in the fire of poison; that is the water of anguish, yet here did the Lord Christ break the lock of death, and with his human soul budded through death in the light of God and thus in his light-life now leads death captive, so that he has become a mockery. For with this lock Lucifer thought to be a master and almighty prince in the wrath; but when the lock was broken the power of the Deity in the light destroyed his kingdom. There he became a captive servant, for God's light and the water of gentleness are his death, for the wrath is killed thereby.

12. Thus have love and light-entered the wrath with the paradisaic element and the water of eternal life, and thus God's wrath has been quenched. For this reason Lucifer now remains within himself as a mere anguishful, wrath-filled fire source, in which his body is a poison and a source of the poison water. And thus he has been thrust out from God's fire into the matrix of the

eternal nature, that is the harsh astringency which generates the eternal darkness. There he carries on the very stern government in the anguishful Mercurius and is thus as one disgraced or cast out who in his origin was a prince. Now he is esteemed no more than an executioner or dishonourable villain who in God's wrath has to be as a hangman who punishes evil when he is bidden to do so by his lord. He has no further power, although he is still a deceiver and would like to lay hands on much so that his kingdom might become great, and that he might possess much and not with little be a mockery. As also a whore thinks, if only there are many whores then I shall not alone be a whore, but I am like others; thus he too desires a great tribe that he may thereby mock God. The devil always lays the blame on God for his fall, saying that God's wrath had thus drawn him and thrust him into such a will of pride that he did not withstand. He thinks if only he might draw many to himself that his kingdom will grow great and that he will get all the more of them who also do as he does and would curse God, but justify themselves. That is his strength and delight in his dark and bitter anguish that he ever stirs up the fire within him and flies out above thrones. So he still regards himself as a lord and king; and though he is evil he is nevertheless a lord over his legions in the wrath in his creature. But with the wrath without his creature he has not power to act, there he must remain as an impotent captive.

13. Understand therefore the human life as being m two forms, one according to the fire of nature, the other according to the fire of light, the which fire burns in the love in which the noble image of God appears. And herein we understand that the will of man should enter into the will of God; thus he passes in the death of Christ and with the soul of Christ through death into the eternal freedom of God, into the light-life, and there he is with God in Christ. The third form of life is the outer life created out of the world, that is of the sun, the stars and elements, the which God's spirit breathed into Adam's nostrils with the spirit of the greater world, when he also became an outer soul, which swims in the

blood and water and burns in the outer enkindled fire, namely in the warmth.

14. This outer life was not to enter into the image, viz. in the inner life, nor was the image to let it enter the inner light (which shines through death and with its power buds in eternal freedom) for the outer life is only a similitude of the inner life. The inner spirit was only to manifest the eternal wonders in the outer mirror (such as in God's wisdom had been beheld in the unground in the divine magia) and to bring them into a figurative mirror, that is a wonder-mirror to God's honour and to the joy of the inner man who is generated of God. But his will was not to enter therein to draw the outer wonders into the image, as we now recognize with sorrow, that man draws into his mind and imagines an earthly treasure thus destroying the pure image of God according to the second principle.

15. For man's will-spirit now enters the earthly being and introduces his love in which the image resides into the earthly being, that is into an earthly treasure, an earthen vessel. Now the image in such an imagination also becomes earthly and passes again into death, and loses God and the Kingdom of Heaven, for its will-spirit remains fixed with its love in the outer life. Now the outer life must die and break up in order that the created image according to the inner kingdom may appear, and thus the will-spirit remains with its love in the outer wonders, and on the dying of the outer life brings these wonders with it before the judgment of God. There the will-spirit will have to pass through fire and the image be tried in the fire. All that is earthly must be burnt off from the image, for it must be quite pure and without spot. Just as the light subsists in the fire, so the will-spirit must also subsist in God's fire, and if it cannot pass unhindered through the fire of God, through death, that same soul image will be spewed out into eternal darkness.

16. And just this is the grievous fall of Adam that he placed his will-spirit in the outer life, that is the external principle, in the false craving, and imagined into the earthly life. Thus he went out from paradise which, through death, buds forth into the

second principle, into the Outer, and thus he entered into death. He had therefore to die, and thus his image was destroyed. This we have inherited from Adam. But we have also inherited the regeneration from the second Adam, Christ, in that we must enter into the incarnation of Christ and go with him into his death and with him out of death bud forth in the paradise world in the eternal substantiality of the freedom of God.

CHAPTER VI

WHAT LUST CAN DO; HOW WE IN ADAM HAVE FALLEN AND IN. CHRIST HAVE BEEN BORN AGAIN; AND THAT IT IS NOT SUCH AN EASY MATTER TO BECOME A TRUE CHRISTIAN

1. THUS we understand that it is due to lust, and that corruption has come out of lust and still does so. For lust is an imaginating in which the imagination insinuates itself into all forms of nature so that they are impregnated with the thing out of which lust springs. By this we understand the outer spirit of man which is a similitude of the inner. It has lusted after the fair image and for its sake has set its imagination on the inner, whence the inner has become tainted. And because it did not immediately feel death it has made room in its will-spirit for the outer. Thus the outer has taken up its lodging in the inner and has finally become the master in the house, and has darkened the inner so that the fair image has faded. Here the fair image fell among murderers, that is, among the harsh spirits of nature and the origin of life. These held the image captive and drew off from it the robe of paradise and left it lying half dead.

2. Now was there need of the Samaritan, Christ. And that is the cause that God became man. If the harm could have been healed through the speaking of a word or a word of forgiveness God would not have become man. But God and paradise were lost and moreover the noble image had been destroyed and made desolate and had to be generated again out of God. Therefore God came with his word which is the centre in the light-life, and became flesh, so that the soul might again receive a divine paradisedwelling. Understand that as Adam's soul had opened the door of the fire-essences and let in the earthly essences (the which source had insinuated itself into the paradise-image and made the image earthly), so God's heart opened the door of the light-essences and clothed the soul with heavenly flesh, and thus the essences of the holy flesh imaginated after the image, after the

soul's essences. Thus the soul was once more impregnated so that with its will-spirit it entered through death into the paradise-life. Hence came the temptation of Christ, that he was tempted to see whether the soul would eat of the Word of the Lord, and could, through death, enter again into God's life. And this was finally fulfilled on the tree of the cross when Christ's soul passed through the fire of wrath, through the stern source, through death and budded forth again in the holy paradise world in which Adam was created. Thus were we men helped again.

3. Therefore it is needful for us that we should draw out our will, mind and heart from all earthly things and turn them into Christ's suffering, dying, death and resurrection, that we continually crucify the old Adam with Christ's death and continually die with sin in the death and dying of Christ and with him continually rise again out of the anguish of death into a new man and bud forth in the life of God. There is no other remedy but this. We must die to the earthly world in our will, and must continually be born again in faith to the new world in the flesh and blood of Christ. We must be born out of Christ's Flesh if indeed we will see the kingdom of God.

4. It is not such an easy matter, but the hardest thing of all, to be a true Christian. The will must become a champion and must fight against the corrupt will. It must sink itself out of the earthly reason into the death of Christ, in God's wrath, and, as a worthy champion, break the power of the earthly will and venture so desperately that it will stake its earthly life on it and not desist until he has broken the earthly will. And that is indeed a stern warfare in which two principles struggle for the mastery. It is no jest: there must be determination to fight for the knightly garland, and no man attains to it unless he be victorious. He must break the power of the earthly will which, however, he is unable to do of his own might. But, if he sink himself out of the earthly reason with his inner will into Christ's death, he will sink through Christ's death, through God's wrath, into the paradise world, into the life of Christ in spite of all opposition of the devil. He must

make his will as it were dead; thus he will live to God and sink into God's love, while yet he lives in the outer kingdom.

5. But I speak of the knightly garland which he will receive in the paradise world when once he penetrates into it. For there the noble seed is sown and he receives the most precious pledge of the Holy Spirit which afterwards leads and guides him. And though in this world he have to walk in a dark valley where the devil and the wickedness of the world always roar over him and often cast the outer man into abominations and thus cover up the noble grain of mustard seed, yet it will not let itself be kept back, but buds forth, and there grows from it a tree in God's kingdom despite all the raging and roaring of the devil and his followers. And the more the noble pearl-tree is crushed down, the more vigorously and mightily it grows. It will not let itself be suppressed even though it should cost the outer life.

6. Therefore, my dear soul, inquire aright after the tree of Christian faith. It does not stand in this world. It must indeed be within thee, but thou with the tree must be with Christ in God, in such a way that this world merely hangs on thee as it also only hung on Christ. But this must not be understood to mean that this world is worth nothing or is unprofitable before God. It is the great mysterium, and man has been created into this world, as a wise ruler of it, that he should disclose all its wonders (which from everlasting are in the sulphur out of which this world with the stars and elements have been created) and to bring them according to his will into forms, figures and images, all to his joy and glory.

7. Man was created entirely free without any law. He had no law but the nature-law alone, that he should not mingle one principle with the other. The inner man was to allow nothing earthly to enter into him, but was to rule all-powerfully over the outer principle. Thus there would have entered into him neither death nor dying, nor could the outer elements have touched him, neither heat nor frost would have touched him. For as the noble image must subsist in the fire, so also that noble image was to rule

throughout the whole man, through all three principles, and govern all and fill all with the source of paradise.

8. But as that might not be and the flesh has become earthly, we must now be generated in the faith, seeing that indeed the earthly life covers the true life. We must therefore put on the right garment called Hope and set our will on hope and always labour at the tree of faith that it may bring forth its fruits, namely the blessed love towards God and our neighbour. A man must be good, not only for his own sake, but also that he may through his example and life amend his neighbour. He must consider that he is a tree in God's kingdom, so that he may bear God's fruit, grow in God's field, that his fruit is for God's table, and that he may clothe his works and wonders in true love and walk in love that he may bring them into God's kingdom. For God is a spirit and faith is also a spirit in God and God has become man in Christ. The faith's spirit is also in Christ born a man. Thus the will-spirit walks truly in God, for it is one spirit with God, and with God works divine works. And though the earthly life cover him so that he does not know the works which he has generated in faith, yet, in the destruction of the earthly life, it is made manifest, for hope is his shrine and a mystery in which the works of faith are sown and also preserved.

CHAPTER VII

TO WHAT END THIS WORLD WITH ALL BEING WAS CREATED, ALSO CONCERNING TWO ETERNAL MYSTERIES; OF THE EXCEEDINGLY FIERCE STRUGGLE IN MAN FOR THE IMAGE, AND WHEREIN THE TREE OF THE CHRISTIAN FAITH STANDS, GROWS AND BEARS FRUIT

1. SINCE man thus stands in a threefold life, each life is a mysterium to the other and each desires the other. For this end the world with all Being has been created, for the divine essentiality desires the mirror or similitude. For this world is a similitude according to God's being, and God is revealed in an earthly similitude. For the wonders of the hidden secrecy might not be disclosed in the angelic world, in the love-birth. But in this world in which love and wrath are mingled, where there is a twofold genetrix, it might be. For all things originated out of the fire root but are surrounded with the water of gentleness, so that it is a lovely being. But since in the angelic world the fire is not known, for the centrum of the genetrix stands in the light and is God's word, the wonders of nature cannot be manifested otherwise than in a spiritual magia, that is, they must be seen in God's wisdom. But as this is almost impossible for the angels and the souls of men to lay hold of, and yet God wills to be known of angels and men, the angelic world yearns for the great wonders to know them which from eternity have been in God's wisdom. And in the earthly similitude these are brought into substance, in figures and images, all of them according to the eternal essences of the centre of nature, so that the wonders may abide for ever. Not however essentially, but in figures, images and similitudes, and in forms. Magical indeed according to the will, but the genetrix is nonetheless in the centre of the wonders, for it has once been awakened out of the fire, -but it will be swallowed up again in the mysterium and stands as a hidden life. Therefore all beings shall be made manifest as a shadow in the angelic world,

but only those which in God's will have been introduced into the mysterium. For there are two mysteries which are eternal, the one in love, the other in wrath. Into whichever of these the will-spirit with its wonders enters, there within also stand all its works and wonders.

2. In the same manner therefore we are to know that the outer vehemently desires the inner, for all runs toward the centre, that is, the origin, and desires freedom.. For in the fire of nature there is anguish and torment; now therefore the formation or image of the gentleness in the source of love wills to be free, and yet may not be free in the source of the fiery essences, until the time when the source divides in the breaking: then each passes into its mysterium. In like manner the fire wants to be free from the water, for water is also the fire's death, and is also a mysterium for it. Similarly we see herewith how the water holds captive the fire, and yet there is no dying in the fire, but it is only a mysterium in the fire, as can be see~ when it breaks out in the water and manifests itself, when it reveals itself out of the centre of its own genetrix. This may be seen in the lightning, and may also be recognized in a stone, which yet is water. We see however chiefly how all forms of nature desire light, for in that desire is generated the oil in which the light becomes known, for it originates from the gentleness.

3. Our life is thus to be known to us, namely, that in us the centre of fire stands open, for the life burns in the fire. And then we have to consider the desire for love which originates in the word of life in the angelic world where God's heart with its desiring stands towards us with its imagining and also draws us into the divine mysterium.

4. And thirdly we must consider the magical kingdom of this world which also burns in us and draws us vehemently into its wonders, for it wills to be manifest. And man was created therein to this end that he should reveal that same mysterium and should bring the wonders to light and into forms according to the eternal wisdom. Now seeing he is to do this and thus burns in a threefold fire, the true spirit, in which the angelic image dwells, has great anxiety and is in great danger, for it walks along a very narrow

path and has two enemies which continually draw it, each of which wants to be in the image and to introduce its source therein. These are the inner and the outer fire; the inner kingdom of wrath and also the outer earthly kingdom of the mirror. Thus the true image stands in the midst in the crush. For the inner kingdom wants to manifest the wonders through the outer one, but because it is too sharp the outer kingdom flees from the inner and grasps at the middle, namely the image, which stands in the freedom of God, and so entwines itself into the image. For it all reaches out to the heart of God as to the centre of the kingdom of joy. Now the image has need to defend itself that it let not in the earthly guest, much less the fiery one. And yet it is generated out of both, that is, the life out of the fire and the wonders out of the outer life. Therefore it is most necessary for man's image that it lead a temperate sober life and not fill itself too full of the outer kingdom, else this will make its indwelling in the noble image.

5. And here we understand the mighty struggle in man for God's image, for there are three that strive for it. First the stern fire-life, secondly the divine life, and thirdly the earthly life. Thus the noble. image stands in the middle and is drawn by three. Now it is needful for it to hide itself in faith in the mysterium of hope and stand still in that mysterium seeing that the devil in the inner fire-life continually rides forth into the outer earthly life in pride, falseness and covetousness, over the noble image, and would bring it into the fire and anguish life and break it. For he always thinks that the place of this world is his kingdom; he will suffer no other image therein. Now the noble image falls into suffering, tribulation, anguish and distress, and at this point a great struggle ensues to fight for the noble knightly garland of God's image. Hence arises prayer that the image may ever go forth with prayer out of the introdueed earthly being, and also out of the proud, hellish abominations, continually enter into God's life, and his love. Thus the true image continually slays the earthly Adam as well as the hellish devil of pride, and must continually stand as a champion. The most necessary thing for it is to wrap itself in

patience, to throw itself under the cross and ever to well up in love, for that is its sword with which it slays the devil and drives out the earthly nature. It has no other sword with which to defend itself than the sweet water of the eternal life; which the proud fierce fire-spirit does not relish, for it is poison to it and it flees from it.

6. Now if we wish rightly to make known the tree of the Christian faith we say: Its root stands in the mysterium of hope, its growth in the love and its body in the laying hold of faith, that is when the image with its earnest desiring penetrates into God's love and grasps the substantiality of God, namely Christ's body. This is then the corpus in which the tree stands, grows and buds and brings forth fruits in patience. All of these fruits belong to the angelic world, they are the food of the soul, of which the soul eats and refreshes its fiery life so that it is changed into the light of gentleness.

7. Thus grows the tree in God's paradise, a tree which the outer man does not know, and which no reason grasps, but to the noble image it is very well known. When the outer life is broken up, the tree is then manifest and all its works follow it in the mysterium of hope into which it has sown. Therefore let no one who will follow God's pilgrim's way purpose to have in this world good and gladsome days with worldly honour, but tribulation, scorn and persecution await him every hour. Here he is only in a vale of misery and must continuously stand in strife, for the devil goes about him like a roaring lion and incites all his children of wickedness against him. He is accounted a fool, he is a stranger to his brother, his mother's house scorns and despises him. He passes along, sows in tribulation, suffers anguish, but there is no one who understands or whose heart is moved thereby. Everyone deems it is his folly which thus plagues him. Thus he remains hidden to the world, for with his noble image he is born, not of the world, but of God. He sows in sorrow and reaps in joy. But who can express the glory which is his reward? Or who will speak of the knightly garland which he attains? Who can express the virgin's crown which the virgin of God's wisdom sets upon him?

Where is there such beauty which surpasses Heaven? Oh noble image! Thou art indeed an image of the Holy Trinity in which God himself dwells. God sets upon thee his fairest jewels that thou mayest eternally rejoice in him.

8. For what then is the nature of this world seeing that it breaks up and only brings man into grief, anguish and misery, moreover into God's wrath, destroys his fair image and clothes him in a monstrous shape? Oh, what great shame will a man have on this account, when at God's judgment-day he will appear thus with a bestial image, not to speak of what follows thereafter, that he shall remain therein eternally. Now will begin a repentance, a groaning and weeping for the lost pledge which cannot in all eternity be recovered, for the image has to stand eternally before the horrible devil and do what Lucifer, the prince of abominations, will.

CHAPTER VIII

IN WHAT MANNER GOD FORGIVES SIN, AND HOW YOU BECOME A CHILD OF GOD

1. MY dear, seeking, eager mind, that hungereth and thirsteth for God's kingdom, do give heed to the ground of what is shown thee. It is indeed not so easy a matter to become a child of God as Babel teaches. There consciences are led into histories, they are flattered with Christ's sufferings and death; there the forgiveness of sins is taught historically as in a worldly court of law, there guilt is remitted through favour, though a man remain a hypocrite at heart. Here it is altogether different; God will have no hypocrites. He does not thus take our sins from us while we cling only to science and comfort ourselves with the sufferings of Christ, but in our conscience remain in the abominations. Scripture says: Ye must be born again or ye will not see the kingdom of God. A man who should flatter himself with Christ's sufferings and death, and appropriate that to himself, but with his will should remain unregenerate in the Adamic man, is like one who comforts himself that his master will bestow his land on him though he be not his son, and though the master have promised to bestow it on the son alone. Thus it is here also Wilt thou possess thy master's land and have it for thine own thou must become his true son, for the son of the maidservant shall not inherit with the son of the free woman. The son of History is a stranger; thou must be born of God in Christ that thou mayest become a true son; then thou wilt be God's child and an heir to the suffering and death of Christ. Christ's death is thy death, his resurrection from the grave is thy resurrection, his ascension thy ascension, and his eternal kingdom thy kingdom. In that thou art born his true son of his Flesh and Blood thou art an heir to all his goods. Thou canst not otherwise be the child and heir of Christ.
2. So long as the earthly kingdom remains in thine image thou art the earthly son of the corrupt Adam. No dissembling avails. Give fair words before God as thou wilt, thou art none the less an alien

child and God's goods are not thy due until thou return with the prodigal son to the father in right true contrition and repentance for thy lost heritage. Then thou must with thy will-spirit go out from this earthly life and break the earthly will; (it hurts to forsake with the mind and will-spirit the treasure once possessed, in which the will-spirit was generated), and thou must enter into God's will-spirit. There thou wilt sow thy seed in God's kingdom and wilt be born again in God as a fruit which grows in God's field, for thy will receives God's power, Christ's body and the new body in God will grow on thee. Then art thou God's child and Christ's goods belong to thee. His merit is thy merit, his suffering, death and resurrection, all are thine, thou art a member of his body, his Spirit is thy spirit, he will lead thee in the right way and all thou doest, thou doest to God. Thou sowest in this world and reapest in God's heaven; thou art God's wonder-work and thou revealest his wonders in the earthly life and drawest them with thy will-spirit into the holy mysterium.

3. Mark this therefore, ye covetous, proud, envious, false judges, ye wicked men, who bring your will and desire into earthly goods, money and possessions, into the sweets of this life and account money and possessions your treasure and set your desire therein, though ye want nonetheless to be God's children; ye stand and dissemble before God that he may forgive you your sins. But with your image ye remain in Adam's skin, in Adam's flesh, ye comfort yourselves thus with Christ's suffering and are but dissemblers. Ye are not God's children, ye must be born in God if ye will be children, else ye deceive yourselves together with your hypocrites who paint deceptive colours before you. They teach, but are not known of God, nor sent to teach. They do so for the belly's sake and for worldly honour, and they are the great whore in Babel who dissemble to God with their lips, but with their heart and will-spirit serve the dragon in Babel.

4. Dear soul, if thou wouldest become God's child, prepare for temptation and tribulation. It is not easy and pleasant to enter into the child-life, especially when reason lies imprisoned in the earthly kingdom. The reason must be broken, and the will go

forth from the reason and sow itself in humble obedience in God's kingdom, as a grain is sown in the field. The will must make itself as it were dead in- reason and give itself up to God; thus the new fruit grows in God's kingdom.

5. Man therefore stands in a threefold life and all belongs to God; the inner fiery essences of the first principle are incorporated with the new body in Christ, so that they may out of God's will flow into Christ's flesh and blood. Their fire is God's fire out of which burn love, gentleness and meekness, whence goes forth the Holy Spirit and helps them sustain the battle against earthly reason as also against the corrupt flesh and the devil's will. Man's yoke of the earthly will becomes easier to him, but he must in this world remain in the strife. For to the earthly life belongs sustenance; this man must seek and yet he may not set his will and heart upon it and cleave to it; he must trust in God, his earthly reason continually falls into doubt that he may suffer lack; it desires continually to see God and yet cannot, for God dwells not in the earthly kingdom but in himself.

6. Therefore reason, because it cannot see God, must be driven into hope; and there doubt runs counter against faith and would destroy hope. Then the earnest will must fight with the true image against the earthly reason. That is painful and it often goes sadly, especially when reason considers the course of this world, and recognizes its will-spirit as foolish in respect of the course of this world. Then scripture says: Be sober, watch, fast and pray that ye may benumb the earthly reason, and make it as it were dead that God's spirit may find place in you. When it appears it soon overcomes the earthly reason and looks with its love and sweetness at the will in its anguish, and each time a fair little branch is then generated out of the tree of faith, and all tribulation and temptation serve God's children for the best. For whenever God ordains for his children that they be brought into anguish and tribulation they stand each time in the birth of a new branch out of the tree of faith. When the Spirit of God appears again it draws up each time a new growth whereat the noble image greatly rejoices. It is only a question of the first serious

onslaught when the earthly tree must be overcome and the noble grain sown in God's field, so that man may learn to know the earthly man. For when the will receives God's light the mirror sees itself in itself, one essence sees the other in the light. Thus the whole man finds himself in himself and knows what he is, which he cannot know in the earthly reason.

7. Therefore let no one think that the tree of Christian faith may be seen or known in the kingdom of this world. The outer reason knows it not, and although the fair tree stands already in the inner man, yet the outer, earthly reason still doubts, for the Spirit of God is to it as foolishness, which it cannot grasp. Although it may happen that the Holy Spirit reveal himself in the outer mirror so that the outer life greatly rejoices therein and becomes trembling for great joy and thinks: Now I have won the worthy guest, now I will believe it, yet there is no perfect continuance therein, for the Spirit of God does not remain evermore in the earthly source. He will have a pure vessel, and when he withdraws into his principle, namely the true image, the outer life becomes despondent and timorous. Therefore the noble image must always be in strife against the outer reason-life, and the more it strives, the greater grows that fair tree, for the image co-operates with God. For just as an earthly tree grows in wind, rain, cold and heat, so also the tree of God's image amid suffering and tribulation, in anguish and pain, in scorn and contempt, and buds forth in God's kingdom and brings forth fruit in patience.

8. Seeing then we know this we should apply our-selves thereto and not let ourselves be held back by any fear or terror, for we shall indeed enjoy and reap to all eternity what we have sown here in anguish and hardship, so that we have comfort eternally. Amen, Hallelujah!

THE END

www.ingramcontent.com/pod-product-compliance
Lightning Source LLC
Chambersburg PA
CBHW071157160426
43196CB00011B/2113